I0614470

POETRY FROM CRESCENT
MOON

Walking In Cornwall
by Ursula Le Guin

Hymns To the Night
by Novalis

Hymns To the Night: In Translation
by Novalis

Flower Pollen: Selected Thoughts
by Novalis

*Novalis: His Life, Thoughts and
Works*
by Novalis

Edmund Spenser: *Heavenly Love:
Selected Poems*
selected and introduced by Teresa
Page

Edmund Spenser: *Amoretti*
edited by Teresa Page

*The Visions of Petrarch and Bellay:
Early Sonnets*
by Edmund Spenser

Robert Herrick: *Delight In
Disorder: Selected Poems*
edited and introduced by M.K.
Pace

Robert Herrick: *Hesperides*
edited and introduced by M.K.
Pace

Robert Herrick: *Upon Julia's
Breasts: Love Poems*
edited and introduced by M.K.
Pace

Sir Thomas Wyatt: *Love For Love:
Selected Poems*
selected and introduced by Louise
Cooper

John Donne: *Air and Angels:
Selected Poems*
selected and introduced by A.H.
Ninham

D.H. Lawrence: *Being Alive:
Selected Poems*
edited with an introduction by
Margaret Elvy

D.H. Lawrence: *Amores*
edited with an introduction by
Margaret Elvy

D.H. Lawrence: *Look! We Have
Come Through!*
edited with an introduction by
Margaret Elvy

D.H. Lawrence: *Love Poems and
Others*
edited with an introduction by
Margaret Elvy

D.H. Lawrence: *New Poems*
edited with an introduction by
Margaret Elvy

D.H. Lawrence: *Symbolic
Landscapes*
by Jane Foster

D.H. Lawrence: *Infinite Sensual
Violence*
by M.K. Pace

Percy Bysshe Shelley: *Paradise of
Golden Lights: Selected Poems*
selected and introduced by
Charlotte Greene

DRAMATIS PERSONÆ

DRAMATIS PERSONÆ

ARTHUR SYMONS

Edited by Jeremy Mark Robinson

CRESCENT MOON

First published 1923. This edition © 2021. Reprint 2024.

Set in Book Antiqua 10 on 14pt.
Designed by Radiance Graphics.

British Library Cataloguing in Publication data

ISBN-13 9781861718136
ISBN-13 9781861719072

CRESCENT MOON PUBLISHING
P.O. Box 1312, Maidstone, Kent, ME14 5XU
Great Britain, www.crmoon.com

CONTENTS

NOTE ON THE TEXT

The text is from *Dramatis Personæ* by Arthur Symons, published by Bobbs-Merrill, Indianapolis, 1923.

Arthur Symons, two portraits
(both National Portrait
Gallery, London).

PUBLISHER'S NOTE

Although it would be presumptuous to introduce the work of Arthur Symons, a word or two about this particular collection may not be out of place. A number of these essays have appeared in representative American and English periodicals, but their preservation here needs no apology as they have already earned a meritorious place in the bibliography of English criticism. The publisher believes, also, that the critical reader must realize the futility of any attempt to correct discrepancies due to the death of contemporaries, or augmentations to their work, lest the essays as originally conceived by the author suffer in spirit.

DRAMATIS PERSONÆ

CONRAD

"The Earth is a Temple where there is going on a Mystery Play, childish and poignant, ridiculous and awful enough in all conscience."

I

Conrad's inexplicable mind has created for itself a secret world to live in, some corner stealthily hidden away from view, among impenetrable forests, on the banks of untraveled rivers. From that corner, like a spider in his web, he throws out tentacles into the darkness; he gathers in his spoils, he collects them like a miser, stripping from them their dreams and visions to decorate his web magnificently. He chooses among them, and sends out into the world shadowy messengers, for the troubling of the peace of man, self-satisfied in his ignorance of the invisible. At the center of his web sits an elemental sarcasm discussing human affairs with a calm and cynical ferocity; "that particular field whose mission is to jog the memories of men, lest they should forget the meaning of life." Behind that sarcasm crouches some ghastly influence, outside humanity, some powerful devil, invisible, poisonous, irresistible, spawning evil for his delight. They guard this secret corner of the world with mists and delusions, so that very few of those to whom the shadowy messengers have revealed themselves can come nearer than the outer edge of it.

Beyond and below this obscure realm, beyond and below human nature itself, Conrad is seen through the veil of the persons of his drama, living a hidden, exasperated life. And it is by his sympathy with these unpermitted things, the "aggravated witch-dance" in his brain, that Conrad is severed from all material associations, as if stupendously uncivilized, consumed by a continual protest, an insatiable thirst, unsatisfied to be condemned to the mere exercise of a prodigious genius.

Conrad's depth of wisdom must trouble and terrify those who read him for entertainment. There are few secrets in the mind of men or in the pitiless heart of nature that he has not captured and made his plaything. He calls up all the dreams and illusions by which men have been destroyed and saved, and lays them mockingly naked. He is the master of dreams, the interpreter of illusions, the chronicler of memory. He shows the bare side of every virtue, the hidden heroism of every vice or crime. He calls up before him all the injustices that have come to birth out of ignorance and self-love. He shows how failure is success, and success failure, and that the sinner can be saved. His meanest creatures have in them a touch of honor, of honesty, or of heroism; his heroes have always some error, weakness, a mistake, some sin or crime, to redeem. And in all this there is no judgment, only an implacable comprehension, as of one outside nature, to whom joy and sorrow, right and wrong, savagery and civilization, are equal and indifferent.

Reality, to Conrad, is non-existent; he sees through it into a realm of illusion of the unknown: a world that is comforting and bewildering, filled with ghosts and devils, a world of holy terror. Always is there some suggestion of a dark region, within and around one; the consciousness that "They made a whole that had features, shades of expression, a complicated aspect that could be remembered by the eye, and something else besides, something invisible, a directing spirit of perdition that dwells within, like a malevolent soul in a detestable body."

"This awful activity of mind" is seen at work on every page, torturing familiar words into strange meanings, clutching at cobwebs, in a continual despair before the unknown. Something must be found, in the most unlikely quarter; a word, a hint, something unsaid but guessed at in a gesture, a change of face. "He turned upon me his eyes suddenly amazed and full of pain, with a bewildered, startled face, as though he had tumbled down from a star." There is a mental crisis in that look: the unknown has suddenly opened.

Memory, that inner voice, stealthy, an inveterate follower; memory, Conrad has found out, is the great secret, the ecstasy and despair which weave the texture of life. A motto from Amiel in one of his books faintly suggests it: "*Qui de nous n'a eu sa terre promise, son jour d'extase et sa fin en exil?*" And the book, *Almayer's Folly*, his first, a rare and significant book, is just that. *An Outcast of the Islands* has the despairing motto from Calderon, that better is it for a man had he never been born. *Lord Jim* is the soul's tragedy, ending after a long dim suffusion in clouds, in a great sunset, sudden and final glory. No man lives wholly in his day; every hour of these suspensive and foreboding days and nights is a part of the past or of the future. Even in a splendid moment, a crisis, like the love scene of Nina and Dain in the woods, there is no forgetfulness. "In the sublime vanity of her kind she was thinking already of moulding a god out of the clay at her feet. ... He spoke of his forefathers." Lord Jim, as he dies, remembers why he is letting himself be killed, and in that remembrance tastes heaven. How is it that no one except Conrad has got to this hidden depth, where the soul really lives and dies, where, in an almost perpetual concealment, it works out its plan, its own fate? Tolstoy, Hawthorne, know something of it; but the one turns aside into moral tracts, and the other to shadows and things spiritual. Conrad gives us the soul's own dream of itself, as if a novelist of adventure had turned Neo-Platonist.

A woman once spoke to me in a phrase I have never forgotten, of Conrad's sullen subjective vision. Sullen is a fine word for the aspect under which he sees land and sea; sullen clouds, a sullen sea. And some of that quality has come to form part of his mind, which is protesting, supremely conscious. He is never indifferent to his people, rarely kind. He sees them for the most part as they reveal themselves in suffering. Now and then he gives them the full price, the glory, but rarely in this life, or for more than a moment. How can those who live in suspense, between memory and foreboding, ever be happy, except for some little permitted while? The world for those who live in it, is a damp forest, where savagery and civilization meet, and in vain try to mingle. Only the sea, when they are out of sight of land, sometimes gives them freedom.

It is strange but true that Conrad's men are more subtly comprehended and more magnificent than his women. There are few men who are seen full length, and many of them are nameless shadows. Aissa and Nina in the earliest books have the fierce charm of the unknown. In *Lord Jim* there is only one glimpse of the painful mystery of a woman's ignorant heart. In *Nostromo* the women are secondary, hardly alive; there is no woman in *The Nigger of the Narcissus*, nor in *Typhoon*, nor in *Youth*. There are some women, slightly seen, in Tales of Unrest, and only one of them, the woman of *The Return*, is actually characterized.

Is there not something of an achievement in this stern rejection of the obvious love-story, the material of almost every novel? Not in a single tale, even when a man dies of regret for a woman, is the woman prominent in the action. Almayer, and not Nina, is the center of the book named after him. And yet Nina is strange, mysterious, enchanting, as no other woman is to be. Afterward they are thrust back out of the story; they come and go like spinners of Destiny, unconscious, ignorant, turning idle wheels, like the two women knitting black wool in the waiting room of the Trading Company's office, "guarding the door of Darkness."

Now, can we conjecture why a woman has never been the center of any of these stories? Conrad chooses his tools and his materials; he realizes that men are the best materials for his tools. It is only men who can be represented heroically upon the stage of life; who can be seen adventuring doggedly, irresistibly, by sheer will and purpose; it is only given to men to attain a visible glory of achievement. He sees woman as a parasite or an idol, one of the illusions of men. He asks wonderingly how the world can look at them. He shows men fearing them, hating them, captivated, helpless, cruel, conquering. He rarely indicates a great passion between man and woman; his men are passionate after fame, power, success; they embrace the sea in a love-wrestle; they wander down unsounded rivers and succumb to "the spell of the wilderness," they are gigantic in failure and triumph; they are the children of the mightiness of the earth; but their love is the love of the impossible. What room is there, in this unlimited world, for women? "Oh, she is out of it – completely. They – the women I mean – are out of it – should be out of it. We must help them to stay in that beautiful world of their own, lets ours gets worse. Oh, she had to be out of it."

There is Karain, "clothed in the vision of unavoidable success," flying before a shadow, comforting himself with the certainty of a charm. There is Kurtz, who returns to barbarism, and Tuan Jim with his sacrifice of life to honor, and even the dying nigger steersman who, shot through by a spear, looks once on his master, "and the intimate profundity of that look which he gave me when he received his hurt remains to this day in my memory – like a claim of distant kinship affirmed in a supreme moment." It is with this agonizing clearness, this pitiless mercy, that Conrad shows us human beings. He loves them for their discontent, for their revolt against reality, for their failure, their atonement, their triumphs. And he loves them best because their love is the love of the impossible; he loves them because they are part of the unknown.

And so, it is *Lord Jim* in which his genius has attained its zenith with *Karain* and *Heart of Darkness* close after it. Consider the marvelous art, the suspense, the evasion of definite statement, the overpowering profundity of it. To begin with, there is the trick, one of Conrad's inextricable tricks of art, by which suspense is scarcely concerned with action, but with a gradually revealed knowledge of what might have happened in the making of a man. Take an instance in *Nostromo*. There is Doctor Monyngham who comes in at the beginning of the book comes and goes briefly up to the three hundredth page; and then suddenly, *à propos* of nothing, the whole history of his troubles, the whole explanation of what has seemed mysterious to him, is given in four pages; whereupon the last sentence, four pages back, is caught up and continued with the words: "That is why he hobbled in distress in the Casa Gould on that morning." Now why is there this kind of hesitation? Why is a disguise kept up so long and thrown off for no apparent reason? It is merely one of his secrets, which is entirely his own; but another of them he has learned from Balzac: the method of doubling or trebling the interest by setting action within action, as a picture is set within a frame. In *Youth* the man who is telling the story to more or less indifferent hearers, times his narrative with a kind of refrain. ... "Pass the bottle," he says whenever a pause seems to be necessary; and, as the tale is ending, the final harmony is struck by an unexpected and satisfying chord: "He drank.... He drank again."

To find a greater novel than *Lord Jim*, we might have to go back to *Don Quixote*. Like that immortal masterpiece, it is more than a novel; it is life itself, and it is a criticism of life. Like Don Quixote, Lord Jim, in his followings of a dream, encounters many rough handlings. He has the same egoism, isolation, and conviction; the same interrupting world about him, the same contempt of reality, the same unconsciousness of the nature of windmills. In Marlow, he has quite a modern Sancho Panza, disillusioned, but following his master. Certainly this narrator of Jim's failures and successes represents them under the obscure guidance of "a strange and melancholy illusion, evolved half-unconsciously like all our illusions, which I suspect only to be visions of remote unattainable truth, seen dimly." He is a soul "drunk with the divine philtre of an unbounded confidence in himself." That illusion is suddenly put to the test; he fails, he goes into the cloud, emerges out of it, is struck gloriously dead.

In *Lord Jim* Conrad has revealed, more finally than elsewhere, his ideal: the ideal of an applauded heroism, the necessity of adding to one's own conviction the world's acceptance and acclamation. In this stupendous work, what secret of humanity is left untold? Only told, is too definite a word. Here is Conrad's creed, his statement of things as they are:

> It is when we try to grapple with another man's need that we perceive how incomprehensible, wavering, and misty are the beings that share with us the sight of the stars and the warmth of the sun. It is as if loneliness were a hard and absolute condition of existence; the envelope of flesh and blood on which our eyes are fixed melts before the outstretched hand, and there remains only the capricious, unconsolable, and elusive spirit that no eye can follow, no hand can grasp.

"Man is amazing, but he is not a masterpiece," says some one in the book, one of the many types and illustrations of men who have fallen into a dream, all with some original sin to proclaim or conceal or justify, men of honor, tottering phantoms clinging to a foul existence, one crowding on another, disappearing, unrealized. All have their place, literally or symbolically, in the slow working-out of the salvation of Tuan Jim. Amazing they may be, but Jim "approaching greatness as genuine as any man ever achieved," with the shame of his "jump" from a sinking ship and his last fearless jump "into the unknown," his last "extraordinary success," when, in one proud and unflinching glance, he beholds "the face of that opportunity which, like an Eastern bride, had come veiled to his side": amazing he may be, but a masterpiece, proved, authentic, justifying Man.

Next after this triumph, Karain is the greatest. It is mysterious, a thing that haunts one by its extreme fascination; and in this, as in all Conrad, there is the trial of life: first the trial, then the failure, finally (but not quite always) the redemption. "As to Karain, nothing could happen to him unless what happens to all – failure and death; but his quality was to appear clothed in the illusion of unavoidable success." And on what a gorgeous and barbaric and changing stage is this obscure tragedy of the soul enacted! There is in it grave splendor. In Conrad's imagination three villages on a narrow plain become a great empire and their ruler a monarch.

To read Conrad is to shudder on the edge of a gulf, in a silent darkness. *Karain* is full of mystery, *Heart of Darkness* of an unholy magic. "The fascination of the abomination – you know," the teller of the story says for him, and "droll thing life is." The whole narrative is an evocation of that "stillness of an implacable brooding over an incalculable intention," and of the monstrous Kurtz who has been bewitched by the "heavy mute spell of the wilderness that seems to draw him to its pitiless breast by the awakening of forgotten and brutal instincts, by the memory of gratified and monstrous passions; and this alone had beguiled his unlawful soul beyond the bounds of permitted aspiration." And it all ends with the cry: "The horror! The horror!" called out in his last despair by a dying man. Gloomy, tremendous, this has a deeper, because more inexplicable, agony than the tragedy of *Karain*. Here, the darkness is unbroken; there is no remedy; body and soul are drawn slowly and inevitably down under the yielding and pestilent swamp. The failure seems irretrievable. We see nature casting out one who had gone beyond nature. We see "the meanness, the torment, the tempestuous anguish of a soul" that, in its last moment of earthly existence, had peeped over the edge of the gulf, with a stare "that could not see the flame of the candle, but was wide enough to embrace the whole universe."

With *Nostromo* we get a new manner and new scenery. The scene is laid in Colombia, the Nuevo Granada of the Spaniards, and the silver mine is its center, and around that fatal treasure-house the whole action moves. The Spanish streets, glittering with heat, with their cool patios, peopled by the Indians, the "whites," a cross between Spanish and native, the Italians, the English, the Indian girls with long dark hair, the Mozenitas with golden combs, are seen under strong sunlight with a vivid actuality more accentuated than in any other of Conrad's scenes. A sinister masquerade is going on in the streets, very unreal and very real. There is the lingering death of Decoud on a deserted island ("he died from solitude, the enemy known to few on this earth, and whom only the simplest of us are fit to withstand"); the horrible agonies of Hirsch; the vile survival of Doctor Monyngham. It is by profound and futile seriousness that these persons and events take on an air of irony, and are so comic as they endure the pains of tragedy.

This strange novel is oddly constructed. It is a narrative in which episode follows episode with little apparent connection. The first half is a lengthy explanation of what the second part is to put into action. It drags and seems endless, and might be defined by a sentence out of the book, where some one "recognized a wearisome impressiveness in the pompous manner of his narrative." Suddenly, with Nostromo's first actualized adventure the story begins, the interest awakens, and it is only now that Nostromo himself becomes actual. He has been suggested by hints, indicated in faint outline. We have been told of his power and influence, we see the admiration which surrounds him, but the man walks veiled. His vanity, evident at the first, becomes colossal: "The man remained astonishingly simple in the jealous greatness of his conceit." Then, as he awakens one morning under the sky, he rises "as natural and free from evil in the moment of waking as a magnificent and unconscious wild beast." The figure greatens in his allegiance to the shining spectre of the treasure, which makes him afraid because "he belonged body and soul to the unlawfulness of his audacity." His death is accidental, but, in Conrad's merciful last words, he has, after his death, the "greatest, the most enviable, the most sinister of his successes. In that true cry of love and grief that seemed to ring aloud from

Punta Mala to Azuera and away to the bright line of the horizon, overhung by a big white cloud shining like a mass of solid silver, the genius of the magnificent Capataz de Caegadores dominated the dark gulf containing his conquests of treasure and love."

II

Conrad's first fame was made by his sea-novels, and the sea is never quite out of any of his books. Who, before or since, could have evoked this picture of heat, stillness and solitude?

In *Typhoon* we are cast into the midst of a terrible outrage of the destructive force of nature:

> something formidable and swift, like the sudden smashing of a vial of wrath. It seemed to explode all round the ship with an overpowering concussion and a rush of great waters, as if an immense dam had been blown up to windward. In an instant the men lost touch of each other. This is the disintegrating power of a great wind; it isolates one from one's kind. ... The motion of the ship was extravagant. Her lurches had an appalling helplessness; she pitched as if taking a header into a void, and seemed to find a wall to hit every time. ... The seas in the dark seemed to rush from all sides to keep her back where she might perish. There was hate in the way she was handled, and a ferocity in the blows that fell. She was like a living creature thrown to the rage of a mob! hustled terribly, struck at, borne up, flung down, leaped upon. ... At last she rose slowly, staggering, as if she had to lift a mountain with her bows.

There have been many writers about the sea, but only Conrad has loved it with so profound and yet untrustful a love. His storms have sublimity, made out of intense attention to detail, often trivial or ludicrous, but heightened into tragedy by the shifting floor and changing background on which is represented the vast struggle of man with the powers of nature. And as he loves the earth only in its extravagances, so he loves the sea most in storm, where love and fear mingle. The tropics, the Malay Archipelago, and the sea in a continual tempest, the ship suffering through a typhoon, or burning itself out on the waters: these are his scenes, these he cherishes in his faithful and unquiet memory. How much is memory, how much is imagination, no one need know or care. They are one; he does not distinguish between them.

Once, in one of the pages of *Lord Jim*, Conrad has confessed himself with perfect frankness. He represents himself receiving a packet of letters which are to tell him the last news of Lord Jim. He goes to the window and draws the heavy curtains.

> The light of his shaded reading-lamp slept like a sheltered pool, his footfalls made no sound on the carpet, his wandering days were over. No more horizons as boundless as hope, no more twilights within the forests as solemn as temples, in the hot quest for the Ever-undiscovered Country over the hill, across the stream, beyond the wave. The hour was striking! No more! No more! – but the opened packet under the lamp brought back the sounds, the visions, the very savor of the past – a multitude of fading faces, a tumult of low voices, dying away upon the shores of distant seas under a passionate and unconsoling sunshine. He sighed and sat down to read.

That is the confession of one who, of foreign race, is an alien, solitary among his memories.

Conrad's stories have no plots, and they do not need them. They are a series of studies in temperaments, deduced from slight incidents; studies in emotion, with hardly a rag to hold together the one or two scraps of action, out of which they are woven. A spider hanging by one leg to his web, or sitting motionless outside it: that is the image of some of these tales, which are made to terrify, bewilder and grip you. No plot ever made a thing so vital as *Lord Jim*, where there is no plot; merely episodes, explanations, two or three events only significant for the inner meaning by which they are darkened or illuminated. I would call this invention, creation; the evasion of what is needless in the plots of most novels. But Conrad has said, of course, the right thing, in a parenthesis: "It had that mysterious, almost miraculous, power of producing striking effects by means impossible of detection, which is the last word of the highest art."

Conrad conceals his astonishing invention under many disguises. What has seemed to some to be untidy in construction will be found to be a mere matter of subtlety, a skilful arresting of the attention, a diverting of it by a new interest thrust in sideways. *Lord Jim* is a model of intelligent disarray.

In the strict sense Conrad is not a novelist: he writes by instinct. And his art is unlike the art of every other novelist. For instance, Meredith or Stendhal make great things out of surface material; they give us life through its accidents, one brilliantly, the other with scrupulous care. Conrad uses detail as illustrations of his ideas, as veils of life, not as any essential part of it. The allusion to him is more real than the fact; and, when he deals with the low or trivial, with Mr. Verloc's dubious shop in the backstreet, it is always a symbol.

Conrad, writing in English, does not always think in English. For, in this man, who is pure Polish, there is a brooding mind, an exalted soul, a fearless intelligence, a merciful judgment. And he has voyaged through many seas of the soul, in which he finds that fascination, the fascination of fear, splendor, and uncertainty, which the water that surrounds the earth had to give him. And he has made for himself a style which is personal, unique, naked English, and which brings into English literature an audacious and profound English speech.

In his sarcasm Conrad is elemental. He is a fatalist, and might say with Sidi Ali Ismayem, in the *Malay Annals*: "It is necessary that what has been ordained should take place in all creatures." But in his fatalism there is a furious revolt against all those evils that must be accepted, those material and mental miseries that will never be removed. His hatred of rule, measure, progress, civilization is unbounded. He sits and laughs with an inhuman laughter, outside the crowd, in a chair of wisdom; and his mockery, persuaded of the incurable horrors of existence, can achieve monstrosity, both logical and ghastly.

In the "simple tale" of *The Secret Agent*, which is a story of horror, in our London of to-day, the central motive is the same as that of the other romances: memory as Nemesis. The man comes to his death because he can not get a visible fear out of his eyes; and the woman kills him because she can not get a more terrible, more actual thing, which she has not seen, but which has been thrust into her brain, out of her eyes. "That particular fiend" drives him into a cruel blunder and her into a madness, a murder, a suicide, which combine into one chain, link after link, inevitably.

The blood-thirstiness of Conrad's "simple story" of modern life, a horror as profound as that of Poe, and manipulated with the same careful and attentive skill, is no form of cruelty, but of cold observation. What is common enough among the half-civilized population of that Malay Peninsula, which forms so much of the material of the earlier novels, has to be transported, by a choice of subject and the search for what is horrible in it, when life comes to be studied in a modern city. The interest is still in the almost less civilized savagery of the Anarchists; and it is around the problem of blood-shedding that the whole story revolves. The same lust of slaughter, brought from Asia to Europe, seems cruder and less interesting as material. There the atmosphere veiled what the gaslight of the disreputable shop and its back-parlor do but make more visible. It is an experiment in realism which comes dangerously near to being sensational, only just avoids it.

The whole question depends upon whether the material horror surpasses that horror of the soul which is never absent from it; whether the dreadful picture of the woman's hand holding the carving-knife, seen reflected on the ceiling by the husband in the last conscious moment before death, is more evident to us than the man's sluggish acquiescence in his crime and the woman's slow intoxication by memory into a crime more direct and perhaps more excusable. It seems, while you are reading it, impossible that the intellect should overcome the pang given to the senses; and yet, on reflection, there is the same mind seen at work, more ruthlessly, more despairingly than ever, turning the soul inside out, in the outwardly "respectable" couple who commit murder, because they "refrained from going to the bottom of facts and motives." Conrad has made a horrible, forgivable, admirable work of art out of a bright tin can, a befouled shovel, and a stained carving knife. He has made of these three domestic objects the symbols of that destroying element, "red in tooth and claw," which turns the wheel on which the world is broken.

MAURICE MAETERLINCK

I

Often, mostly at night, a wheel of memory seems to turn in my head like a kaleidoscope, flashing out the pictures and the visions of my own that I keep there. The same wheel turned in my head when I was in Dieppe with Charles Conder, and it turned into these verses:

> There's a tune burns, bums in my head,
> And I hear it beat to the sound of my feet,
> For that was the tune we used to walk to
> In the days that are over and dead.
>
> Another tune turns under and over.
> And it turns in my brain as I think again
> Of the days that are dead, and the ways she walks now,
> To the self-same tune, with her lover.

I see, for instance, Mallarmé, with his exquisite manner of welcome, as he opens the door to me on the fourth floor of the Rue de Rome; I hear Jean Moréas thunder out some verses of his own to a waitress in a Bouillon Duval, whose name was Celimène, who pretended to understand them; Stuart Mérill at the Rue Ballier, Henri de Regnier silent under his eye-glass in one of the rooms of the *Mercerie de France*; Maurice Maeterlinck in all the hurry of a departure, between two portmanteaux. That was, I suppose, one of the most surprising meetings I ever had; for, as a matter of fact, one night in Fountain Court, it was in 1894 – I was equally surprised when I opened his *Alladine et Palamides* which he had sent me with a dedication. After that time I saw him, during several years, fairly often in Paris and once in Rome, in 1903, when one performance was given of his *Joyzelle* – the most unsatisfactory performance I ever saw, and of certainly an unsatisfactory play. Nervous as he always was – he used, for one thing, to keep a loaded revolver always beside him in his bedroom – he shirked the occasion and went to Naples. I have never forgotten the afternoon when he read to me in his house in Paris whole pages of *Monna Vanna*. After I had left the house, I said to a certain lady who was with me: "Rhetoric, nothing but rhetoric! It may be obviously dramatic; but the worst of it is, all the magic and mystery of his earlier plays had vanished: there is logic rather than life."

It is very unfortunate for a man to be compared to Shakespeare even by his enemies, when he is only twenty-seven and has time before him. That is what has happened to Maurice Maeterlinck. Two years ago the poet of *Serres Chaudes* was known to only a small circle of amateurs of the new; he was known as a young Belgian of curious talent who had published a small volume of vague poems in monotone. On the appearance of *La Princesse maleine*, in the early part of 1890, Maeterlinck had an unexpected "greatness thrust upon him" by a flaming article of Octave Mirbeau, the author of that striking novel *Sébastian Roch* in the *Figaro* of August 24th. "Maurice Maeterlinck," said this uncompromising enthusiast,

> "*nous a donné l'oeuvre la plus géniale de ce temps, et la plus extraordinaire et la plus naive aussi, comparable – et oserai-je le dire? – supérieure en beauté à ce qu'il y a de plus beau dans Shakespeare.... plus tragique que 'Macbeth,' plus extraordinaire de pensée que 'Hamlet.'*"

In short, there was no Shakespearean merit in which *La*

Princesse Maleine was lacking, and it followed that the author of *La Princesse Maleine* was the Shakespeare of our age – the Belgian Shakespeare. The merits of Maeterlinck were widely discussed in France and Belgium, and it was not long before the five-act drama was followed by two pieces, each in one act, called *L'Intruse* and *Les Aveugles*. In May, 1891, *L'Intruse* was given by the Théâtre d'Art at the Vaudeville on the occasion of the benefit of Paul Verlaine and Paul Gauguin.

He is not entirely the initiator of this impressionistic drama; first in order of talent, he is second in order of time to another Belgian, Charles van Lerberghe, to whom *Les Aveugles* is dedicated. It was Van Lerberghe (in *Les Flaireurs*, for example) who discovered the effect which might be obtained on the stage by certain appeals to the sense of hearing and of sight, newly directed and with new intentions. But what is crude and even distracting in *Les Flaireurs* becomes an exquisite subtlety in *L'Intruse*. In *La Princesse Maleine*, in *L'Intruse*, in *Les Aveugles*, in *Les Sept Princesses*, Maeterlinck has but one note, that of fear – the "vague spiritual fear" of imaginative childhood, of excited nerves, of morbid apprehension. In *La Princesse Maleine* there is a certain amount of action – action which is certainly meant to reinvest the terrors of Macbeth and of Lear. In *L'Intruse* and *Les Aveugles* the scene is stationary, the action but reflected upon the stage, as if from some other plane. In *Les Sept Princesses* the action, such as it is, is "such stuff as dreams are made of," and is literally, in great part, seen through a window. From first to last it is not the play, but the atmosphere of the play, that is "the thing." In the creation of this atmosphere Maeterlinck shows his particular skill; it is here that he communicates to us the nouveau frisson, here that he does what no one has done before.

La Princesse Maleine, it is said, was written for a theater of marionettes, and it is, certainly, with the effect of marionettes that these sudden, exclamatory people come and go. Maleine, Hjalmar, Uglyane – these are no characters, these are no realizable persons; they are a mask of shadows, a dance of silhouettes behind the white sheet of the "Chat Noir," and they have the fantastic charm of these enigmatical semblances – "luminous, gem-like, ghost-like" – with, also, their somewhat mechanical eeriness. Maeterlinck has recorded his intellectual debt to Villiers de l'Isle Adam, but it was not from the author of *Axel* that he learned his method. The personages of Maeterlinck – are only too eloquent, too volubly poetical. In their mystical aim Villiers and Maeterlinck are at one; in their method there is all the difference in the world. This is how Sara, in *Axel*, speaks: –

Songe! Des coeurs condamnés à ce supplice de pas m'aimer! ne sont-ils pas assez infortunés d'être d'une telle nature?

But Maleine has nothing more impressive to say than this: –

Mon Dieu! mon Dieu! comme je suis malade! Et je ne sais pas ce que j'ai; – et personne ne sait ce que le médecin ne sait pas ce que j'ai; ma nourrice ne sait pas ce que j'ai; Hjalmar ne sait pas ce que j'ai.

That these repetitions lend themselves to parody is obvious; that they are sometimes ridiculous is certain; but the principle which underlies them is at the root of much of the finest Eastern poetry - notably in the Bible. The charm and the impressiveness of monotony is one of the secrets of the East; we see it in their literature, in their dances, we hear it in their music. The desire of the West is after variety, but as variety is the most tiring of all excesses, we are in the mood for welcoming an experiment in monotone. And therein lies the originality, therein also the success of Maeterlinck.

In comparing the author of *La Princesse Maleine* with Shakespeare, Mirbeau probably accepted for a moment the traditional Shakespeare of grotesque horror and violent buffoonery. There is in *Maleine* something which might be called Elizabethan – though it is Elizabethan of the school of Webster and Tourneur rather than of Shakespeare. But in *L'Intruse* and *Les Aveugles* the spiritual terror and physical apprehension which are common to all Maeterlinck's work have changed, have become more interior. The art of both pieces consists in the subtle gradations of terror, the slow, creeping progress of the nightmare of apprehension. Nothing quite like it has been done before – not even by Poe, not even by Villiers. A brooding poet, a mystic, a contemplative spectator of the comedy of death – that is how Maeterlinck presents himself to us in his work, and the introduction which he has prefixed to his translation of *L'Ornement des Noces Spirituelles* of Ruysbroeck l'Admirable shows how deeply he has studied the mystical writers of all ages, and how much akin to theirs is his own temper. Plato and Plotinus, Saint Bernard and Jacob Boehme, Coleridge and Novalis – he knows them all, and it is with a sort of reverence that he sets himself to the task of translating the astonishing Flemish mystic of the thirteenth century, known till now only by the fragments translated into French by Ernest Hello from a sixteenth-century Latin version. This translation and this introduction help to explain the real character of Maeterlinck's dramatic work – dramatic as to form, by a sort of accident, but essentially mystical. As a dramatist Maeterlinck has but one note – that of fear; he has but one method – that of repetition. This is no equipment for a Shakespeare, and it will probably be some time before Maeterlinck can recover from the literary damage of so incredible a misnomer.

In the preface to the first volume of the collected edition, which should be read with attention by all who are interested in knowing Maeterlinck's opinion of his own work, we are told: –

> *Quant aux deux petites pièces… je voudrais qu'il n'y eut aucun malentendu à leur endroit. Ce n'est pas parce qu'elles sont postérieures qu'il y faudrait chercher une évolution ou un nouveau désir. Ce sont, à proprement parler, de petits jeux de scène, de courts poèmes du genre assez malheureusement appelé "opéra-comique" destinés à fournir, aux musiciens qui les avaient demandés, un thème convenable à des développements lyriques. Ils ne prétendent à rien d'avantage, et l'on se méprendrait sur mes intentions si l'on y voulait trouver par surcroît de grandes arrière-pensées morales ou philosophiques.*

Maeterlinck may be taken at his word, and, if we take him at his word, we shall be the less disappointed. The two new plays are slight; they have neither the subtlety of meaning nor the strangeness of atmosphere which gives their quality of beauty and force to *Pelléas et Mélisande* and to *Les Aveugles*. *Soeur Béatrice* is a dramatic version of the legend which Davidson told effectively in the*Ballad of a Nun; Ariane et Barbe-Bleue* is a new reading of the legend of Blue-Beard. Both are written in verse, although printed as prose. It may be remembered that Maeterlinck once admitted that *La Princesse Maleine* was meant to be a kind of *verse libre*, and that he had originally intended to print it as verse. As it stands now it is certainly not verse in any real sense, where – as *Soeur Béatrice* is written throughout on the basis of the Alexandrine, although without rhyme. The mute *e* is, as in most modern French verse, sometimes sounded and sometimes not sounded; short lines are frequently interspersed among the lines of twelve syllables. Here are a few lines, taken at random, and printed as verse; –

> *Tu ne me réponds pas? Je n'entends pas ton souffle…*
> *Et tes genoux fléchissent…. Viens, viens,*
>   *n'attendons pas*
> *Que l'aurore envieuse tende ses pièges d'or*
> *Par les chemins d'azur qui mènent au bonheur.*

That is perfectly regular twelve-syllable verse with the exception of the second line, where the final *ent of fléchissent* is slurred. Twelve-syllable unrhymed verse is almost as disconcerting and unknown in English as in French, but it has been used, with splendid effect, by Blake, and it is a metre of infinite possibilities. The metre of *Ariane et Barbe-Bleue* (as Maeterlinck has finally decided to call it) is vaguer and more capricious; some of it is in twelve-syllable verse, some in irregular verse, and some in what can not be called verse at all. Take, for instance: –

Il parait qu'on pleurait dans les rues. – Pourquoi est-elle venue? On m'a dit qu'elle avait son idée. Il n'aura pas celle-ci.

The form in French is not, to our ears, successfully achieved; it seems to take a hesitating step upon the road which Paul Fort, in his *Ballades Françaises* has tramped along so vigorously, but in so doubtful a direction. Fort has published several volumes, which have been much praised by many of the younger critics, in which verse is printed as verse – verse which is sometimes rhymed and sometimes unrhymed, sometimes regular and sometimes irregular; and along with this verse there is a great deal of merely rhythmical prose, which is not more like verse than any page of *Salammbo*, or *À Rebours*, or *L'Étui de Nacre*. Now it seems to us that this indiscriminate mingling of prose and verse is for the good neither of prose nor of verse. It is a breaking down of limits without any conquest of new country. The mere printing of verse as prose, which Maeterlinck has favored, seems to us a travesty unworthy of a writer of beautiful prose or of beautiful verse.

Le Temple Enseveli is by no means equal, as literature or as philosophy, to *Le Trésor des Humbles*, or even to *La Sagesse et la Destinée*, but it is, like everything which Maeterlinck writes, full of brooding honesty of thought and of a grave moral beauty of feeling. It is the work of a thinker who "waits patiently," like a Christian upon divine grace, upon the secret voices which come to us out of the deepest places in our nature. He is absolutely openminded, his trust and his skepticism are alike an homage to truth. If what he has to say to us is not always "*la sagesse même*," it is at least the speech of one who has sought after wisdom more heedfully than any other writer of our time.

Le Double Jardin is a collection of essays which form a kind of postscript to *Le Temple Enseveli*. They are somewhat less abstract, perhaps a little more casual, than the essays in that book, and are concerned with subjects as varied as *The Wrath of the Bee*, *The Motor-Car*, and *Old-fashioned Flowers*. Maeterlinck has never written anything in prose more graceful, more homely, and more human than some of these pages, particularly those on flowers. In *The Leaf of Olive* and in *Death and the Crown* he carries speculation beyond the limits of our knowledge, and "thinks nobly," not of the soul alone, but also of the intelligence of man in its conflict with the deadly, unintelligent oppositions of the natural forces of the world. Such pages are fortifying, and we can not but be grateful for what is plausible in their encouragement. But the larger part of the book is made up of notes by the way, which have all the more charm because they are not too systematically arranged.

All, it is true, have some link of mutual relation, and proceed from a common center. It is curious to see this harmonizing instinct at work in the present arrangement of the essay now called *Éloge de l'Épée*. The main part of this essay was published in the *Figaro* in 1902 under the title *La Défense de l'Épée*. In the *Figaro* it began with a merely topical reference: –

> *L'autre jour, dans un article charmant, Alfred Capus prévoyait la fin de l'honneur, du moins de "l'honneur salle d'armes" et des instruments qui le protègent.*

Then followed two paragraphs questioning, a little vaguely,

> *si nous vivions dans une société qui nous protège suffisamment pour nous enlever, en toutes circonstances, le droit le plus doux et le plus cher à l'instinct de l'homme – celui de se faire justice à soi-même.*

In the essay as we now read it the topical reference has disappeared, and more than three pages are occupied by a discussion of abstract right, of essential justice, which seems to set, strangely and unexpectedly, a solid foundation under a structure not visibly resting on any foundation sufficient for its support. As the essay now stands it has its place in a system of which it becomes one more illustration.

Few of the essays in this book will be read with more interest than that on *The Modern Drama*. It is a development of the ideas already suggested by Maeterlinck in two prefaces. In asking where, under the conditions of modern life, and in the expression of modern ideas, we can find that background of beauty and of mystery which was like a natural atmosphere to Sophocles and to Shakespeare, he is asking, not indeed answering, a question which is being asked just now by all serious thinkers who are concerned with the present and the future of the drama. This suggestive essay should be contrasted and compared with a not less suggestive, but more audaciously affirmative essay, *De l'Évolution du Théâtre*, given as a lecture by André Gide, and reprinted at the beginning of the volume containing his two latest plays *Saul* and *Le Roi Candaule*. Everything that Gide writes is full of honest, subtle and unusual thought, and this consideration of the modern drama, though it asks more questions, not answering them, seems also to answer a few of the questions asked by Maeterlinck.

II

Le Trésor des Humbles is in some respects the most important, as it is certainly the most purely beautiful, of Maeterlinck's works. Limiting himself as he did in his plays to the rendering of certain sensations, and to the rendering of these in the most disembodied way possible, he did not permit himself to indulge either in the weight of wisdom or the adornment of beauty, each of which would have seemed to him (perhaps wrongly) as an intrusion. Those web-like plays, a very spider's work of filminess, allowed you to divine behind them one who was after all a philosopher rather than a playwright. The philosopher could but be divined, he was never seen. In these essays he has dropped the disguise of his many masks. Speaking without intermediary, he speaks more directly, with a more absolute abandonment of every convention of human reserve, except the reserve of an extreme fastidiousness in the choice of words simple enough and sincere enough to convey exactly his meaning, more spontaneously, it would seem, than any writer since Emerson. From Emerson he has certainly learned much; he has found, for instance, the precise form in which to say what he has to say, in little essays, not, indeed, so disconnected as Emerson's, but with a like care to say something very definite in every sentence, so that that sentence might stand by itself, without its context, as something more than a mere part of a paragraph. But his philosophical system, though it has its essential links with the great mystical system, which has developed itself through many manifestations, from Plotinus and Porphyry downward, is very much his own, and owes little to anything but his own meditation; and whether his subject is *La Beauté Intérieure* or *Les Femmes, Les Avertis* or *Le Tragique Quotidien*, it is with the same wisdom, certainty and beauty that he speaks. The book might well become the favorite reading of those persons to whom beauty must come with a certain dogmatism, if it is to be accepted for what it is. It reveals the inner life, with a simplicity which would seem the most obvious if it were not the rarest of qualities. It denies nothing, but it asserts many things, and it asserts nothing which has not been really seen.

In the preface to the first volume of his *Théâtre*, Maeterlinck takes us very simply into his confidence, and explains to us some of his intentions and some of his methods. He sees in *La Princesse Maleine* one quality, and one only: "*une certaine harmonie épouvantée et sombre.*" The other plays, up to *Aglavaine et Sélysette*, "*présentent une humanité et des sentiments plus précis, en proie à des forces aussi inconnues, mais un peu mieux dessinées.*" These unknown forces, "*au fond desquelles on trouve l'idée du Dieu chrétien, mêlée à celle de la fatalité antique,*" are realized, for the most part, under the form of death. A fragile, suffering, ignorant

▶ 42

humanity is represented struggling through a brief existence under the terror and apprehension of death. It is this conception of life which gives these plays their atmosphere, indeed their chief value. For, as we are rightly told, the primary element of poetry is

l'idée que la poète se fait de l'inconnu dans lequel flottent les êtres et les choses qu'il évoque, du mystère qui les domine et les juge et qui préside à leurs destinées.

This idea it no longer seems to him possible to represent honestly by the idea of death, and he asks: What is there to take its place?

Pour mon humble part, après les petits drames que j'ai énumérés plus haut, il m'a semblé loyal et sage d'écarter la mort de ce trône auquel il n'est pas certain qu'elle ait droit. Déjà, dans le dernier, que je n'ai pas nommé parmi les autres, dans "Aglavaine et Sélysette," j'aurais voulu qu'elle cédât à l'amour, à la sagesse ou au bonheur une part de sa puissance. Elle ne m'a pas obéi, et j'attends, avec la plupart des poètes de mon temps, qu'une autre force se révèle.

There is a fine and serious simplicity in these avowals, which show the intellectual honesty of Maeterlinck's dramatic work, its basis in philosophical thought. He is not merely a playwright who has found a method, he is a thinker who has to express his own conception of the universe, and therefore concerns literature. He finds that conception changing, and, for the moment, he stands aside, waiting. "The man who never alters his opinion," said Blake, "is like standing water, and breeds reptiles of the mind."

Aglavaine et Sélysette is the most beautiful play that Maeterlinck has yet written; it is as beautiful as *Le Trésor des Humbles*. Hitherto, in his dramatic prose, he has deliberately refrained from that explicit beauty of phrase which is to be found in almost every sentence of the essays. Implicit beauty there has been from the first, a beauty of reverie in which the close lips of his shadowy people seem afraid to do more than whisper a few vague words, mere hints of whatever dreams and thoughts had come to them out of the darkness. But of the elaborate beauty of the essays, in which an extreme simplicity becomes more ornate than any adornment, there has been, until now, almost nothing. In *Aglavaine et Sélysette* we have not merely beauty of conception and atmosphere, but writing which is beautiful in itself, and in which meditation achieves its own right to exist, not merely because it carries out that conception, or forms that atmosphere. And at the same time the very essence of the drama has been yet further spiritualized. Maeterlinck has always realized, better than any one else, the significance, in life and art, of mystery. He has realized how unsearchable is the darkness out of which we have but just stepped, and the darkness into which we are about to pass. And he has realized how the thought and sense of that twofold darkness invade the little space of light in which, for a moment, we move; the depth to which they shadow our steps, even in that moment's partial escape. But in some of his plays he would seem to have apprehended this mystery as a thing merely or mainly terrifying – the actual physical darkness surrounding blind men, the actual physical approach of death as a stealthy intruder into our midst; he has shown us people huddled at a window, out of which they almost feared to look, or beating at a door, the opening of which they dreaded. Fear shivers through these plays, creeping across our nerves like a damp mist coiling up out of a valley. And there is beauty certainly in this "vague spiritual fear;" but certainly a lower kind of beauty than that which gives its supreme pathos to *Aglavaine et Sélysette*. Here is mystery which is also pure beauty, in these delicate approaches of intellectual pathos, in which suffering and death and error become transformed into something almost happy, so full is it of strange light.

And, with this spiritualizing of the very substance of what had always been so fully a drama of things unseen, there comes, as we have said, a freer abandonment to the instinctive desire of the artist to write beautifully. Having realized that one need not be afraid of beauty, he is not afraid to let soul speak to soul in language worthy of both. And, curiously, at the same time he becomes more familiar, more human. Sélysette is quite the most natural character that Maeterlinck has ever drawn, as Aglavaine is the most noble. Méléandre is, perhaps, more shadowy than ever, but that is because he is deliberately subordinated in the composition, which is concerned only with the action upon one another of the two women. He suffers the action of these forces, does not himself act; standing between them as man stands between the calling of the intellectual and the emotional life, between the simplicity of daily existence, in which he is good, affectionate, happy, and the perhaps "immoral" heightening of that existence which is somewhat disastrously possible in the achievement of his dreams. In this play, which touches so beautifully and so profoundly on so many questions, this eternal question is restated; of course, not answered. To answer it would be to find the missing word in the great enigma; and to Maeterlinck, who can believe in nothing which is not mystery, it is of the essence of his philosophy not to answer his own question.

EMILY BRONTË

It is one hundred years to a month – I write in August – that Emily Brontë was born; she was born in August, 1818, and died December 19th, 1848, at the age of thirty. The stoic in woman has been seen once only, and that in the only woman in whom there is seen the paradox of passion without sensuousness. She required no passionate experience to endow her with more than a memory of passion. Passion was alive in her as flame is alive in the earth. Her poems are all outcries, as her great novel, *Wuthering Heights*, is one long outcry. Rossetti in 1854 wrote: "I've been greatly interested in *Wuthering Heights*, the first novel I've read for an age, and the best (as regards power and style only) for two ages, except *Sidonia*. But it is a fiend of a book. The action is laid in hell – only it seems places and people have English names there." He is not altogether right in what he says, and yet there is hell in the heart of Heathcliff, that magnificent and malevolent gypsy, who, to my mind, can only be compared with Borrow's creations in *Lavengro* and *The Romany Rye* – such as the immortal Jasper Petilengro and the immoral Ursula – and with the lesser creations of Meredith's in *The Adventures of Harry Richmond* (in spite of the savage and piteous and fascinating Kiomi – I have seen a young gypsy girl of this name the other day, tragical).

When Charlotte says of Emily that what "her mind had gathered of the real concerning the people around her was too exclusively confined to their tragic and terrible traits, out of which she created Earnshaw and Catherine, and that having formed these beings, she did not know what she had done," there is no doubt that on the whole she is right. For these spirits are relentless and implacable, fallen and lost spirits, and it is only in this amazing novel that I find maledictions and curses and cries of anguish and writhings of agony and raptures of delight and passionate supplications, such as only abnormal creatures could contrive to express, and within the bounded space of the moors, made sad by somber sunrises and glad by radiant sunsets. It is sad colored and desolate, but when gleams of sunlight or of starlight pierce the clouds that hang generally above it a rare and sunny beauty comes into the bare outlines, quickening them with living splendor.

In the passionately tragic genius of Emily I find a primitive nature-worship; so strangely primitive that that wonderful scene of mad recrimination between the dying Catherine and the repentant Heathcliff, when she cries "I forgive you! Forgive me!" and he answers: "Kiss me again; and don't let me see your eyes. I forgive what you have done to me. I love *my* murderer – but *yours?* How can I?" is almost comparable with a passage in *Macbeth* where Banquo speaks of "the temple-haunting Martlet" and its loved masonry which preludes Lady Macbeth's entrance from under the buttresses as the delicate air bears witness to the incarnate murder that swarms, snake-like, hidden under grass. Something of Emily's saturnine humor comes into the mouth of the Calvinistic farm-servant, whose jests are as grim and as deadly and as plague-like as the snow-storms that make winter unendurable.

Yes, this creator has, in herself and in her imagination, something solitary and sorrowful – that of a woman who lived, literally, alone – and whose genius had no scorn. She, who believed in the indestructible God within herself, was silenced forever; herself and her genius which had moved as a wind and moved as the sea in tumult and moved as the thunderclouds in fury upon the tragical and perilous waters of passion that surround "the topless towers" of *Wuthering Heights.*

In one who, like Emily Brontë, was always dying of too much life, one can imagine the sensitive reticences, the glowing eyes, and the strain of the vehemences of that inner fire that fed on itself, which gave her her taciturnity. "It is useless to ask her; you get no answers. The awful point was that, while full of ruth for others, on herself she had no pity; the spirit was inexorable to the flesh; from the trembling hand, the unnerved limbs, the fading eyes, the same service was exacted as they had rendered in health."

"The spirit inexorable to the flesh:" there is the whole secret of what in her life was her genius. Alone with herself – with her soul and her body – she allows herself no respite: for she was always of an unresting nature. So in the words of Pater – who told me of his enormous admiration for her prose – "we are all *condamnés à mort avec des sursis indéfinis*; we have our interval and then our place knows us no more." How she spent these "intervals" must be forever unknown. Not in high passions, I imagine, nor in wisdom, nor in care for material things; but in moods of passion, in intellectual excitement, in an inexhaustible curiosity, in an ironical contemplation "of the counted pulses of a variegated, dramatic life." But never, I am certain, was she ever capable – as she watches the weaving and unweaving of herself – of the base corruption of what his existence was to Beardsley. "That he should be so honest with his fear," I have written of him, "that he should sit down before its face and study it feature by feature: that he should never turn aside his eyes for more than one instant, make no attempt to escape, but sit at home with it, travel with it, see it in his mirror, taste it in the sacrament: that is the marvellous thing, and the sign of his fundamental sincerity in life and art."

Emily Brontë's passionate and daring genius attains this utmost limit of tragedy, and with this a sense – an extreme sense – of the mystery of terror which lurks in all the highest poetry as certainly in her lyrical prose; a quality which distinguishes such prose and verse from all that is but a little lower than the highest. Her genius is somber in the sense that Webster's is, but much less dramatic. Neither his tragedies nor her novel are well-constructed; and in her case something is certainly lacking; for her narrative is dominated by sheer chance, and guided by mere accident. And I think that she, with her sleepless imagination, might have said as the child Giovanni in Webster's Tragedy says: "I have not slept these six nights. When do the dead walk?" and is answered: "When God shall please." When in disguise she sings of the useless rebellions of the earth, rarely has a more poignant cry been wrenched out of "a soul on the rack" – that is to say since Santa Teresa sang: –

> A soul in God hidden from sin,
> What more desires for thee remain,
> Save but to love, and love again
> And, all on flame, with love within,
> Love on, and turn to love again?

than this stanza:

> O! dreadful is the shock – intense the agony –
> When the ear begins to hear, and the eye begins to see;
> When the pulse begins to throb, the brain to think again,
> The soul to feel the flesh and the flesh to feel the chain.

At times there is a tragic sublimity in her imagination, which gathers together, as it were, the winds from the world's four quarters, that howled in winter nights across the moor around the house she lived in. Indeed the very storm of her genius hovers in the air between things sublime and things hideous. "There never was such a thunderstorm of a play," said Swinburne on Cyril Tourneur's *Revenger's Tragedy*. I am inclined to add: "There never was such a thunderstorm of a novel as *Wuthering Heights*." And it is blood-stained with the blood of the roses of sunsets; the heavy atmosphere is sultry as the hush and heat and awe of midnoon;

sad visions appear with tragic countenances, fugitives try in vain to escape from the insane brooding of their consciences. And there are serviceable shadows; implacable self-devotions and implacable cruelties; vengeances unassuaged; and a kind of unscrupulous ferocity is seen not only in Heathcliff but in one of his victims. And there are startling scenes and sentences that, once impressed on the memory, are unforgettable: as scarlet flowers of evil and as poisonous weeds they take root in one.

ON ENGLISH AND
FRENCH FICTION

I

Certainly the modern English novel begins with that elaborate masterpiece, *Tom Jones*, of Henry Fielding. And it seems to me that his genius is contained, on the whole, in that one book; in which he creates living people; the very soil is living. His hero is the typical sullen, selfish, base-born, stupid, sensual, easily seduced and adventurous youth, with whom his creator is mightily amused. The very Prefaces are full of humorous wisdom; copied, I suppose, from Montaigne. The typically wicked woman is painted almost as Hogarth might have painted her. It is quite possible that she may have a few touches, here and there, of Lady Wishfort, who, wrote Meredith, "is unmatched for the vigour and pointedness of the tongue. It spins along with a final ring, like the voice of Nature in a fury, and is, indeed, racy eloquence of the elevated fishwife."

Fielding has a strong sense of the vigilant comic, which is the genius of thoughtful laughter, but never serving as a public advocate. Contempt can not be entertained by comic intelligence. Blifil is essentially the grossly and basely animal creature, who is also a villain, and who has his part in the plot; indeed one scandalous scene in which he is discovered is laughable in the purely comic sense.

Jonathan Wild presents a case of peculiar distinction, when that man of eminent greatness remarks on the unfairness of a trial in which the condemnation has been brought about by twelve men of the opposite party; yet it is immensely comic to hear a guilty villain protesting that his own "party" should have a voice in the Law. It opens an avenue into a villain's ratiocination, as in Lady Booby's exclamation when Joseph defends himself: "Your *virtue!* I shall never survive it!" Fielding can be equally satiric and comic: can raise laughter but never move pity. And it is as he evokes great spirits that Meredith cries: "O for a breath of Aristophanes, Rabelais, Voltaire, Cervantes, Fielding, Molière! These are spirits that, if you know them well, will come when you do call."

After Fielding comes Thackeray, and his *Vanity Fair* is the second masterpiece in modern fiction. It is the work of a man of the world, keenly observant of all the follies and virtues and vices and crimes and splendors, of crimes and of failures, of his neither moral nor immoral Fair. He takes his title from John Bunyan; but in originality he is almost equal with Fielding. "As the Manager of the Performance sits before the curtain on the boards, and looks into the Fair, a feeling of profound melancholy comes over him in his survey of the bustling place." Such is the moral, if you like; at any rate the whole Show "is accompanied by appropriate scenery and brilliantly illuminated with the author's own candles." At the end the Finis: "Ah! *Vanitas Vanitatum!* Which of us is happy in this world? Which of us has his desire? or, having it, is satisfied? – Come children, let us shut up the box and the puppets, for our play is played out."

There is no question that Becky Sharp is not derived from Balzac's Lisbeth in *La Cousine Bette,* but at what a distance, when once you think of the greatest of all novelists, who has the fortune to be French, and of Thackeray, who has the fortune (at times the misfortune) of being English. When we thing of Becky she startles us by her cynical entrance: she inherits from her parents bad qualities. Her first epigram sums her up. "Revenge may be wicked, but it's natural. I'm no angel." She fascinates Lord Pitt, Rawdon Crawley and Lord Steyne in a way Lisbeth never does. Lisbeth's fascination is that of the evil-doer; she is envious, spiteful, malicious, a lying hypocrite; always deliberately bent on having her own way, always for evil purposes: so that she, in her sinister effrontery, causes the ruin of many of the lives she thrives on, feigns to help, deludes; only, she never deludes as Valérie Marnette does. We have only to say: "Valérie!" and the woman is before us. As for Valérie: "*Elle était belle comme sont belles les femmes assez belles, pour être belles en dormant;*" a sentence certainly lyrical. Lisbeth's character has "*Une dose du mordant parisien.*" Unmarried, she is monstrous, her snares are inevitable, her dissimulation impenetrable. But she is never given a scene so consummately achieved in its sordid and voluptuous tragedy as the scene in *Vanity Fair* when Rawdon enters his house at midnight, and finds Becky dressed in a brilliant toilet, her arms and her fingers sparkling with bracelets and rings, and the brilliants in her breast which Steyne had given her. "He had her hand in his, and was bowing to kiss it, when Becky started up with a faint scream as she caught sight of Rawdon's white face." And, as the writer adds, with an entire sense of the tragic and comic drama that is over: "All her lies and her schemes, all her selfishness and her wiles, all her wit and all her genius had come to this bankruptcy."

I have never had any actual admiration for the novels of George Eliot; she had her passing fame, her popularity, her success; people compared her prose – wrongly – with the poetry of Mrs. Browning; and, as for her attempts at verse, the less said of them the better. In favor of my opinion I quote this scathing sentence of Swinburne: "Having no taste for the dissection of dolls, I shall leave Daniel Deronda in his natural place above the ragshop door; and having no ear for the melodies of a Jew's harp, I shall leave the Spanish Gypsy to perform on that instrument to such audience as she may collect." Certainly Charlotte Brontë excelled George Eliot in almost every quality; the latter having, perhaps, more knowledge and culture, but not for a moment comparable with Charlotte's purity of passion, depth and fervor of feeling, inspiration, imagination and a most masterly style.

As for her *Romola*, I find it almost an elaborate failure in the endeavor to create the atmosphere of the period of Savonarola – that amazing age when the greatest spirits of the world were alive and producing works of unsurpassable genius – and in her too anatomical demonstration of the varying vices and virtues of Tito: for she has none of that strange subtlety that a writer of novels must possess to delineate how this human soul may pass in the course of decomposition into some irremediable ruin. She is too much of the moralist to be able to present this character as a necessary and natural figure, such as far greater writers have had no difficulty in doing. She presents him – rather after the fashion of George Sand, as a fearful and warning example. Think, for a moment, – the comparison is all but impossible, – of this attempt at characterization with Browning's Guido Franceschini; for in his two monologues every nerve of the mind is touched by the patient scalpel, every joint and vein of the subtle and intricate spirit laid bare and divided. Compare this also with Cenci: the comparison has been made by Swinburne, with an equal praise of two masterpieces, *The Cenci* of Shelley and *The Ring and the Book* of Browning. Both Cenci and Franceschini are cunningly drawn and colored so as to be absolute models of the highest form of realism: as cunningly colored and drawn as the immortal creation of Madame Bovary.

Take, for instance, the character of Rochester in *Jane Eyre*. It is incomparable of its kind; an absolutely conceived living being, who has enough nerves and enough passion to more or less extinguish the various male characters in George Eliot's novels. That Maggie Tulliver, in *The Mill on the Floss*, the finest of her novels, can be moved to any sense but that of bitter disgust and sickening disdain by a thing – I will not write, a man – of Stephen Guest's character, is a lamentable and an ugly case of shameful failure; for as Swinburne says, "The last word of realism has surely been spoken, the last abyss of cynicism has surely been sounded and laid bare." And I am glad to note here that he dismisses her with this reference to three great French writers; using, of course, his invariable ironical paradoxes. "For a higher view and a more cheery aspect of the sex, we must turn back to those gentler teachers, those more flattering painters of our own – Laclos, Stendhal and Merrimée; we must take up *La Double Méprise* – or *Le Rouge et le Noir* – or *Les Liaisons Dangereuses.*"

The genius of George Meredith is unquestionable; he was as great a creator, in fact a greater creator, than any other English novelist; yet his fascination is not, I think, quite explicable. Not since the Elizabethans have we had so flame-like a life possessing the wanton body of a style. Our literature has not a more vividly entertaining book than *The Shaving of Shagpat* – I have the rare first edition of 1856 in my possession – nor has the soul of a style been lost more spectacularly. And with this fantastic, learned, poetic, passionate, intelligent style, a style which might have lent itself so well to the making of Elizabethan drama, Meredith has set himself the task of writing novels of contemporary life; nor can it be wondered that every novel of his breaks every rule which could possibly be laid down for the writing of a novel. Why has his prose so irresistible a fascination for so many of us, as it certainly has? I find Meredith breaking every canon of what are to me the laws of the novel; and yet I read him in preference to any other novelist.

Meredith first conceives that the novelist's prime study is human nature and his first duty to be true to it. Moreover, being an artist, he is not content with simple observations; there must be creation, the imaginative fusion of the mass of observed fact. The philosophy of his seeking is only another name for intuition, analysis, imaginative thought. He has comprehension of a character from height to depth through that "eye of steady flame," which he attributes to Shakespeare, and which may be defined in every great artist. He sees it, he beholds a complete nature, at once and in entirety. His task is to make others see what he sees. But this can not be done at a stroke. It must be done little by little, touch upon touch, light upon shade, shade upon light. The completeness, as seen by the seer or creator – the term is the same – must be microscopically investigated, divided into its component parts, produced piece by piece, and connected visibly. It is this that is meant when we talk of analysis; and the antithesis between analysis and creation is hardly so sheer as it seems. Partly through a selection of appropriate action, partly through the revealing casual speech, the imagined character takes palpable form: finally it does, or it should, live and breathe before the reader with some likeness of the hue and breadth of actual life. But there is a step farther, and it is this step that Meredith is strenuous to take. You have the flesh, animate it with spirit, with soul. If this is an unworthy aim, condemn Shakespeare. This is Meredith's, and it is this and no other consummation that he prays for in demanding philosophy in fiction.

The main peculiarity of Meredith's style is this: he thinks, to begin with, before writing – a singular thing, one must observe, for the present day. Then, having certain definite thoughts to express, and thoughts frequently of a difficult remoteness, he is careful to employ words of a rich and fruitful significance, made richer and more fruitful by a studied and uncommon arrangement. His sentences are architectural; and it is natural in reading him to cry out at the strangeness. Strange, certainly; often obscure, often tantalizing; more often magnificent and somber and strong and passionate, his wit is perhaps too fantastical, too remote, too allusive; partly because it is subtly ironical; perhaps most of all because it is shrewdly stinging to our prejudices. Still, everywhere, the poet, struggling against the bondage of prose, flings himself on every opportunity of evading his bondage. It is thus by the very quality that is his distraction – perhaps because he always writes English as if it were a learned language – that Meredith holds us, by the intensity of his vision of a world which is not our world, by the energy of genius which has done so much to achieve the impossible.

II

Prose is the language of what we call real life, and it is only in prose that an illusion of external reality can be given. Compare the whole process and existence of character in a play of Shakespeare and in a novel of Balzac. I choose Balzac among novelists because his mind is nearer to what is creative in the poet's mind than that of a novelist, and his method nearer to the method of the poet. Take King Lear and take Père Goriot. Goriot is a Lear at heart, and he suffers the same tortures and humiliations. But precisely where Lear grows up before the mind's eye into a vast cloud and shadowy mountain of trouble, Goriot grows downward into the earth and takes root there, wrapping the dust about all his fibers. Lear may exchange his crown for the fool's bauble, knowing nothing of it; but Goriot knows well enough the value of every bank-note that his daughters rob him of. In that definiteness, that new power of "stationary" emotion in a firm and material way, lies one of the great opportunities of prose.

The genius of prose is essentially different from the "genius of poetry;" and that is the reason why writers like De Quincy and Ruskin trespassed, as thieves do, on forbidden ground. It is much better to pick forbidden fruit and to eat thereof, and be as stealthy as the traveler in Blake's deliciously wicked poem who steals from the unloved lover the woman he loves:

Soon after she has gone from me
A traveller came by,
Silently, invisibly:
He took her with a sigh.

The moral of it is "Never seek to sell thy love;" but such writers as those I have referred to tread fallen fruit ruthlessly under foot and therefore ought to be thrust out of the garden they have robbed. Both tried to write prose as if they were writing verse, and both failed; Ruskin ruined by his fatal facility and De Quincy by his cultivating eloquence in rhetoric. Certain prose writers have written lyrical prose, because their genius at times drove them to do so, and with an absolute success. One finds such passages in Shakespeare and Blake and Pater and Lamb; in certain pages of Balzac and of Flaubert and of Meredith and of Conrad. Yet, in what I must call lyrical prose, there is a certain rhythm, but not that of rhymed verse; that is to say, if the inspiration were the same, the mediums are different: the rhythm of prose that has no meter and the rhythm of verse that has meter.

Take, for instance, Peacock, who was neither a great prose writer nor a great poet, but whose novels are unique in English, and are among the most scholarly, original and entertaining prose writings of the century.

> A strain too learned for a shallow age,
> Too wide for selfish bigots, let his page
> Which charms the chosen spirits of the time
> Fold itself up for the serener clime
> Of years to come, and find its recompense
> In that just expectation.

So Shelley praises him, who was certainly aware of Peacock's clever scraps of rhyming that are like no other verse; the masterpiece being the comically heroic *War-Song of Dinar Valor*, which the author defines as "the quintessence of all war songs that were ever written, and the sum and substances of all the appetences, tendencies and consequences of military." This learned wit, his satire upon the vulgarity of progress (in which he is one with Baudelaire and one with Meredith) are more continuously present in his prose than in his verse; yet his characters are caricatures, they speak a language that is not ours; they are given sensational adventures, often comical in the extreme; and in these pages plenty of nonsense and of laughter and of satire and of serious prose with an undercurrent of bitter cynicism. He treats all his creatures cruelly, and I can not help seeing the reason why Richard Garnett admired his prose so much: that there is something curiously alike and unlike in their humor.

Garnett himself told me, as I always thought, that *The Twilight of the Gods* was far and away the best book he had written. In France Marcel Schwob and André Gide have done certain things comparable in their way with these learned inventions, these ironic "criticisms of life," these irreverent classical burlesques in which religion, morality, learning, and all civilization's conventions, are turned topsy-turvy, and presented in the ridiculousness of their unaccustomed attitude. But no modern man in England has done anything remotely comparable with them, and neither Schwob nor André Gide has heaped mockery so high as in *Abdullah the Adite*, and remained as sure a master of all the reticences of art and manners. This learned mockery has an undefinable quality, macabre, diabolical, a witchcraft of its own, which I can find in no other writer.

To return to the question of rhythm, the rhythm of prose, for one thing, is physiological, the rhythm of poetry is musical. There is in every play of Ibsen a rhythm perfect of its kind, but it is the physiological rhythm of prose. The rhythm of a play of Shakespeare speaks to the blood like wine or music: it is with exultation, with intoxication, that we see or read *Antony and Cleopatra* or even *Richard II*; it gives us exactly the same intoxication and the same exultation when we hear Vladimir de Pachmann play the piano, when we hear Wagner's *Tristan*. But the rhythm of a play of Ibsen is like that of a diagram in Euclid; it is the rhythm of logic, and it produces in us the purely mental exaltation of a problem solved.

III

Is not a criticism of primary ideas, the only kind of criticism, when one considers it, that is really worth writing? A critic may tell us that So-an-So has written a charming book, that it is the best of his charming books, that it is better or worse than another book by another writer with whom we see no necessity to compare him, that it is, in short, an "addition to literature;" well and good, here is some one's opinion, perhaps right, perhaps wrong; not very important if right, not easy to disprove if wrong. But let him tell us, in noting the precise quality of *À Rebours*, and its precise divergence from the tradition of naturalism: "*Il ne s'agissait plus tant de faire entrer dans l'art, par la représentation, l'extériorité brute, que de tirer de cette extériorité même des motifs de rêve et de la révélation intérieure;*" let him tell us in discussing the question of literary sincerity that a certain writer "*est sincère, non parce qu'il avoue toute sa pensée, mais parce qu'il pense tout son aveu:*" has he not added to the very substance of our thought, or touched that substance with new light?

The curious thing in regard to Benjamin Constant is that there was not a single interest, out of the many that occupied his life, which he did not destroy by some inconsequence of action, for no reason in the world, apparently, except some irrational necessity of doing exactly the opposite of what he ought to have done, of what he wanted to do. So he creates *Adolphe* so much of himself in it, and makes him say, in a memorable sentence, "*Je me reposais, pour ainsi dire, dans l'indifférence des autres, de la fatigue de son amour.*" He was never tired of listening to himself, and the acute interest of his Journal consists in the absolute sincerity of its confessions, and at the same time the scrutinizing self-consciousness of every word that is written down. "*Il y a en moi deux personnes, dont l'en observe l'autre.*" So cold-hearted is he that when perhaps his best friend, Mademoiselle Talma, is dying, he spends day and night by her bedside, overwhelmed with grief; and he writes in his Journal: "*Y étudie la mort.*" So out of this distressing kind of reality which afflicts the artist, he creates his art, *Adolphe*, a masterpiece of psychological narrative, from which the modern novel of analysis may have been said to have arisen, which is simply a human document in which he has told us the story of his liaison with the writer of *Corinne*. She made him suffer for he writes: *"Tous les volcans sont moins flamboyants qu'elle."* He suffers, as his hero does, because he can neither be intensely absorbed, nor, for one moment, indifferent; that very spirit of analysis which would seem to throw some doubt on the sincerity of his passion, does but intensify the acuteness with which he feels it. It is the turning of the sword in a wound. He sums up and typifies the artistic temperament at its acutest point of weakness; the temperament which can neither resist, nor dominate, nor even wholly succumb to, emotion; which is forever seeking its own hurt, with the persistence almost of mania; which, if it ruins other lives in the pursuit, as is supposed, of artistic purposes, gains at all events no personal satisfaction out of the bargain; except, indeed, when one has written *Adolphe*, the satisfaction of having lived unhappily for more than sixty years, and left behind one a hundred pages that are still read with admiration, sixty years afterward.

Flaubert, possessed of an absolute belief that there exists but one way of expressing one thing, one word to call it by, one adjective to qualify, one verb to animate it, gave himself to superhuman labors for the discovery, in every phrase, of that word, that verb, that adjective. And the desperate certitude in his spirit always was: "Among all the expressions in the world, all forms and turns of expression, there is but *one* – one form, one mode – to express all I want to say." He desired, above all things, impersonality; and yet, in spite of the fact that he is the most impersonal of novelists, the artist is always felt; for as Pater said: "his subjectivity must and will color the incidents, as his very bodily eye selects the aspects of things." Yet again, in spite of the fact that Flaubert did keep *Madame Bovary* at a great distance from himself, we find in these pages the analyst and the lyric poet in equilibrium. It is the history of a woman, as carefully observed as any story that has ever been written, and observed in surroundings of the most extraordinary kind. He creates Emma cruelly, morbidly, marvelously; he creates in her, as Baudelaire says, the adulterous woman with a depraved imagination. *"Elle se donne"* he writes, *"magnifiquement, généreusement, d'une manière toute masculine, à des drôles qui ne sont pas ses égaux, exactement comme les poètes se livrent a des drôlesses."*

As Flaubert invented the rhythm of every sentence I choose this one from the novel I have referred to, this magnificently tragic sentence: *"Et Emma se mit à rire, d'un rire atroce, frénétique, désespéré, croient voir la face hideuse du misérable qui se dressait dans les ténèbres éternelles comme un épouvantant."* Aeschylus might have put such words as these on the lying and crying lips of Clytemnestra in her atrocious speech after she has slain Agamemnon. With this compare a sentence I translate from Petrus Bórel. "I have often heard that certain insects were made for the amusement of children: perhaps man also was created for the same pleasures of superior beings, who delight in torturing him, and disport themselves in his groans." This is a sentence which might almost have been written by Hardy, so clearly does it state, in an image like one of his own, the very center of his philosophy. Take, for example, these sentences in *The Return of the Native*: "Yet, upon the whole, neither the man nor the woman lost dignity by sudden death. Misfortune had struck them gracefully, cutting off their erratic histories with a catastrophic dash."

Swinburne, who invariably overpraises Victor Hugo, over-praises his atrocious novel *L'Homme qui rit*. But I forgive him everything when he writes such Baudelairean sentences as these:

Bakilphedro, who plays the part of devil, is a bastard begotten by Iago upon his sister, Madame de Merteuil; having something of both, but diminished and degraded; wanting, for instance, the deep daemonic calm of their lifelong patience. He has too much heat of discontent, too much fever and fire, to know their perfect peace of spirit, the equable element of their souls, the quiet of mind in which they live and work out their work at leisure. He does not sin at rest, there is somewhat of fume and fret in his wickedness. There is the peace of the devil, which passeth all understanding.

Certainly, for an absolutely diabolical dissection of three equally infamous characters, this is unsurpassable. Iago is not entirely malignant, nor is he abjectly vile, nor is he utterly dishonest: he is supreme in evil, and almost as far above vice as he is beyond virtue. He has not even a fleshly desire for Desdemona: yet he is the impassioned villain who "spins the plot." Can one conceive, as Swinburne conjectures, "something of Iago's attitude in hell – of his unalterable and indomitable posture for all eternity?" As for Madame Merteuil she is, in *Les Liaisons dangereuses*, not only a counterfoil for Valmont, but a spirit of almost inconceivable malignity; yet she is not as abnormal as Iago. She has a sublime lack of virtue, with an immense sense of her seductiveness. There is no grandeur in her evil, as there is in Valmont's. In the longest letter she writes, that Baudelaire praises, she confesses herself with so curious a shamelessness as to intrigue one. In composing this for her Laclos shows the most sinister side of his genius. He shows her sterility, her depraved imagination, her deceit and her dissimulations: rarely the humiliations she has endured. As she is resolved on the ruin of Valmont she writes in this fashion: "*Séduite par votre réputation, il me semblait que vous manquiez à ma gloire; je brûlais de vous combattre corps à corps.*" She is not even a criminal, not even the symbol of one of the poisonous women of the Renaissance, who smiled complacently after an assassination. Her nature is perverted by the lack of the intoxication of crime. The imagination which stands to her in the place of virtue has brought its revenge, and for her, too, there is only the release of death.

"*Tout les livres sont immoraux,*" wrote Baudelaire in his notes on this book: certainly a sweeping paradox, for there is much less immorality in Laclos' novel than in Rabelais or in Swift or in Aristophanes. Still as he wrote this book in the time of the French

Revolution, there was more than enough of hell-creating material in the age of Robespierre and Marat and Danton and Mirabeau, who wrote the infamous *Erotika Biblion*. It is amusing to note that in Perlet-Malassis's reprint in 1866 the writer of a preface dated 1832 says: *"Le style de Mirabeau, par cette vive puissance de la pensée que resplendit de son propre éclat sans rien emprunter aux ornements de l'art, s'élève dans cet ouvrage jusqu'aux beautés les plus sublimes."* Exactly a year before Mirabeau's book appeared Laclos printed his novel; and, for what I must call the sublimity of casuistry, here is one consummate sentence of Valmont's. *"Je ne sortais de ses bras que pour tomber à ses genoux, pour lui jurer un amour éternel, et, il faut tout avouer, je pensais ce que je disais."*

IV

George Borrow has always had a curious fascination for me: for this man, half Cornish and half French, with his peculiar kind of genius – such as one generally finds in mixed blood – is both creative and inventive, normal and abnormal, perverse and unpassionate, obscure and grimly humorous. I was very young when I read his masterpiece *Lavengro* (1851) in its original three volumes, from which I got my first taste for a sort of gypsy element in literature. The reading of that book did many things for me. It absorbed me from the first page with a curiously personal appeal, as of some one akin to me: the appeal, I suppose, to what was wild in my blood.

What Borrow really creates is a by no means undiscovered world: I mean the world of the Gypsies; yet he is the first to discover their peculiar characteristics, their savagery and uncivilization; he gives them life, in their tents, on the road, along the hedges; he makes them speak, in their pure and corrupted dialects, much as they always speak, but nearly always with something of Borrow in them. They are imaginative: he gives them part of his imagination. They are not subtle, nor is he; they are not complex, he at times is complex; he paints their morality and immorality almost as Hogarth might have done.

In regard to the sense of fear, you find it in Shakespeare, in Balzac, everywhere; but never I think more intensely than in the chapters in *Lavengro* describing Borrow's paroxysm of fear in the dingle. There is nothing of the kind, in any language, equal to those pages of Borrow; they go deep down into some "obscure night of the soul;" they are abnormal. It is "the screaming horror" that takes possession of him.

> The evil one was upon me; the inscrutable horror which I had felt from boyhood had once more taken possession of me. I uttered wild cries. I sat down with my back against a thorn-bush; the thorns entered my flesh, and when I felt them, I pressed harder against the bush: I thought the pain of the flesh might in some degree counteract the mental agony; presently I felt them no longer – the power of the mental horror was so great that it was impossible, with that upon me, to feel my pain from the thorns.

Borrow writes as if civilization did not exist, and he obtains, in his indirect way, an extraordinary directness. Really the most artificial of writers, he is always true to that "peculiar mind and system of nerves" of which he was so well aware, and which drove him into all sorts of cunning ways of telling the truth, and making it at once bewildering and convincing.

I have often wondered why Robert Louis Stevenson was almost invariably looked on as a man of genius. He had touches of it, certainly; and therein lies part of the secret of his captivating the heart; why, quite by himself, he ranks with writers like Thoreau and with Dumas (one for a certain seductiveness of manner, the other for his extravagant passion for miraculous adventures); and why he appeals to us, not only from his curious charm as a literary vagrant – to some of us an irresistible charm – and from the exhilaration of the blood which he causes in us, and from the actual fever of his prose, and for his inhuman sense of life's whimsical distresses, of its cruelties and maladies and confusions, but from a certain gypsy and wayward grace, so like a woman's, that can thrill to the blood often more instantly than in the presence of the august perfection of classic beauty.

His style, as he admits, is never wholly original; a "sedulous ape," as he once humorously named himself, that aped the styles of Baudelaire and Hawthorne and Lamb and Hazlitt; and that never, except rarely and by certain happy accidents in his rejection of words and using some of them as if no one had ever used them before, attains the inevitable perfection of Baudelaire's prose style, nor the quintessential and exultant and tragic style of Lamb, which has, beyond any writer preeminent for charm, salt and sting; nor Montaigne's malign trickery of style, his roving imagination, his preoccupation with himself, who said so splendidly: "I have no other end in writing but to discover myself, who also shall peradventure be another thing to-morrow."

As in a tragic drama so in a tragic novel we must not forbid an artist in fiction to set before us strange instances of inconsistency and eccentricity in conduct as well as in action; but we require of him that he should make us feel such aberrations to be as clearly inevitable as they are certainly exceptional. Balzac has done that and Flaubert and Goncourt and Maupassant and Conrad. All these, at their greatest, are inevitable; only no novelist is ever consistently great. Reade's Griffith Gaunt is not, as he ought to have been, inevitable; for what is tragic and pathetic and eccentric in his character is flawed by the writer's failure in showing what ought to have been the intolerable and irresistible force of the temptation; his art is an act of envy, therefore a base act, and has none of the grandeur of Othello's jealousy, which makes one love him the more for that, more even because he is unconscious of Iago's poisoned tongue. Leontes excites our repulsion: he is a coward, selfish and deluded and ignoble.

At his finest I find in Charles Reade certain adventures almost worthy of Dumas; only he never had that overflowing negro-like genius of the French novelist; who can be tedious at times, and can write very badly when he likes, for he never had much of a style. Yet, with all his suspense and the suddenness of his vivid action and of the living conversation of furiously living creatures, he does really carry us along in an amazing way; equally in the tragic figure Edmund Dantès as in those of d'Artagnan and Aramis and Porthos. Among Reade's many faults is the inability to blot when he ought to have blotted, to abstain, as he too often did not, from ostentation and self-praise, by the fact that he can not always get far enough away from what to him was the pernicious atmosphere of the stage.

The Picture of Dorian Gray (1891) is partly made out of Wilde himself, partly out of two other men, both of whom are alive. Not being creative he was cruel enough to mix his somewhat poisonous color after the fashion of an impressionistic painter, and so to give a treble reflection of three different temperaments instead of giving one. In any case, as Pater wrote: "Dorian himself, though a quite unsuccessful experiment in Epicureanism, in life as a fine art, is (till his inward spoiling takes visible effect suddenly, and in a moment, at the end of his story) a beautiful creature."

His peculiar kind of beauty might be imaged by a strangely colored Eastern vessel, and hidden within it, a few delicate young serpents. For he has something of the coiled up life of the serpents, in his poisonous sins; sins he communicates to others, ruining their youthful lives with no deliberate malice, but simply because he can not help it. He has no sense of shame, even in his most ignoble nights. Sin is a thing that writes itself across a man's face; but secret vices can not be concealed; one sees them in the mere ironical curl of sinister lips, or in the enigmatical lifting of an eyelid. He has made the devil's bargain, but not in the sense in which Faustus sells his soul to Satan; yet he is always entangled in the painted sins, the more and more hideous aspects, of his intolerably accusing portrait, taken, certainly, in Wilde's usual manner, from *La Peau de Chagrin* of Balzac; only, and therein lies the immense difference, the man's life never shrinks, but the very lines and colors of his painted image shrivel, until the thing itself – the thing he has come to hate as one hates hell – has its revenge.

A passion for caprice, a whimsical Irish temperament, a love of art for art's sake – it is in such qualities as these that I find the origin of the beautiful force of estheticism, the exquisite echoes of the poems, the subtle decadence of *Dorian Gray*, and the paradoxical truths, the perverted common sense of the *Intentions*. Certainly, as Pater realized, Wilde, with his hatred of the bourgeois seriousness of dull people, has always taken refuge from commonplace in irony. Life, to him, even when he is most frivolous, ought not to be realism, but a following after art: a provoking enough phrase for those who are lost to the sense of suggestiveness. He is conscious of the charm of grateful echoes, and is always original in his quotations.

In Wilde we see a great spectacular intellect, to which, at last, pity and terror have come in their own person, and no longer as puppets in a play. In its sight, human life has always been something created on the stage; a comedy in which it is the wise man's part to sit aside and laugh, but in which he may also disdainfully take part, as in a carnival, under any mask. The unbiased, scornful intellect, to which humanity has never been a burden, comes now to be unable to sit aside and laugh, and it has worn and looked behind so many masks that there is nothing left desirable in illusion. Having seen, as the artist sees, further than morality, but with so partial an eyesight as to have overlooked it on the way, it has come at length to discover morality, in the only way left possible, for itself. And, like most of those who have "thought themselves weary," have made the adventure of putting thought into action, it has had to discover it sorrowfully, at its own inevitable expense. And now, having so newly become acquainted with what is pitiful, and what seems most unjust, in the arrangements of mortal affairs, it has gone, not unnaturally, to an extreme, and taken on the one hand, humanitarianism, on the other realism, at more than their just valuation in matters of art. It is that old instinct of the intellect; the necessity to carry things to their farthest point of development, to be more logical than either art or life, two very wayward and illogical things, in which conclusions do not always follow from premises.

Swinburne's *Love's Cross Currents* appeared originally under what is now its sub-title *A Year's Letters*, in a weekly periodical, long since extinct, called *The Tattler*, from August 25th to December 29th, 1877. It was written under the pseudonym of Mrs. Horace Manners, and was preceded by a letter "To the Author," supposed to come from some unnamed publisher or literary adviser, who returns her manuscript to the lady with much faultfinding on the ground of morality. The letter ends:

> I recommend you, therefore, to suppress, or even to destroy, this book, for two reasons: It is a false picture of domestic life in England, because it suggests as possible the chance that a married lady may prefer some chance stranger to her husband, which is palpably and demonstrably absurd. It is also, as far as I can see, deficient in purpose and significance. Morality, I need not add, is the soul of art; a picture, poem, or story must be judged by the lesson it conveys. If it strengthens our hold upon fact, if it heightens our love of truth, if it rekindles our ardour for the right, it is admissible as good; if not, what shall we say of it?

The two final sentences of the first chapter, now omitted, are amusing enough to seem characteristic: "For the worldling's sneer may silence religion, but philanthropy is a tough fox and dies hard. The pietist may subside on attack into actual sermonising, and thence into a dumb agony of appeal against what he hears – the impotence of sincere disgust; but infinite coarse chaff will not shut up the natural lecturer; he snuffs sharply at all implied objection, and comes up to time again, gasping, verbose and resolute." But is there not a certain needless loss in the omission of two or three of the piquant passages in French? One is on the woman of sixty who *"seule sait mettre du fard moral sans jurer avec."*

There is another passage in French which comes out of page 220; it is not clear why, for it is sprightly enough, as this is also, which drops out of page 175: "*Ce sang répandu, voyez-vous, mon enfant, c'était la monnaie de sa vertu.*" I said I should have preferred it without the small change. "*'Mais, avec de la grosse monnaie on n'achète jamais rien qui vaille,' she said placidly.*" Then follows, as we now have it: "*C'était décidément une femme forte.*" Such, so slight, and at times so uncalled for, are the changes in this "disinterment" of "so early an attempt in the great art of fiction or creation."

In defending the form of his story in letters, Swinburne invokes the names of Richardson and Laclos and "the giant genius of Balzac." But the *Mémoires des deux jeunes Mariées* is full of firm reality, *Pamela* is full of patient analysis, and *Les Liaisons dangereuses* is full of reality, analysis, and a hard brilliant genius for psychology. Swinburne may have found in Laclos a little of his cynicism, though for that he need have gone no further than Stendhal, who is referred to in these pages, significantly. Some one says of some one: "I'd as soon read the *Chartreuse de Parme* as listen to her talk long; it is Stendhal diluted and transmuted." But neither in Laclos nor in Stendhal did he find that great novelist's gift which both have: that passion for life, and for the unraveling of the threads of life. His people and their doings are spectral, lunar; all the more so because their names are "Redgie," Frank, and only rarely Amicia; and because they talk schoolboy slang as schoolboys and French drawing-room slang as elderly people. They are presented by brilliant descriptive or satiric touches; they say the cleverest things of one another; they have a ghostly likeness to real people which one would be surprised that Swinburne should ever have tried to get, had he not repeated the same hopeless experiment in his modern play *The Sisters*, which sacrifices every possible charm of poetry or deep feeling to such a semblance; to so mere a mimicry of every-day speech and manners. There is more reality in any mere Félise or Fragoletta than in the plausible polite letter-writers. It is impossible to care what they are doing or have done; not easy indeed, without close reading, to find out; and, while there is hardly a sentence which we can not read with pleasure for its literary savor, its prim ironic elegance, there is not a page which we turn with the faintest thrill of curiosity. A novel which lacks interest may have every formal merit of writing, but it can not have merit as a novel. The novel professes to show us men and women, alive and in action: the one thing vitally interesting to men and women.

ON CRITICISM

Criticism is a valuation of forces, and it is indifferent to their direction. It is concerned with them only as force, and it is concerned only with force in its kind and degree.

The aim of criticism is to distinguish what is essential in the work of a writer; and in order to do this, its first business must be to find out where he is different from all other writers. It is the delight of the critic to praise; but praise is scarcely a part of his duty. He may often seem to find himself obliged to condemn; yet condemnation is hardly a necessary part of his office. What we ask of him is, that he should find out for us more than we can find out for ourselves: trace what in us is a whim or leaning to its remote home or center of gravity, and explain why we are affected in this way or that way by this or that writer. He studies origins in effects, and must know himself, and be able to allow for his own mental and emotional variations, if he is to do more than give us the records of his likes and dislikes. He must have the passion of the lover, and be enamored of every form of beauty; and, like the lover, not of all equally, but with a general allowance of those least to his liking. He will do well to be not without a touch of intolerance: that intolerance which, in the lover of the best, is an act of justice against the second-rate. The second-rate may perhaps have some reason for existence: that is doubtful; but the danger of the second-rate, if it is accepted "on its own merits," as people say, is that it may come to be taken for the thing it resembles, as a wavering image in water resembles the rock which it reflects.

Dryden, a poet who was even greater as a critic than as a poet, said, "True judgment in poetry, like that in painting, takes a view of the whole together, whether it be good or not; and where the beauties are more than the faults, concludes for the poet against the little judge." Here, in this decision, as to the proportions of merit and demerit in a work, is the critic's first task; it is one that is often overlooked by careful analysts, careless of what substance they are analyzing. What has been called the historical method is responsible for a great deal of these post-mortem dissections. How often do we not see learned persons engaged in this dismal occupation, not even conscious that they are fumbling among the bones and sinews of the dead. Such critics will examine the signs of life with equal gravity in living insignificances. But to the true critic a living insignificance is already dead.

And so, as in a dead man all the virtues go for nothing, no merit, no number of merits, of a secondary kind, in a writer who has been adjudged "not to exist," can avail anything. The critic concerns himself only with such as do exist. One of these, it may be, exists for a single book out of many books, a single poem out of many volumes of verse; an essay, an epigram, the preface to a book, a song out of a play. No perfect thing is too small for eternal recollection. But there are other writers who, though they have never condensed all their quality into any quite final achievement, live by a kind of bulk, live because there is in them something living, which refuses to go out. It is in his judgment of these two classes of writers, the measure of his skill in finding vital energy concentrated or diffused, in a cell or throughout an organism, that the critic is most likely to show his own quality. Charles Lamb is one of the greatest critics of Shakespeare, but the infallibility of his instinct as a critic is shown, not so much when he writes better about *Lear* than any one had ever written about *Lear*, but when he reveals to us, for the first time, the secret of

Ford, the mainspring of Webster.

Criticism, when it is not mere talk about literature, concerns itself with the first principles of human nature and with fundamental ideas. There is a quite valuable kind of critic to whom a book is merely a book, who is interested in things only as they become words, in emotions only as they add fine raptures to printed pages. To such critics we owe rules and systems; when they tabulate or elucidate meter or any principle of form they are doing a humble but useful service to artists. Their comments on books are often pleasant reading, sometimes turning into a kind of literature, essays which we are content to read for their own charm. But there is hardly anything idler than literary criticism which is a mere describing and comparing of books, a mere praise and blame of this and that writer and his work. When Coleridge writes a criticism of Shakespeare, he is giving us his deepest philosophy, in a manner in which we can best apprehend it. Criticism with Goethe is part of his view of the world, his judgment of human nature, and of society. With Pater, criticism is quickened meditation; with Matthew Arnold, a form of moral instruction or mental satire. Lamb said in his criticism more of what he had to say of "what God and man is," with more gravity and more intensity, than in any other part of his work.

And thus it is that, while there is a great mass of valuable criticism done by critics who were only critics, the most valuable criticism of all, the only quite essential criticism, has been done by creative writers, for the most part poets. The criticism of a philosopher, Aristotle's, comes next to that of the poets, but is never that winged thing which criticism, as well as poetry, can be in the hands of a poet. Aristotle is the mathematician of criticism, while Coleridge is the high priest.

When Dryden said "poets themselves are the most proper, though, I conclude, not the only critics," he was stating a fact which many prose persons have tried, though vainly, to dispute. Baudelaire, in a famous passage of his essay on Wagner, has said with his invariable exactitude, "It would be a wholly new event in the history of the arts if a critic were to turn himself into a poet, a reversal of every psychic law, a monstrosity; on the other hand, all great poets become naturally, inevitably, critics. I pity the poets who are guided solely by instinct; they seem to me incomplete. In the spiritual life of the former there must come a crisis when they would think out their art, discover the obscure laws in consequence of which they have produced, and draw from this study a series of precepts whose divine purpose is infallibility in poetic production. It would be impossible for a critic to become a poet, and it is impossible for a poet not to contain a critic." And in England we have had few good poets who have not on occasion shown themselves good critics. What is perhaps strange is, that they have put some of their criticism into verse, and made it into poetry. From the days when Lydgate affirmed of Chaucer that "he of English in making was the best," to the days when Landor declared of Browning:

"Since Chaucer was alive and hale,
No man hath walk'd along our roads with step
So active, so inquiring eye, or tongue
So varied in discourse;"

down, indeed, to the present days, when Swinburne has repaid Landor all his praise of poets, almost every English poet has been generously just to his contemporaries, and almost every poet has found the exact word of definition, of revelation, which the prose critics were laboriously hunting for, or still more laboriously writing round. To take a single example, could anything be more actually critical, in the severest sense of the word, than these lines of Shelley on Coleridge, lines which are not less admirable as verse than as criticism?

You will see Coleridge; he who sits obscure
In the exceeding lustre and the pure
Intense irradiation of a mind
Which, with its own internal lightning blind,
Flags wearily through darkness and despair

A cloud-encircled meteor of the air,
A hooded eagle among blinking owls.

Those seven lines are not merely good criticism: they are final; they leave nothing more to be said. Criticism, at such a height, is no longer mere reasoning; it has the absolute sanction of intuition.

And, it will be found, the criticism of poets, not only such as is expressed, deliberately or by the way, in verse, but such as is set down by them in essays, or in letters, however carefully or casually, remains the most valuable criticism of poetry which we can get; and, similarly, the opinion of men of genius on their own work and on their own form of art, whatever it may be, is of more value than all the theories made by "little judges." The occasional notes and sayings of such men as Blake and Rossetti are often of more essential quality than their more ordered and elaborate comments. The essence they contain is undiluted. They are what is remembered over from a state of inspiration; and they are to be received as reports are received from eye-witnesses, whose honesty has already proved itself in authentic deeds.

The *Biographia Literaria* is the greatest book of criticism in English, and one of the most annoying books in any language. The thought of Coleridge has to be pursued across stones, ditches, and morasses; with haste, lingering, and disappointment; it turns back, loses itself, fetches wide circuits, and comes to no visible end. But you must follow it step by step; and if you are ceaselessly attentive, will be ceaselessly rewarded.

When Coleridge says, in this book, that "the ultimate end of criticism is much more to establish the principle of writing than to furnish rules how to pass judgment on what has been written by others," he is defining that form of criticism in which he is supreme among critics. Lamb can be more instant in the detection of beauty; Pater can make over again an image or likeness of that beauty which he defines, with more sensitive precision; but no one has ever gone deeper down into the substance of creation itself, or more nearly reached that unknown point where creation begins. As poet, he knows; as philosopher, he understands; and thus, as critic, he can explain almost the origin of creation.

THE DECADENT MOVEMENT
IN LITERATURE

The latest movement in European literature has been called by many names, none of them quite exact or comprehensive – Decadence, Symbolism, Impressionism, for instance. It is easy to dispute over words, and we shall find that Verlaine objects to being called a Decadent, Maeterlinck to being called a Symbolist, Huysmans to being called an Impressionist. These terms, as it happens, have been adopted as the badge of little separate cliques, noisy, brainsick young people who haunt the brasseries of the Boulevard Saint-Michel, and exhaust their ingenuities in theorizing over the works they can not write. But, taken frankly as epithets which express their own meaning, both Impressionism and Symbolism convey some notion of that new kind of literature which is perhaps more broadly characterized by the word Decadence. The most representative literature of the day – the writing which appeals to, which has done so much to form, the younger generation – is certainly not classic, nor has it any relation with that old antithesis of the Classic, the Romantic. After a fashion it is no doubt a decadence; it has all the qualities that mark the end of great periods, the qualities that we find in the Greek, the Latin, decadence: an intense self-consciousness, a restless curiosity in research, an over-subtilizing refinement upon refinement, a spiritual and moral perversity. If what we call the classic is indeed the supreme art – those qualities of perfect simplicity, perfect sanity, perfect proportion, the supreme qualities – then this representative literature of to-day, interesting, beautiful, novel as it is, is really a new and beautiful and interesting disease.

Healthy we can not call it, and healthy it does not wish to be considered. The Goncourts, in their prefaces, in their *Journal*, are always insisting on their own pet malady, *la névrose*. It is in their work too, that Huysmans notes with delight *le style tacheté et faisandé* – high-flavored and spotted with corruption – which he himself possesses in the highest degree. "Having desire without light, curiosity, without wisdom, seeking God by strange ways, by ways traced by the hands of men; offering rash incense upon the high places to an unknown God, who is the God of darkness" – that is how Ernest Hello, in one of his apocalyptic moments, characterizes the nineteenth century. And this unreason of the soul – of which Hello himself is so curious a victim – this unstable equilibrium, which has overbalanced so many brilliant intelligences into one form or another of spiritual confusion, is but another form of the *maladie fin de siècle*. For its very disease of form, this literature is certainly typical of a civilization grown over-luxurious, over-inquiring, too languid for the relief of action, too uncertain for any emphasis in opinion or in conduct. It reflects all the moods, all the manners, of a sophisticated society; its very artificiality is a way of I being true to nature: simplicity, sanity, proportion – the classic qualities – how much do we possess them in our life, our surroundings, that we should look to find them in our literature – so evidently the literature of a decadence?

Taking the word Decadence, then, as most precisely expressing the general sense of the newest movement in literature, we find that the terms Impressionism and Symbolism define correctly enough the two main branches of that movement. Now Impressionist and Symbolist have more in common than either supposes; both are really working on the same hypothesis, applied in different directions. What both seek is not general truth merely, but *vérité vraie*, the very essence of truth – the truth of appearances to the senses, of the visible world to the eyes that see it; and the truth of spiritual things to the spiritual vision. The Impressionist, in literature as in painting, would flash upon you in a new, sudden way so exact an image of what you have just seen, just as you have seen it, that you may say, as a young American sculptor, a pupil of Rodin, said to me on seeing for the first time a picture of Whistler's, "Whistler seems to think his picture upon canvas – and there it is!" Or you may find, with Sainte-Beuve, writing of Goncourt, the "soul of the landscape" – the soul of whatever corner of the visible world has to be realized. The Symbolist, in this new, sudden way, would I flash upon you the "soul" of that which can be apprehended only by the soul – the finer sense of things unseen, the deeper meaning of things evident. And naturally, necessarily, this endeavor after a perfect truth to one's impression, to one's intuition – perhaps an impossible endeavor – has brought with it, in its revolt from ready-made impressions and conclusions, a revolt from the ready-made of language, from the bondage of traditional form, of a form become rigid. In France, where this movement began and has mainly flourished, it is Goncourt who was the first to invent a style in prose really new, impressionistic, a style which was itself almost sensation. It is Verlaine who has invented such another new style in verse.

The work of the brothers De Goncourt – twelve novels, eleven or twelve studies in the history of the eighteenth century, six or seven books about art, the art mainly of the eighteenth century and of Japan, two plays, some volumes of letters and of fragments, and a *Journal* in six volumes – is perhaps, in its intention and its consequences, the most revolutionary of the century. No one has ever tried so deliberately to do something new as the Goncourts; and the final word in the summing up which the survivor has placed at the head of the *Préfaces et Manifestes* is a word which speaks of *tentatives, enfin, où les deux frères ont à faire du neuf, ont fait leurs efforts pour doter les diverses branches de la littérature de*

quelque chose que n'avaient point songé à trouver leurs prédécesseurs.
And in the preface to *Chérie*, in that pathetic passage which tells of
the two brothers (one mortally stricken, and within a few months
of death) taking their daily walk in the Bois de Boulogne, there is
a definite demand on posterity. "The search after *reality* in
literature, the resurrection of eighteenth-century art, the triumph
of *Japonisme* – are not these," said Jules, "the three great literary
and artistic movements of the second half of the nineteenth
century? And it is we who brought them about, these three
movements. Well, when one has done that, it is difficult indeed
not to be *somebody* in the future." Nor, even, is this all. What the
Goncourts have done is to specialize vision, so to speak, and to
subtilize language to the point of rendering every detail in just
the form and color of the actual impression. Edmond de Goncourt
once said to me – varying, if I remember rightly, an expression
he had put into the *Journal* – "My brother and I invented an
opera-glass: the young people nowadays are taking it out of our
hands."

An opera-glass – a special, unique way of seeing things – that
is what the Goncourts have brought to bear upon the common
things about us; and it is here that they have done the
"something new," here more than anywhere. They have never
sought "to see life steadily, and see it whole:" their vision has
always been somewhat feverish, with the diseased sharpness of
over-excited nerves. "We do not hide from ourselves that we have
been passionate, nervous creatures, unhealthily impressionable,"
confesses the *Journal*. But it is this morbid intensity in seeing and
seizing things that has helped to form that marvelous style – "a
style perhaps too ambitious of impossibilities," as they admit – a
style which inherits some of its color from Gautier, some of its fine
outline from Flaubert, but which has brought light and shadow
into the color, which has softened outline in the magic of
atmosphere. With them words are not merely color and sound,
they live. That search after *l'image peinte, l'épithète rare*, is not (as
with Flaubert) a search after harmony of phrase for its own sake;

it is a desperate endeavor to give sensation, to flash the impression of the moment, to preserve the very heat and motion of life. And so, in analysis as in description, they have found a way of noting the fine shades; they have broken the outline of the conventional novel in chapters, with its continuous story, in order to indicate – sometimes in a chapter of half a page – this and that revealing moment, this or that significant attitude or accident or sensation. For the placid traditions of French prose they have had but little respect; their aim has been but one, that of having (as M. Edmond de Goncourt tells us in the preface to *Chérie*) "une langue rendant nos idées, nos sensations, nos figurations des hommes et des choses, d'une façon distincte de celui-ci ou de celui-là, une langue personnelle, une langue portant notre signature."

What Goncourt has done in prose – inventing absolutely a new way of saying things, to correspond with that new way of seeing things which he has found – Verlaine has done in verse. In a famous poem, *Art Poétique*, he has himself defined his own ideal of the poetic art:

> *Car nous voulons la Nuance encor,*
> *Pas la Couleur, rien que la Nuance!*
> *Oh! la Nuance seule fiance*
> *Le rêve au rêve et la flûte au cor!*

Music first of all and before all, he insists; and then, not color, but *la nuance*, the last fine shade. Poetry is to be something vague, intangible, evanescent, a winged soul in flight "toward other skies and other loves." To express the inexpressible he speaks of beautiful eyes behind a veil, of the palpitating sunlight of noon, of the blue swarm of clear stars in a cool autumn sky; and the verse in which he makes this confession of faith has the exquisite troubled beauty – *sans rien en lui qui pèse ou qui pose* – which he commends as the essential quality of verse. In a later poem of poetical counsel he tells us that art should, first of all, be absolutely clear, absolutely sincere: *L'art mes enfants, c'est d'être absolument soi-même*. The two poems, with their seven years' interval – an interval which means so much in the life of a man like Verlaine – give us all that there is of theory in the work of the least theoretical, the most really instinctive, of poetical innovators. Verlaine's poetry has varied with his life; always in excess – now furiously sensual, now feverishly devout – he has been constant only to himself, to his own self-contradictions. For, with all the violence, turmoil and disorder of a life which is almost the life of a modern Villon, Paul Verlaine has always retained that childlike simplicity, and, in his verse, which has been his confessional, that fine sincerity, of which Villon may be thought to have set the example in literature.

Beginning his career as a Parnassian with the *Poèmes Saturniens*, Verlaine becomes himself, in the *Fêtes Galantes*, caprices after Watteau, followed, a year later, by *La Bonne Chanson*, a happy record of too confident a lover's happiness. *Romances sans Paroles*, in which the poetry of Impressionism reaches its very highest point, is more *tourmenté*, goes deeper, becomes more poignantly personal. It is the poetry of sensation, of evocation; poetry which paints as well as sings, and which paints as Whistler paints, seeming to think the colors and outlines upon the canvas, to think them only, and they are there. The mere magic of words – words which evoke pictures, which recall sensations – can go no further; and in his next book, *Sagesse*, published after seven years' wanderings and sufferings, there is a graver manner of more deeply personal confession – that "sincerity, and the impression of the moment followed to the letter," which he has defined in a prose criticism on himself as his main preference in regard to style. "Sincerity, and the impression of the moment followed to the letter," mark the rest of Verlaine's work, whether the sentiment be that of passionate friendship, as in *Amour*; of love, human and divine, as in *Bonheur*; of the mere lust of the flesh, as in *Parallèlement* and *Chansons pour Elle*. In his very latest verse the quality of simplicity has become exaggerated, has become, at times, childish; the once exquisite depravity of style has lost some of its distinction; there is no longer the same delicately vivid "impression of the moment" to render. Yet the very closeness with which it follows a lamentable career gives a curious interest to even the worst of Verlaine's work. And how unique, how unsurpassable in its kind, is the best! "*Et tout le reste est littérature!*" was the cry, supreme and contemptuous, of that early *Art Poétique*; and, compared with Verlaine at his best, all other contemporary work in verse seems not yet disenfranchised from mere "literature." To fix the last fine shade, the quintessence of things; to fix it fleetingly; to be a disembodied voice, and yet the voice of a human soul: that is the ideal of Decadence, and it is what Paul Verlaine has achieved.

And certainly, so far as achievement goes, no other poet of the actual group in France can be named beside him or near him. But in Stéphane Mallarmé, with his supreme pose as the supreme poet, and his two or three pieces of exquisite verse and delicately artificial prose to show by way of result, we have – the prophet and pontiff of the movement, the mystical and theoretical leader of the great emancipation. No one has ever dreamed such beautiful, impossible dreams as Mallarmé; no one has ever so possessed his soul in the contemplation of masterpieces to come. All his life he has been haunted by the desire to create, not so much something new in literature, as a literature which should itself be a new art. He has dreamed of a work into which all the arts should enter, and achieve themselves by a mutual interdependence – a harmonizing of all the arts into one supreme art – and he has theorized with infinite subtlety over the possibilities of doing the impossible. Every Tuesday for the last twenty years he has talked more fascinatingly, more suggestively, than any one else has ever done, in that little room in the Rue de Rome, to that little group of eager young poets. "A seeker after something in the world, that is there in no satisfying measure, or not at all," he has carried his contempt for the usual, the conventional, beyond the point of literary expression, into the domain of practical affairs. Until the publication, quite recently, of a selection of *Vers et Prose*, it was only possible to get his poems in a limited and expensive edition, lithographed in facsimile of his own clear and elegant handwriting. An aristocrat of letters, Mallarmé has always looked with intense disdain on the indiscriminate accident of universal suffrage. He has wished neither to be read nor to be understood by the bourgeois intelligence, and it is with some deliberateness of intention that he has made both issues impossible. Catulle Mendès defines him admirably as "a difficult author," and in his latest period he has succeeded in becoming absolutely unintelligible. His early poems, L'Après-midi d'un Faune, Herodiade, for example, and some exquisite sonnets, and one or two fragments of perfectly polished verse, are written in a language which has nothing in common with every-day language – symbol within symbol, image within image; but symbol and image achieve themselves in expression without seeming to call for the necessity of a key. The latest poems (in which punctuation is sometimes entirely suppressed, for our further bewilderment) consist merely of a sequence of symbols, in which every word must be taken in a sense with which its ordinary significance has nothing to do. Mallarmé's contortion of the French language, so far as mere style is concerned, is curiously similar to the kind of depravation which was undergone by the Latin language in its decadence. It is, indeed, in part a reversion to Latin phraseology, to the Latin construction, and it has made, of the clear and flowing French language, something irregular, unquiet, expressive, with sudden surprising felicities, with nervous starts and lapses, with new capacities for the exact noting of sensation. Alike to the ordinary and to the scholarly reader, it is painful, intolerable; a jargon, a massacre. Supremely self-confident, and backed, certainly, by an ardent following of the younger generation, Mallarmé goes on his way, experimenting more and more audaciously, having achieved by this time, at all events, a style wholly his own. Yet the chef-d'œuvre inconnu seems no nearer completion, the impossible seems no more likely to be done. The two or three beautiful fragments remain, and we still hear the voice in the Rue de Rome.

Probably it is as a voice, an influence, that Mallarmé will be remembered. His personal magnetism has had a great deal to do with the making of the very newest French literature; few literary beginners in Paris have been able to escape the rewards and punishments of his contact, his suggestion. One of the young poets who form that delightful Tuesday evening coterie said to me the other day, "We owe much to Mallarmé, but he has kept us all back three years." That is where the danger of so inspiring, so helping a personality comes in. The work even of Henri de Regnier, who is the best of the disciples, has not entirely got clear from the influence that has shown his fine talent the way to develop. Perhaps it is in the verse of men who are not exactly following in the counsel of the master – who might disown him, whom he might disown – that one sees most clearly the outcome of his theories, the actual consequences of his practise. In regard to the construction of verse, Mallarmé has always remained faithful to the traditional syllabic measurement; but the freak or the discovery of *le vers libre* is certainly the natural consequence of his experiments upon the elasticity of rhythm, upon the power of resistance of the cæsura. *Le vers libre* in the hands of most of the experimenters becomes merely rhymeless irregular prose. I never really understood the charm that may be found in this apparent structureless rhythm until I heard, not long since, Dujardin read aloud the as yet unpublished conclusion of a dramatic poem in several parts. It was rhymed, but rhymed with some irregularity, and the rhythm was purely and simply a vocal effect. The rhythm came and went as the spirit moved. You might deny that it was rhythm at all; and yet, read as I heard it read, in a sort of slow chant, it produced on me the effect of really beautiful verse. But *vers libres* in the hands of a sciolist are the most intolerably easy and annoying of poetical exercises. Even in the case of *Le Pèlerin Passionné* I can not see the justification of what is merely regular syllabic verse lengthened or shortened arbitrarily, with the Alexandrine always evident in the background as the foot-rule of the new metre. In this hazardous experiment Jean Moréas, whose real talent lies in quite another direction, has brought nothing into literature but an example of deliberate singularity for singularity's sake. I seem to find the measure of the man in a remark I once heard him make in a *café*, where we were discussing the technique of meter: "You, Verlaine!" he cried, leaning across the table, "have only written lines of sixteen syllables; I have written lines of twenty syllables!" And turning to me, he asked anxiously if Swinburne had ever done that – had written a line of twenty syllables.

That is indeed the measure of the man, and it points a criticism upon not a few of the busy little *littérateurs* who are founding new *revues* every other week in Paris. These people have nothing to say, but they are resolved to say something, and to say it in the newest mode. They are Impressionists because it is the fashion, Symbolists because it is the vogue, Decadents because Decadence is in the very air of the cafés. And so, in their manner, they are mile-posts on the way of this new movement, telling how far it has gone. But to find a new personality, a new way of seeing things, among the young writers who are starting up on every hand, we must turn from Paris to Brussels – to the so-called Belgian Shakespeare, Maurice Maeterlinck.

In truth, Maeterlinck is not a Shakespeare, and the Elizabethan violence of his first play is of the school of Webster and Tourneur rather than of Shakespeare. As a dramatist he has but one note, that of fear; he has but one method, that of repetition.

The window, looking out upon the unseen – an open door, as in *L'Intruse*, through which Death, the intruder, may come invisibly – how typical of the new kind of symbolistic and impressionistic drama which Maeterlinck has invented! I say invented, a little rashly. The real discoverer of this new kind of drama was that strange, inspiring, incomplete man of genius whom Maeterlinck, above all others, delights to honor, Villiers de l'Isle-Adam. Imagine a combination of Swift, of Poe, and of

Coleridge, and you will have some idea of the extraordinary, impossible poet and cynic who, after a life of brilliant failure, has left a series of unfinished works in every kind of literature; among the finished achievements one volume of short stories, *Contes Cruels*, which is an absolute masterpiece. Yet, apart from this, it was the misfortune of Villiers never to attain the height of his imaginings, and even *Axël*, the work of a lifetime, is an achievement only half achieved. Only half achieved, or achieved only in the work of others; for, in its mystical intention, its remoteness from any kind of outward reality, *Axël* is undoubtedly the origin of the symbolistic drama. This drama, in Villiers, is of pure symbol, of sheer poetry. It has an exalted eloquence which we find in none of his followers. As Maeterlinck has developed it, it is a drama which appeals directly to the sensations – sometimes crudely, sometimes subtly – playing its variations upon the very nerves themselves. The "vague spiritual fear" which it creates out of our nervous apprehension is unlike anything that has ever been done before, even by Hoffman, even by Poe. It is an effect of atmosphere – an atmosphere in which outlines change and become mysterious, in which a word quietly uttered makes one start, in which all one's mental activity becomes concentrated on something, one knows not what, something slow, creeping, terrifying, which comes nearer and nearer, an impending nightmare.

As an experiment in a new kind of drama, these curious plays do not seem to exactly achieve themselves on the stage; it is difficult to imagine how they could ever be made so impressive, when thus externalized, as they are when all is left to the imagination. *L'Intruse*, for instance, seemed, as one saw it acted, too faint in outline, with too little carrying power for scenic effect. But Maeterlinck is by no means anxious to be considered merely or mainly as a dramatist. A brooding poet, a mystic, a contemplative spectator of the comedy of death – that is how he presents himself to us in his work; and the introduction which he has prefixed to his translation of *L'Ornement des Noces Spirituelles*, of Ruysbroeck l'Admirable, shows how deeply he has studied the mystical writers of all ages, and how much akin to theirs is his own temper. Plato and Plotinus, Saint Bernard and Jacob Boehm, Coleridge and Novalis – he knows them all, and it is with a sort of reverence that he sets himself to the task of translating the astonishing Flemish mystic of the thirteenth century, known till now only by the fragments translated into French by Ernest Hollo from a sixteenth-century Latin version. This translation and this introduction help to explain the real character of Maeterlinck's dramatic work – dramatic as to form, by a sort of accident, but essentially mystical.

Partly akin to Maeterlinck by race, more completely alien from him in temper than it is possible to express, Joris Karl Huysmans demands a prominent place in any record of the Decadent movement. His work, like that of the Goncourts, is largely determined by the *maladie fin de siècle* – the diseased nerves that, in his case, have given a curious personal quality of pessimism to his outlook on the world, his view of life. Part of his work – *Marthe, Les Sœurs Vatard, En Ménage, À Vau-l'Eau* – is a minute and searching study of the minor discomforts, the commonplace miseries of life, as seen by a peevishly disordered vision, delighting, for its own self-torture, in the insistent contemplation of human stupidity, of the sordid in existence. Yet these books do but lead up to the unique masterpiece, the astonishing caprice of *À Rebours*, in which he has concentrated all that is delicately depraved, all that is beautifully, curiously poisonous, in modern art. *À Rebours* is the history of a typical Decadent – a study, indeed, after a real man, but a study which seizes the type rather than the personality. In the sensations and ideas of Des Esseintes we see the sensations and ideas of the effeminate, over-civilized, deliberately abnormal creature who is the last product of our society: partly the father, partly the offspring, of the perverse art that he adores. Des Esseintes creates for his solace, in the wilderness of a barren and profoundly uncomfortable world, an artificial paradise. His Thébaïde raffinée is furnished elaborately for candle-light, equipped with the pictures, the books, that satisfy his sense of the exquisitely abnormal. He delights in the Latin of Apuleius and Petronius, in the French of Baudelaire, Goncourt, Verlaine, Mallarmé, Villiers; in the pictures of Gustave Moreau, of Odilon Redon. He delights in the beauty of strange, unnatural flowers, in the melodic combination of scents, in the imagined harmonies of the sense of taste. And at last, exhausted by these spiritual and sensory debauches in the delights of the artificial, he is left (as we close the book) with a brief, doubtful choice before him – madness or death, or else a return to nature, to the normal life.

Since *À Rebours*, Huysmans has written one other remarkable book, *Là-Bas*, a study in the hysteria and mystical corruption of contemporary Black Magic. But it is on that one exceptional achievement, *À Rebours*, that his fame will rest; it is there that he has expressed not merely himself, but an epoch. And he has done so in a style which carries the modern experiments upon language to their furthest development. Formed upon Goncourt and Flaubert, it has sought for novelty, *l'image peinte*, the exactitude of color, the forcible precision of epithet, wherever words, images, or epithets are to be found. Barbaric in its profusion, violent in its emphasis, wearying in its splendor, it is – especially in regard to things seen – extraordinarily expressive, with all the shades of a painter's palette. Elaborately and deliberately perverse, it is in its very perversity that Huysmans' work – so fascinating, so repellent, so instinctively artificial – comes to represent, as the work of no other writer can be said to do, the main tendencies, the chief results, of the Decadent movement in literature.

Joseph Conrad

Maurice Maeterlinck (before 1905)

The Brontë sisters, by their brother Bramwell, c. 1834

Dante Gabriel Rossetti, Self-Portrait, 1847,
National Portrait Gallery, London

Paul Verlaine by Eugène Carrière

Stéphane Mallarmé by Félix Nadar

J.-K. Huysmans

Francesco Melzi, Portrait of Leonardo, after 1510, Windsor

THE ROSSETTIS

William Michael Rossetti, who has just died, survived his brother, Dante Gabriel Rossetti, by thirty-seven years, dying at the age of eighty-nine. Not really a man of letters, in the essential sense, his verse, as Gabriel said, "Always going back on the old track," he had a certain talent of his own; for he edited an excellent edition of Blake's Poems, and a creditable edition of Shelley, the first critical edition of his poems.

He was the first Englishman who ever dared to print a Selection from Whitman's *Leaves of Grass*, – in 1868; and, in spite of having to exclude such passages as he considered indecent, the whole book was a valuable contribution to our literature.

There is no question that Michael was not invaluable to Gabriel; indeed, during the whole of the tragic and wonderful life of that man of supreme genius; not only because he dedicated his *Poems* of 1870 to one "who had given them the first brotherly hearing;" not only because, had not Michael been with him at the British Museum on the ever-memorable and unforgettable date of April 30, 1847, he had never bought the imperishable *MS. Book of Blake*, borrowing for this purchase ten shillings from his brother; but also because when Rossetti, after his wife's death, had his manuscript volume of poems exhumed in October, 1869, he did the right thing, both in his impetuous act in burying them beside his dead wife and in his silence with his brother – who was really aware of the event – so that his own tortured nerves might have some respite.

Still, I have never forgotten how passionately Eleanore Duse said to me, in 1900:

> Rossetti's eyes desire some feverish thing, but the mouth and chin hesitate in pursuit. All Rossetti is in that story of his *MS.* buried in his wife's coffin. He could do it, he could repent of it; but he should have gone and taken it back himself: he sent his friends.

In one of Dante Gabriel Rossetti's invaluable notes on Poetry, he tells us that to him "the leading point about Coleridge's work is its human love." That Rossetti, whose face indicated voluptuousness brooding thoughtfully over destiny, was intensely sensitive, is true; and this made him a sort of medium to forces seen and unseen. Yet, I think, he wanted in life more than most men of such genius as he had wanted. For, as Watts-Dunton said: "He was the slave of his imagination – an imagination of a power and dominance such as I have never seen equalled. Of his vividness, no artistic expression of his can give any notion. He had not the smallest command over it." That is one of the reasons why, with all his affection for his brother Michael, the chasm between them was immense – a chasm no dragon-created bridge could ever span; Gabriel had in him, perhaps, too much of "chasm-fire": his genius was too flame-fledged for earth's eternity, to have ever had one wing of it broken by an enemy's shaft.

No modern poet ever had anything like the same grasp upon whatever is essential in poetry that Rossetti had; for all that he wrote or said about Art has in it an absolute rightness of judgment; and, with these, as absolutely, an intellectual sanity. Here is one principle of artistic creation stated with instantaneous certainty: "Conception, *fundamental brain work*, that is what makes the difference in all art. Work your metal as much as you like, but first take care that the gold was worth working." But it is, strangely enough, that at the beginning of a review of Hake's *Parables and Tales* he says the final, the inevitable words on creation and on what lies in the artist's mind before the act of creation:

> The first and highest is that where the work has been all mentally "cartooned," as it were, beforehand by a process intensely conscious, but patient and silent – an occult evolution of life: then follows the glory of wielding words, and we see the hand of Dante, as the hand of Michelangelo – or almost as that quickening hand which Michelangelo has dared to embody – sweep from left to right, fiery and final.

In 1862, Rossetti took possession of his famous house, 10 Cheyne Walk, Chelsea, where he lived to the end of his life, and whose joint occupants were, for a certain length of time, George Meredith, Swinburne and William Michael Rossetti, who left the house in 1874, the year in which he married Lucy Madox Brown.

That four men of individualities so utterly different, and, in some senses, aggressive, or at least assertive, should have been able to live together in closeness of continuous intimacy, from which there was hardly an escape, was barely conceivable. Yet it was in this house that Swinburne wrote many of his *Poems Ballads*, part of his book on Blake and his masterpiece, *Atalanta in Calydon*. There Meredith finished his masterpiece in the matter of tragic and passionate verse, *Modern Love*. There is nothing like it in the whole of English poetry, nor did he ever achieve so magnificent a vivisection of the heart in verse as in these pages – in which he created a wonderful style, acid, stinging, bitter-sweet, poignant – where these self-torturing and cruel lovers weave the amazing web of their disillusions as they struggle, open-eyed, against the blindness of passion.

The poem laughs while it cries.

Swinburne, who was, I think, on the whole, less susceptible in regard to abusive attacks on his books than Meredith or Rossetti, vindicates himself, and superbly, in the pamphlet I have before me: *Notes on Poems and Reviews* (1866). He has been accused of indecency and immorality and perversity; and is amazed to find that *Anactoria* "has excited, among the chaste and candid critics of the day, or hour, or minute, a more vehement reputation, a more virtuous horror, a more passionate appeal, than any other of my writing. I am evidently not virtuous enough to understand them. I thank Heaven that I am not. *Ma corruption rougirait de leur pudeur.*"

In regard to *Laus Veneris*, I turn for a moment to W. M. Rossetti's *Swinburne's Poems and Ballads: A criticism* (1866) which, on the whole, is uncommonly well written, to one of those passages where he betrays a kind of Puritanism in his Italian blood; saying that the opening lines were, apart from any question of sentiment, much overdone. "That is a situation (and there are many such in Swinburne's writings) which we would much rather see touched off with the reticence of a Tennyson: he would probably have given one epithet, or, at the utmost, one line, to it, and it would at least equally have haunted the memory." I turn from this to Swinburne on Tennyson, as for instance: "At times, of course, his song was then as sweet as ever it has sounded since; but he could never make sure of singing right for more than a few minutes or stanzas." And – what is certainly true – that Vivien's impurity is eclipsed by her incredible and incomparable vulgarity. "She is such a sordid creature as plucks men passing by the sleeve."

Now the actual origin of *Laus Veneris* came about when Swinburne, with Rossetti, bought the first edition of Fitzgerald's wonderful version of *Omar Khayyam*. "We invested," Swinburne writes, "in hardly less than six-penny-worth apiece, and on returning to the stall next day, for more, found that we had sent up the market to the sinfully extravagant price of two-pence, an imposition which evoked from Rossetti a fervent and impressive remonstrance." Swinburne went down to stay with Meredith in the country with the priceless book; and, before lunch, they read, alternately, stanza after stanza. The result was that, after lunch, Swinburne went to his room and came down to Meredith's study with his invariable blue paper and wrote there and then thirteen stanzas of *Veneris*, that end with the lines:

Till when the spool is finished, lo I see
His web, reeled off, curls and goes out like steam.

His only invention was the certainly cunning one of inserting a rhyme after the second line of each stanza, which is not in the version.

Swinburne's re-creation of the immortal legend of Venus and her Knight, certainly – though certainly unknown to W. M. Rossetti – owes also much of its origin from Swinburne's inordinate admiration of *Les Fleurs du Mal*, by Baudelaire. Its origin, in a certain sense only; that is of the influence of one poet on the other. For, as he says:

> It was not till my poem was completed that I received from the hands of its author the admirable pamphlet of Charles Baudelaire on Wagner's *Tannhauser*. If anyone desires to see, expressed in better words than I can command, the conception of the mediæval Venus which it was my aim to put into verse, let him turn to the magnificent passage in which Baudelaire describes the fallen goddess, grown diabolic among eyes that would not accept her as divine.

I need not reiterate the extraordinary influence that Baudelaire always had on Swinburne; seen most of all in *Poems and Ballads* and recurring at intervals in later volumes of his verse. Both had in their genius, a certain abnormality, a certain perversity, a certain love of depravity in the highest sense of the word.

Swinburne, who had a fashion of overpraising many writers, such as Hugo, so that his prose is often extravagant and the criticism as unbalanced as the praise, dedicated his finest book, "*William Blake*," to W. M. Rossetti, in words whose almost strained sense of humility – a way really in which he often showed the intensity of his pride – makes one wonder how he could have said: "I can but bring you brass for the gold you send me; but between equals and friends there can be no question of barter. Like Diomed, I take what I am given and offer what I have."

What Swinburne had – his genius – he never gave away lavishly; here he is much too lavish. "There is a joy in praising" might have been written for him, and he communicates to us, as few writers do, his own sense of joy in beauty. It is quite possible to be annoyed by many of the things he has said, not only about literature, but also about religion, and morals and politics. But he has never said anything on any of these subjects which is not generous, and high-minded, and, at least for the moment, passionately and absolutely sincere.

It is almost cruel to have to test one sentence of the man of talent with one sentence of the man of genius. I chose these from the *Notes on the Royal Academy Exhibition* they wrote together in 1868, which I have before me, in the form of a printed pamphlet. "If everybody tells me that the picture of A, of which this pamphlet says nothing, merits criticism, or that the picture of B, praised for color, claims praise on the score of drawing also, I shall have no difficulty in admitting the probable correctness of these remarks; but, if he adds that I am blamable for the omissions, I shall feel entitled to reply that A's picture and B's draughts-manship were not and indeed never were in the bond."

How honestly that is written and how prosaically, "Pale as from poison, with the blood drawn back from her very lips, agonized in face and limbs with the labor and the fierce contention of old love with new, of a daughter's love with a bride's, the fatal figure of Medea pauses a little on the funereal verge of the wood of death, in act to pour a blood-like liquid into the soft opal-coloured hollow of a shell." How princely that praise of Sandys rings in one's ears, lyrical prose that quickens the blood! But the greater marvel to me is that Swinburne in his *Miscellanies*, of 1866, should have quoted two sentences of Rossetti on Shakespeare's Sonnets and ended by saying: "These words themselves deserve to put on immortality: there are none truer or nobler, wiser or more memorable in the whole historic range of highest criticism." I can only imagine it as that of an arrow in flight: only, it loses the mark.

It was when Christina Rossetti was living at 30 Torrington Square that I spent several entrancing hours with her. She had still traces of her Italian beauty; but all the loveliness had gone out of her, so subtly and so delicately painted by Gabriel when she was young. The moment she entered, dressed simply and severely, she bowed, almost curtsied, with that old-fashioned charm that since her time has gone mostly out of the world. Her face lit up when she spoke of Gabriel: for between them was always love and admiration. His genius, to her, both as a poet and a painter, invariably received her elaborate and unstinted praise.

She told me that Gabriel had said to her: "*The Convent Threshold* is a very splendid piece of feminine ascetic passion; and, to me, one of your greatest poems is that on France after the Siege – *To-Day for me.*" And that Swinburne specially loved *Passing away, saith the world, passing away*. It always seems to me that as she had read Leopardi and Baudelaire, the thought of death had for her the same fascination; only it is not the fascination of attraction, as with the one, nor repulsion, as with the other, but of interest, sad but scarcely unquiet interest in what the dead are doing underground, in their memories, if memory they have, of the world they have left.

Yet this fact is of curious interest, knowing the purity of her imagination, that when Swinburne sent her his *Atalanta in Calydon* she crossed out in ink one line:

"*The supreme evil, God.*"

Swinburne himself told me of his amazement and amusement when he happened to turn to this page while he was looking through the copy he had sent her.

It was one of Gabriel Rossetti's glories to paint luxurious women, surrounded by every form of luxury. And some of them are set to pose in Eastern garments, with caskets in their hands and flames about them, looking out with unsearchable eyes. His colors, before they began to have, like his forms, an exaggeration, a blurred vision which gave him the need of repainting, of depriving his figures of life, were as if charmed into their own places; they took on at times some strange and stealthy and startling ardors of paint, with a subtle fury.

By his fiery imagination, his restless energy, he created a world: curious, astonishing, at first sight; strange, morbid, and subtly beautiful. Everything he made was chiefly for his own pleasure; he had a contempt for the outside world, and his life was so given up to beauty, in search for it and in finding of it, that one can but say not only that his life was passion consumed by passion, as his nerves became more and more his tyrants (tyrants, indeed, these were, more formidable and more alluring and more tempting than even the nerves confess), but also that, to put it in the words of Walter Pater: "To him life is a crisis at every moment."

There was in him, as in many artists, the lust of the eyes. And as others feasted their lust on elemental things, as in Turner's *Rain, Steam and Speed*, as in Whistler's *Valparaiso*, as in the *Olympia* of Manet, as in a *Décors de Ballet* of Degas, so did Rossetti upon other regions than theirs. He had neither the evasive and instinctive genius of Whistler, nor Turner's tremendous sweep of vision, nor the creative and fiercely imaginative genius of Manet. But he had his own way of feasting on forms and visions more sensuous, more nervously passionate, more occult, perhaps, than theirs.

Yet, as his intentions overpower him, as he becomes the slave and no longer the master of his dreams, his pictures become no longer symbolic. They become idols. Venus, growing more and more Asiatic as the moon's crescent begins to glitter above her head, and her name changes from Aphrodite into Astarte, loses all the freshness of the waves from which she was born, and her own sorcery hardens into a wooden image painted to be the object of savage worship.

Dreams are no longer content to be turned into waking

realities, taking the color of the daylight, that they may be visible to our eyes, but they remain lunar, spectral, a dark and unintelligible menace.

CONFESSIONS AND COMMENTS

I

I met George Moore, during a feverish winter I spent in Paris in 1890, at the house of Doctor John Chapman, 46 Avenue Kleber; who at one time, before he settled there, had been the Proprietor and then Editor of *The Westminster Review*. In his review appeared in 1886 Pater's wonderful and fascinating essay on Coleridge; in 1887 his penetrating and revealing essay on Wincklemann. "He is the last fruit of the Renaissance, and explains in a striking way its motives and tendencies."

At that time I had heard a good deal of Moore; I had read very few of his novels; these I had found to be entertaining, realistic, and decadent; and certainly founded on modern French fiction. He made little or no impression on me on that occasion; he was Irish and amusing. Our conversation was probably on Paris and France and French prose. He gave me his address, King's Bench Walk, Inner Temple, and asked me to call on him after my return to London.

I was born, "like a fiend hid in a cloud," cruel, nervous, excitable, passionate, restless, never quite human, never quite normal and, from the fact that I have never known what it was to have a home, as most children know it, my life has been in many ways a wonderful, in certain ways a tragic one: an existence, indeed, so inexplicable even to myself, that I can not fathom it. If I have been a vagabond, and have never been able to root myself in any one place in the world, it is because I have no early memories of any one sky or soil. It has freed me from many prejudices in giving me its own unresting kind of freedom; but it has cut me off from whatever is stable, of long growth in the world.

When I came up to London, in 1889, I was fortunate enough to take one room in a narrow street, named Fountain Court. In 1821 Blake left South Molton Street for Fountain Court, where he remained for the rest of his life. The side window looked down through an opening between the houses, showing the river and the hills beyond; Blake worked at a table facing the window. At that time I had only seen the Temple; so that when I entered it for the first time in my life, to call on Moore, I was seized by a sudden fascination which never left me. I questioned him as to the chances I might have of finding rooms there; he wisely advised me to look at the outside of the window of the barber's shop, where notices of vacant flats were put up. Finally I saw: "Fountain Court: rooms to let." I immediately made all the necessary inquiries; and found myself in March, 1871, entire possessor of the top flat, which had a stone balcony from which I looked down on a wide open court, with a stone fountain in the middle. I lived there for ten years. My most intimate friends were, first and foremost, Yeats, then Moore: all three of us being of Celtic origin.

My intercourse with Moore was mostly at night; that is, when I was not wandering in foreign countries or absorbed in much more animal and passionate affairs. I dedicated to him *Studies in Two Literatures* 1897; the dedication was written in Rome, which begins: "My dear Moore, Do you remember, at the time when we were both living in the Temple, and our talks used to begin with midnight, and go on until the first glimmerings of dawn shivered among the trees, yours and mine; do you remember how often we have discussed, well, I suppose, everything which I speak of in these studies in the two literatures which we both chiefly care about." It ends: "I think of our conversations now in Rome, where, as in those old times in the Temple, I still look out of my window on a fountain in a square; only, here, I have the Pantheon to look at, on the other side of my fountain."

George Moore, whose *Pagan Poems* were a mixture of atrociously rhymed sensations, abnormal and monstrous, decadent and depraved, not without a sense of luxury and of color, and yet nothing more than feverish fancies and delirious dreams, has in some way fashioned a French sonnet which is an evident imitation of Mallarmé's. Only, between these writers is, as it were, an abyss. It has been Mallarmé's distinction to have always aspired after an impossible liberation of the soul of literature from what is fretting and constraining in "the body of that death" which is the mere literature of words. Finally come his "last period" – after the jewels of Hérodiade, which scattered and recaptured sudden fire, – in which his spirit wandered in an opaque darkness; as for instance, in the sonnet, made miraculously out of the repetition of two rhymes – "onyx lampadophore" – or, by preference, one that begins:

Une dentelle s'abolit.

Here, then, is Moore's sonnet to Edouard Dujardin.

La chair est bonne de l'alose
Plus fine que celle du bar,
Mais la Loire est loin et je n'ose
Abandonner Pierre Abélard.

Je suis un esclave de l'art;
La sage Héloise se pose
Sans robe, sans coiffe et sans fard,
Et j'oublie aisément l'alose.

Mais je vois la claire maison –
Arbres, pelouses et statue.
Du jardin, j'entend ta leçon:

Raison qui sauve, foi qui tue,
Autels éclabousses du son
Que verse une idole abattue.

I find in Moore's *Confessions* these sentences: "A year passed; a year of art and dissipation – one part art, two parts dissipation. And we thought there was something very thrilling in leaving the Rue de la Gaieté, returning to my home to dress, and presenting our spotless selves to the élite. And we succeeded very well, as indeed all young men do who waltz perfectly and avoid making love to the wrong woman." I should have preferred to read those sentences in French rather than in English; they are essentially Parisian and of the *grands Boulevards*; only, the end of the last sentence must have been suggested from some cynical phrase written by Balzac. Add to this the egoism of the Irishman: after that, what more do we need in the way of comparisons?

That Balzac is the greatest, the most profound, thinker in French literature after Blaise Pascal, is certain. Only, he had a more creative genius than any novelist, a genius unsurpassable and unsurpassed; in proof of which – if such a proof were actually required – I give these sentences of Baudelaire translated by Swinburne. "To me it had always seemed that it was his chief merit to be a visionary, and a passionate visionary; all his characters are gifted with the ardours of life which animated himself. In a word, every one in Balzac, down to the very scullions, has genius. Every mind is a weapon loaded to the muzzle with will. It is actually Balzac himself." Somewhere, he compares Shakespeare with Balzac; and adds: "Balzac asserts, and Balzac cannot blunder or lie. He has that wonderful wisdom, never at fault on its own ground, which made him not simply the chief of dramatic story, but also the great master of morals."

No critic could for one instant apply to any of George Moore's novels the phrase of "grand spiritual realism." A realist he always has been; a realist, who, having founded himself on French novelists, has really, in certain senses, brought something utterly new into English fiction. Luckily, he is Irish; luckily, he lived the best years of his youth in Paris. His prose shows the intense labor with which he produced every chapter of every novel; in fact, there is too much of the laborious mind in all his books. He was right in saying in *Avowals*: "Real literature is concerned with description of life and thoughts of life rather than with acts. He must write about the whole of life and not about parts of life, and he must write truth and not lies." The first sentence expresses the writer's sense of his own prose in his novels: and yet there is always a lot of vivid action in them. Only the greatest novelists have written about the whole of life: Balzac, Tolstoi, Cervantes, for instance; but the fact is that Balzac is always good to reread, but not Tolstoi: I couple two giants. Goriot, Valérie Marneffe, Pons, Landsch are called up before us after the same manner as Othello or Don Quixote; Balzac stakes all on one creation, exactly as Shakespeare stakes all in one creation.

Writing on Joseph Conrad, I referred to one of his tricks – which seem inextricable tricks of art – which he learned from Balzac: the method, which he uses in *Youth*, of doubling or trebling the interest by setting action within action, as certain pictures are set within certain frames. It is astonishing to find the influence Balzac had on Conrad, partly when suspense is scarcely concerned with action, partly in his involved manner of relating events. In Balzac I often find that some of his tales, like Conrad's, grow downwards out of an episode at the end; in some the end is told first, the beginning next – which was a method Poe often used – and last of all in the middle; for instance, in *Honorine*.

Writing of Zola I said:

> Zola has defined art, very aptly, as nature seen through a temperament. The art of Zola is nature seen through a formula. He observes, indeed, with astonishing closeness, but he observes in support of preconceived ideas. And so powerful is his imagination that he has created a whole world which has no existence anywhere but in his own brain, and he has placed there imaginary beings, so much more logical than life, in the midst of surroundings which are themselves so real as to lend almost a semblance of reality to the

embodied formulas who inhabit them.

As I have said that George Moore might be supposed to be a lineal descendant of Zola, it seems to me that in many ways his method is almost the same as Zola's; only, they have different theories; both observe with immense persistence; but their manner of observation, after all, is only that of the man in the street; while, on the contrary, the Goncourts create with their nerves, with their sensations, with their noting of the sensations, with the complex curiosities of a delicately depraved instinct. The strange woman in *La Faustin* is one of Goncourt's most fascinating creations: Germinie Lacerteux, his most sordidly depraved animal; and in the Preface to that novel, in 1864, they were right in saying: "*Aujourd'hui que le Roman s'élargit et grandit, qu'il commence à être la grande forme sérieuse, passionnée, vivante, de l'Étude littéraire et de enquête sociale, qu'il devient, par l'analyse et par la recherche psychologique, l'Histoire morale contemporaine.*" They were the first, I believe, to invent an entirely new form, a breaking-up of the plain, straightforward narrative into chapters, which are generally disconnected, and sometimes no more than six sentences: as, for instance, in that perverse, decadent, delicately depraved study of the stages in the education of the young Parisian girl, *Chérie* (for all its "immodesty") was an admirable thing, and a model for all such studies. Only, when I have to choose, after Balzac, the most wonderfully created woman in any novel, the vision of Emma Bovary starts before me – a woman, as I have said somewhere (with none of the passionate certainty of Charles Baudelaire) who is half vulgar and half hysterical, incapable of a fine passion; her trivial desires, her futile aspirations after second-hand pleasures and second-hand ideals, give to Flaubert all that he wants: the opportunity to create beauty out of reality.

I have always had a great admiration of Camille Lemonnier, who brought something rare, exotic and furiously animal into Flemish prose; as in his masterpiece, *Un Mâle*, where he reveals in an astonishing fashion those peasants who are so brutal, yet so subtly and rudely apprehended, in their instincts: these peasants who are the most elemental of human beings. He has none of Hardy's sinister and dejected vision of life; who often seems closer to the earth than to men and women, and who sees women and men out of the eyes of wild creatures; whose peasants have been compared with Shakespeare's. Lemonnier's women and men have in them something mysterious, dramatic, tragic: in their loves and hatreds, in their crimes and joys, they have something of the mysterious force which germinates in the furrows which they turn.

Pater, who hated every form of noise and of extravagance, who disliked whatever seemed to him either sordid or morbid, guarded himself from all these and from many other things by the wary humor that protects the sensitive. So, in his reviews of Wilde and of Moore, he is always very much on his guard as to the manner of expounding his individual opinions; saying of Wilde that his *Dorian Gray* "may fairly claim to go with that of Edgar Poe, and with some good French work of the same kind, done – probably – in more or less conscious imitation of it." So in praising Moore's clever book, he refers to his "French intuitiveness and gaillardise;" saying that he is "a very animating guide to the things he loves, and in particular to the modern painting of France," that (here he uses his wary humor) "these chapters have, by their very conviction, their perverse conviction, a way of arousing the general reader, lost perhaps in the sleep of conventional ideas," that, to and with "the reader may now judge fairly of Moore's manner of writing; may think perhaps there is something in it of the manner of the artists he writes of."

One of the most original pictures of Degas is *L'Absinthe*, which represents Desboutins in the *café* of the *Nouvelle Athènes* seated beside a woman. Moore says "Desboutins always came to the *café* alone, as did Manet, Degas, Darentz. Desboutins is thinking of his dry points; the woman is incapable of thought. If questioned about her life she would probably answer, *Je suis à la coule.*" To my mind Degas gives in this picture, in a more modern way than Manet, an equal vision of reality. Desboutins, the Bohemian painter, sits there in a mood of grim dissatisfaction; he is just as living as the depraved woman who sits beside him – before the glass of absinthe that shines like an enormous and sea-green jewel – with eyes in which much of her shameful earthiness is betrayed, without malice, without pity.

I open at random, the pages of *Confessions of a Young Man* where there is a reference to the *café* of the *Nouvelle Athènes*, Place Pigalle; where the writer confesses more of himself than on any other page of his book.

> I am a student of ball rooms, bar rooms, streets and alcoves. I have read very little; but all I read I can turn to account, and all I read I remember. To read freely, extensively, has always been my ambition, and my utter inability to study has always been to me a subject of grave inquietude, – study, as contrasted with a general and haphazard gathering of ideas taken in flight. But in me, the impulse is so original to frequent the haunts of men that it is irresistible, conversation is the breath of my nostrils, I watch the movement of life, and my ideas spring from it uncalled for, as buds from branches. Contact with the world is in me the generating force; without it what invention I have is thin and sterile, and it grows thinner rapidly, until it dies away utterly, as it did in the composition of my unfortunate *Roses of Midnight.*

I turn from those sentences to Casanova, whose *Memoirs* are one of the most wonderful autobiographies in the world; who, always passionate after sensations, confesses, in his confessions, the most shameless things that have ever been written: one to whom woman was, indeed, the most important thing in the world, but to whom nothing in the world was indifferent. He was, as he professes, always in love – at least, with something. Being of origin Venetian and Spanish, he had none of the cold blooded libertinism of Valmont in *Les Liaisons Dangereuses* of Laclos. Baudelaire, in two of his sweeping Paradoxes, said of this book: "*Ce livre, s'il brûle, ne peut brûler qu'à la manière de la glace. Tous les livres sont immoraux.*" Casanova, himself, is the primitive type of the Immoralist, in certain senses of the abnormal Immoralist. His latest reincarnation is an André Gide's *L'Immoraliste*; a book perverse and unpassionate.

Now, let us return to the modern writer's Confessions. Whether Moore has read the whole of Casanova or not, there are curiously similar touches in both these writers; as, for instance, in the word "alcoves, streets, ballrooms." Instead of the modern "barrooms" use the word *cafés*. One essential difference is that Casanova had a passion for books: the more essential one is, that Casanova was born to be a vagabond and a Wanderer over almost the whole of Europe, that he had tasted all the forbidden fruits of the earth, and that he had sinned with all his body – leaving, naturally, the soul out of the question.

Every great artist has tasted the sweet poison of the Forbidden Fruit. The Serpent, the most "subtile" of all the Beasts, gave an apple he had gathered from the Tree of the Knowledge of Good and Evil to Eve; she having eaten it and having given one to Adam, both saw they were naked, and, with nakedness, Sin entered into the World. Now, what was stolen from the Garden of God has, ever since, been the one temptation which it is almost impossible to resist. For instance Shakespeare stole from Marlowe, Milton stole from Shakespeare, Keats stole from Virgil, Swinburne stole from Baudelaire and Crashaw, Browning stole from Donne; as for Wagner, having stolen a motet from Vittorio which he used, almost note for note in *Parsifal*, also from Palestrina and his school, and from Berlioz and from Liszt, it is impossible to say what he did not steal. Oscar Wilde stripped, as far as he could, all the fruit he could gather from the orchards of half a dozen French novelists; besides those of Poe and of Pater. Gabrielle d'Annunzio has stolen as thoroughly as Wilde; in fact, the whole contents of certain short stories. As for George Moore, he has been guilty of as many thefts as these; only he has concealed his thefts with more stealth. Henry James said to some one of my acquaintance: "Moore has an absolute genius for picking other men's brains." That saying is as final as it is fundamental.

Rossetti said: "There ought to be always, double of oneself, the self-critic, who should be one always with the poet." The legend of the Doppelgänger haunted him; the result of which is *How They Met Themselves*, where two lovers wandering in a wood come on their doubles, apparitions who, casting their perilous eyes on them sidewise, vanish. It is mysterious and menacing. Pater uses the same symbol: three knights as they hear the night-hawk, are confronted by their own images, but with blood, all three of them, fresh upon the brow, or in the mouth. "It were well to draw the sword, be one's enemy carnal or spiritual; even devils, as all men know, taking flight at its white glitter through the air. Out flashed the brave youths' swords, still with mimic counter-motion, upon nothing – upon the empty darkness before them." These revenants are ghost-like and flame-like: they are the symbols of good and evil; the symbols of the haunting of one uneasy conscience. Balzac, Blake, Hawthorne, saw them in visions; the moderns, such as Maupassant and Moore, must always ignore them.

The novel and the prose play are the two great imaginative forms which prose has invented for itself. Prose is the language of what we call real life, and it is only in prose that an illusion of external reality can be given. And, in any case, the prose play, the novel, come into being as exceptions and are invented by men who can not write plays in verse. Only in the novel and the prose play does prose become free to create, free to develop to the utmost limits of its vitality. Perhaps the highest merit of prose consists in this, that it allows us to think in words. But art, in verse, being strictly and supremely on art, begins by trans-forming. Indeed, there is no form of art which is not an attempt to capture life, to create life over again.

The rhythm of poetry is musical; the rhythm of prose is physiological. For this reason Ibsen's prose is like that of a diagram in Euclid; it is the rhythm of logic, and it produces in us the purely mental exaltation of a problem solved. Swinburne, writing on Wilkie Collins's *Armadale*, declares that the heroine who dies of her own will by her own crime, had an American or a Frenchman introduced her, no acclamation would have been too vehement to express their gratitude! "But neither Feuillet nor Hawthorne could have composed and constructed such a story; the ingenuity spent on it may possibly be perverse, but is certainly superb." As I have never read one line of Feuillet I am no judge of his merit as a novelist. Hawthorne had a magical imagination, a passion for "handling sin" purely; he was haunted by what is obscure and abnormal in that illusive region which exists on the confines of evil and good; his opinion of woman was that she "was plucked out of a mystery, and had its roots still clinging to her." Sin and the Soul, those are the problems he has always before him; Sin, as our punishment; the Soul, in its essence, mist-like and intangible. He uses his belief in witchcraft with admirable effect, the dim mystery which clings about haunted houses, the fantastic gambols of the soul itself, under what seems like the devil's own promptings.

In the whole of Moore's prose there is no such magic, no such mystery, no such diabolism; he is not so lacking in imagination as in style. He has always been, with impressive inaccuracy, described as the English Zola; at the outset of his career he gained a certain notoriety not unlike Zola's; his novels are not based on theories, as some of Zola's are. Moore always knew how to make a cunning plot, to make some of his compositions masterly, and how to construct his characters – which, to a certain extent, are living people, really existent, as their surroundings. As I say further on: "Compare with any of Zola's novels the amazingly clever novel of Moore, *A Mummer's Wife*, which goes with several other novels which are – well – *manqués*, in spite of their ability, their independence, their unquestionable merits of various kinds." The style always drags more than the action. Vivid, sensual, not sensuous, often perverse, never passionate; written with a curious sense of wickedness, of immorality, of vice; extraordinary at times in some of the scenes he evokes in one or several chapters; always with the French element; his prose exotic, morbid, cruel, as cruel as this catsuit of the passions, has in it a certain scorn and contempt of mediocrities, which can be delivered with the force of a sledge-hammer that strikes an anvil and shoots forth sparks.

II

George Moore has been described, with impressive inaccuracy, as the English Zola. At what was practically the outset of his career he gained a certain notoriety; which did him good, by calling public attention to an unknown name; it did him harm, by attaching to that name a certain stigma. In a certainly remote year, but a year we all of us remember, there were strange signs in the literary Zodiac. There had been a distinctly new growth in the short story, and along with the short story ("poisonous honey stolen from France") came a new license in dealing imaginatively with life, almost permitting the Englishman to contend with the writers of other nations on their own ground; permitting him, that is to say, to represent life as it really is. Foreign influences, certainly, had begun to have more and more effect upon the making of such literature as is produced in England nowadays; we had a certain acceptance of Ibsen, a popular personal welcome of Zola, and literary homage paid to Verlaine. What do these facts really mean? It is certain that they mean something.

The visit of Zola, for instance – how impossible that would have been a little while ago! A little while ago we were opening the prison doors for the publishers who had ventured to bring out translations of *Nana* and *La Terre*; now we open the doors of the Guildhall for the author of *Nana* and *La Terre*; and the same pens, with the same jubilance, chronicle both incidents. To the spectator of the comedy of life all this is merely amusing; but to the actor in the tragic comedy of letters it means a whole new *repertoire*. Not so very many years ago George Moore was the only novelist in England who insisted on the novelist's right to be true to life, even when life is unpleasant and immoral; and he was attacked on all sides.

The visit of Paul Verlaine, too – unofficial, unadvertised, as it was – seemed to be significant of much. In the first place, it showed, as in the case of Zola, a readiness on the part of some not unimportant section of the public to overlook either personal or literary scandal connected with a man of letters who has done really remarkable work. But the interest of Verlaine's visit was much more purely literary than that of Zola; his reception was in no sense a concession to success, but entirely a tribute to the genius of a poet.

I find that William Watson published only one tiny volume of verse, the barren burlesque of *The Eloping Angels*, which should never have been printed, and a book of prose, *Excursions in Criticism*, the criticism and the style being alike as immature and unbalanced as his verse is generally mature and accomplished; while Mr. Le Gallienne has forsaken the domesticity of the muse, to officiate, in *The Religion of a Literary Man*, as the Canon Farrar of the younger generation. The most really poetic of the younger poets, W. B. Yeats, who has yet to be "discovered" by the average critic and the average reader, has this year published a new volume of verse, *The Countess Kathleen*, as well as a book of prose stories, *The Celtic Twilight*, and, in conjunction with Edwin J. Ellis, a laborious study in the mysticism of William Blake. Yeats' work, alone among recent work in verse, has the imaginative quality of vision; it has the true Celtic charm and mystery; and while such admirable verse as Watson's, such glowing verse as Thompson's, are both superior, on purely technical grounds, to Yeats', neither has the spontaneous outflow of the somewhat untrained singing-voice of the younger poet.

Another writer of verse who has not yet been estimated at his proper value, John Davidson, has also published a new book of poems, *Fleet Street Eclogues*, and a book of prose, *A Random Itinerary*. It is difficult to do justice to Davidson, for he never does justice to himself. His verse is always vivid and striking; at its best it has a delightful quality of fantastic humor and quaint extravagance; but it is singularly uneven, and never, in my opinion, at its best in purely modern subjects. The *Random Itinerary* is a whole series of happy accidents; but there are gaps in the series. Davidson strikes one as a man who might do almost anything; why, then, does he not do it?

Now, these paradoxical digressions have brought me back to the question of Zola and Moore, and of the realistic novel. Moore's were based on no theories; Zola's on certain theories, really a view of humanity which he adopted as a formula: "Nature seen through a temperament;" a definition supposed to be his definition of all art; which it most certainly is not. Yet nothing, certainly, could be more exact and expressive as a definition of the art of Huysmans.

Zola has made up his mind that he will say everything without omitting a single item; so that his vision is the vision of the mediocre man; and his way of finding out in a slang dictionary that a filthy idea can be expressed by an ingeniously filthy phrase in *Argot*, is by no means desirable. Every one knows two sentences in that supreme masterpiece, *Madame Bovary*, how that detail, brought in without the slightest emphasis of the husband turning his back at the very instant when his wife dies, is a detail of immense psychological value; it indicates to us, at the very beginning of the book, just the character of the man about whom we are to read so much. Zola would have taken at least two pages to say that, and, after all, he would not have said it.

Compare with any of Zola's novels the amazingly clever novel of Moore, *A Mummer's Wife*, which goes with several other novels which are – well – *manqués*, in spite of their ability, their independence, their unquestionable merits of various kinds. *A Mummers Wife* is admirably put together, admirably planned and shaped; the whole composition of the book is masterly. The style may drag, but not the action; the construction of a sentence may be uncertain, but not the construction of a character. The actor and his wife are really living people; we see them in their surroundings, and we see every detail of those surroundings. Here, of course, he would never have made Zola's stupid mistake; but can one imagine for a moment – I certainly can not – the writer of this novel writing, creating, (if I may dare use the word) two such sentences of Flaubert, which I quote in their original? *"Huit jours après, comme elle étendait du linge dans sa cour, elle fut prise d'un crachement de sang, et le lendemain, tandis que Charles avait le dos tourné pour fermer le rideau de la fenêtre, elle dit: 'Ah! Mon Dieu!' poussa un soupir et s'évanouit. Ella était morte."*

George Moore's *Modern Painting* is full of injustices, brutality and ignorances; but it is full also of the most generous justice, the most discriminating sympathy, and the genuine knowledge of the painter. It is hastily thought out, hastily written; but here, in these vivid, direct, unscrupulously logical pages, you will find some of the secrets of the art of painting, let out, so to speak, by an intelligence all sensation, which has soaked them up without knowing it. Yet, having begun by trying to paint, and having failed in painting, and so set himself to the arduous task of being a prose-writer, he is often, in spite of his painter's accuracy as to "values" and "technique" and so on, unreliable.

For, being neither creative as a novelist nor as a critic, he has nothing, as a matter of course, of two among many essential qualities: vision and divination. Take, for instance, a few pages anywhere in *L'Art Romanesque* of Baudelaire, or from his prose on Delacroix, on Constantine Guys, on Wagner, on Daumier, on Whistler, on Flaubert, and on Balzac – where he is always supreme and consummate, "fiery and final" – and place these beside any chosen pages of Moore's prose on either Balzac or on Whistler, and you will see all the difference in the world: as I have said above, between the creative and the uncreative criticism.

Had Walter Pater devoted himself exclusively to art criticism, there is no doubt that, in a sense, he would have been a great art critic. There are essays scattered throughout his work, as in the Botticelli where he first introduces Botticelli to the modern world, as in the Leonardo da Vinci – in which the simplest words take color from each other by the cunning accident of their placing in the sentences, the subtle spiritual fire kindling from word to word creates a masterpiece, a miracle in which all is inspiration, all is certainty, all is evocation, and which, in the famous page on *La Gioconda*, rises to the height of actually lyrical prose – in which the essential principles of the art of painting are divined and interpreted with extraordinary subtlety. In the same sense all that Whistler has written about painting deserves to be taken seriously, and read with understanding. Written in French, and signed by Baudelaire, his truths, and paradoxes reflecting truths, would have been realized for what they are. He fought for himself, and spared no form of stupidity: for, in Whistler, apart from his malice, his poisonous angers, taste was carried to the point of genius, and became creative.

George Moore's literary career has been singularly interesting; his character as a writer is very curious. A man who respects his art, who is devoted to literature, who has a French eye for form, he seems condemned to produce work which is always spotted with imperfection. All his life he has been seeking a style, and he has not yet found one. At times he drops into style as if by accident, and then he drops style as if by design. He has a passionate delight in the beauty of good prose; he has an ear for the magic of phrases; his words catch at times a troubled expressive charm; yet he has never attained ease in writing, and he is capable of astounding incorrectness – the incorrectness of a man who knows better, who is not careless and yet who can not help himself. Yet the author of *A Mummer's Wife*, of *The Confessions of a Young Man*, of *Impressions and Opinions*, has more narrowly escaped being a great writer than even he himself, perhaps, is aware.

FRANCIS THOMPSON

I

If Crashaw, Shelley, Donne, Marvell, Patmore and some other poets had not existed, Francis Thompson would be a poet of remarkable novelty. Not that originality, in the strictest sense, is always essential to the making of a poet. There have been poets who have so absolutely lived in another age, whose whole soul has been so completely absorbed by a fashion of writing, perhaps a single writer, belonging to an earlier century, that their work has been an actual reincarnation of this particular time or writer. Chatterton, for instance, remains one of the finest of English poets, entirely on account of poems which were so deliberately imitative as to have been passed off as transcripts from old manuscripts. Again, it is possible to be deftly and legitimately eclectic, as was Milton, for example. Milton had, in an extraordinary degree, the gift of assimilating all that he found, all that he borrowed. Often, indeed, he improved his borrowed goods; but always he worked them into the pattern of his own stuff, he made them part of himself; and wisdom is justified of her children. Now Thompson, though he affects certain periods, is not so absorbed in any one as to have found his soul by losing it; nor is he a dainty borrower from all, taking his good things wheresoever he finds them. Rather, he has been impressed by certain styles, in themselves incompatible, indeed implying the negation of one another – that of Crashaw, for instance, and that of Patmore – and he has deliberately mixed them, against the very nature of things. Thus his work, with all its splendors, has the impress of no individuality; it is a splendor of rags and patches, a very masque of anarchy. A new poet announces himself by his new way of seeing things, his new way of feeling things; Thompson comes to us a cloudy visionary, a rapturous sentimentalist, in whom emotion means colored words, and sight the opportunity for a bedazzlement.

The opening section of the book *Love in Dian's* Lap is an experiment in Platonic love. The experiment is in itself interesting, though here perhaps a little too deliberate; in its bloodless ecstasy it recalls *Epipsychidion*, which is certainly one of the several models on which it has been formed; it has, too, a finely extravagant courtliness, which belongs to an older school of verse as here: –

Yet I have felt what terrors may consort
In women's cheeks, the Graces' soft resort;
My hand hath shook at gentle hands' access,
And trembled at the waving of a tress;
My blood known panic fear, and fled dismayed,
Where ladies' eyes have set their ambuscade.
The rustle of a robe hath been to me
The very rattle of love's musketry;
Although my heart hath beat the loud advance,
I have recoiled before a challenging glance,
Proved gay alarms where warlike ribbons dance.
And from it all, this knowledge have I got, –
The whole, that others have, is less than they have not;
All which makes other women noted fair,
Unnoted would remain and overshone in her.

Finer, in yet a different style, is the poem *To a Poet Breaking Silence*, of which we may quote the opening lines: –

Too wearily had we and song
Been left to look and left to long,

Yea, song and we to long and look,
Since thine acquainted feet forsook
The mountain where the Muses hymn
For Sinai and the Seraphim.

Now in both the mountains' shine
Dress thy countenance, twice divine!
From Moses and the Muses draw
The Tables of thy double Law!
His rod-born fount and Castaly
Let the one rock bring forth for thee,
Renewing so from either spring
The songs that both thy countries sing:
Or we shall fear lest, heavened thus long,
Thou should'st forget thy native song,
And mar thy mortal melodies
With broken stammer of the skies.

Next after these poems of spiritual love come certain odes and lyrical pieces: one *To the Dead Cardinal of Westminster*, modeled, as to form, on Marvell's great ode: *A Judgment in Heaven*, in which we are permitted to see the angels "as they pelted each other with handfuls of stars" – the most clotted and inchoate poem in the volume; together with *A Corymbus for Autumn* and *The Hound of Heaven* which are the finest things Thompson has done. Here, with all his extravagance, which passes from the sublime to the ridiculous with all the composure of a madman, Thompson has grappled with splendid subjects splendidly. He can, it is true, say:–

Against the red throb of the sunset-heart
I laid my own to beat;

but he can also say (with a solemn imagery which has its precise meaning as well as its large utterance): –

I dimly guess what Time in mists confounds;
Yet ever and anon a trumpet sounds
From the hid battlements of Eternity,
Those shaken mists a space unsettle, then

Round the half-glimpsed turrets slowly wash again;
But not ere him who summoneth
I first have seen, enwound
With glooming robes purpureal, cypress-crowned;
His name I know, and what his trumpet saith.

Here, as ever, Thompson indulges in his passion for poly-syllables – "the splendent might of thy conflagrate fancies," for example; but forced words are less out of place in poems which, in the best sense of the word, are rhapsodies, than in poems such as those on children, which fill the last section of the book, and in which one may read of "a silvern segregation, globed complete," of "derelict trinkets of the darling young," and so forth. The last piece of all, *To Monica Thought Dying*, is written in downright imitation of Patmore; but how far is it, in its straining after fine effects of sound, its straining after fine effects of pathos, from the perfect justice of expression which Patmore has found in such poems as *The Toys* and *Poor Child!* for an equally perfect sentiment of the pathetic! That a writer who at his best is so fiery and exuberant should ever take Patmore for a model, should really try to catch even his tricks of expression, is very curious, and shows, as much as any other single characteristic, the somewhat external quality of Thompson's inspiration. A poet with an individuality to express, seeking for an individual form of expression, could scarcely, one fancies, have been drawn by any natural affinity so far away from himself and his main habitudes. Grashaw and Patmore – we come back to the old antagonism – can a man serve two such masters? Imagine Patmore rewriting, according to his own standard of composition, *The Flaming Heart*, or Crashaw treating in his own way the theme of *Deliciae Sapientiae de Amore!* Here and there, too, in Thompson's work, are reminiscences of Rossetti; as here: –

Yea, in that ultimate heart's occult abode
To lie as in an oubliette of God.

And the influence of Shelley is felt from the first line to the last. Yet, in spite of all this, Thompson has something, unquestionably, of "fine frenzy," not always quite under his own control; he amazes by his audacity, and delights by the violence with which he would fain storm Parnassus. His verse has generally fervor, a certain lyric glow, a certain magnificence; it has abundant fancy, and its measure of swift imagination. But the feast he spreads for us is a very Trimalchio's feast – the heaped profusion, the vaunting prodigality, which brings a surfeit; and, unlike Trimalchio, it could not be said of him *Omnia domi nascuntur.*

Verse, unless it is in some measure ecstasy, can not be poetry. But it does not follow that in verse the most fervid ecstasy is the best poetry. If, indeed, for "fervid" be substituted "fervidly expressed," it is quite the contrary. Coventry Patmore has pointed out that the sign of great art is peace, a peace which comes of the serene, angelic triumph over mortal tumults, and those less essential raptures which are after all flames of the earth's center. Francis Thompson has the ecstasy; but unfortunately he has not realized that ecstasy, if it is to be communicated from the soul to the soul, and not merely from the mouth to the ear, must be whispered, not shouted.

If a man's style is the man – his innermost self, as we may suppose, revealing itself in the very words he uses – Thompson, in a more special sense than almost any other writer, is seen in his language. He is that strange phenomenon, a verbal intelligence. He thinks in words, he receives his emotions and sensations from words, and the rapture which he certainly attains is a rapture of the disembodied word. It is not that his verse is without meaning, that in taking care of the sound he allows the sense (poor orphan!) to take care of itself. He has a meaning, but that meaning, if it has not a purely verbal origin, is at all events allowed to develop under the direct suggestion of the words which present themselves to interpret it. His consciousness is dominated by its own means of expression. And what is most curious of all is that, while Thompson has a quite recognizable manner, he has not achieved a really personal style. He has learned much, not always with wisdom, and in crowding together Cowley, Crashaw, Donne, Patmore, to name but a few of many, he has not remembered that to begin a poem in the manner of Crashaw, and to end it in the manner of Patmore, is not the same thing as fusing two alien substances into a single new substance. Styles he has, but not style. This very possession by the word has, perhaps, hindered him from attaining it. Fine style, the style in which every word is perfect, rises beautifully out of a depth into which words have never stretched down their roots. Intellect and emotion are the molders of style. A profound thought, a profound emotion, speaks as if it were unconscious of words; only when it speaks as if unconscious of words do the supreme words issue from its lips. Ornament may come afterward: you can not begin with ornament. Thompson, however, begins with ornament.

Unhappily, too, Thompson's verse is certainly fatiguing to read, and one of the reasons why it is so fatiguing is that the thought that is in it does not progress; it remains stationary. About the fragile life which cries somewhere in its center he builds up walls of many colored bricks, immuring his idea, hiding it, stifling it. How are we to read an ode of many pages in which there is no development, not even movement? Stanza is heaped upon stanza, page is piled upon page, and we end where we began. The writer has said endless things about something but never the thing itself. Poetry consists in saying the thing itself.

But this is not the only reason why it is fatiguing to read Thompson's verse. To read it is too much like jolting in a springless cart over a plowed field, about noontide, on a hot summer day. His lines, of which this is typical, –

Pulp the globed weight of juiced Iberia's grape,

are so packed with words that each line detains the reader.

Not merely does Thompson prefer the line to the stanza or the paragraph, he prefers the word to the line. He has failed to remember that while two and two make four, four are not necessarily better than two – that because red is brighter than gray, red is not necessarily the better color to use whenever one wants to use a color. He hears the brass in the orchestra sounding out loudly over the strings and he therefore suppresses the strings. He has a bold and prolific fancy, and he pampers his fancy; yet prodigality is not abundance, nor profusion taste. He is without reticence, which he looks upon as stint or as penury. Having invited his guests to his feast, he loads their plates with more than they can eat, forcing it upon them under the impression that to do otherwise is to be lacking in hospitality.

Yet, after all, the feast is there – Trimalchio's if you will, but certainly not a Barmecide's. Thompson has a remarkable talent, he has a singular mastery of verse, as the success of his books is not alone in proving. Never has the seventeenth-century phrasing been so exactly repeated as in some of his poems. Never have Patmore's odes been more scrupulously rewritten, cadence for cadence; Thompson's fancy is untiring, if sometimes it tires the reader; he has, not exactly at command, but not beyond reach, an eager imagination. No one can cause a more vaguely ardent feeling in the sympathetic reader, a feeling made up of admiration and of astonishment in perhaps equal portions. There are times when the fire in him bums clear through its enveloping veils of smoke, and he writes passages of real splendor. Why then does he for the most part wrap himself so willingly in the smoke?

II

In Francis Thompson's first volume of poems, I pointed out some of the sources of the so-called originality of all that highly colored verse – Crashaw, Shelley, Donne, Marvell, Patmore, Rossetti – and I expressed a doubt whether a writer who could allow himself to be so singularly influenced by such singularly different writers could be really, in the full sense of the term, a new poet. The book before me confirms my doubt. Thompson is careful to inform his readers that "this poem, though new in the sense of being now for the first time printed, was written some four years ago, about the same date as the *Hound of Heaven* in my former volume." Still, as he takes the responsibility of printing it, and of issuing it by itself, it may reasonably be assumed that he has written nothing since which he considers to be of higher quality.

The book consists of one long and obscure rhapsody in two parts. Why it should ever begin, or end, or be thus divided, is not obvious, nor, indeed, is the separate significance of most of the separate pages. It begins in a lilt of this kind: –

> The leaves dance, the leaves sing,
> The leaves dance in the breath of Spring.
>> I bid them dance,
>> I bid them sing,
>> For the limpid glance
>> Of my ladyling;
> For the gift to the Spring of a dewier spring,
> For God's good grace of this ladyling!

But the rhythm soon becomes graver, the lines charged with a more heavily consonnated burden of sound, as, for instance, in the opening of the second part: –

> And now, thou elder nursling of the nest,
> Ere all the intertangled west
>> Be one magnificence
> Of multitudinous blossoms that o'er-run
> The flaming brazen bowl o' the burnished sun

Which they do flower from
How shall I 'stablish *thy* memorial?

"I who can scarcely speak my fellows' speech," the writer adds, with more immediate and far-reaching truth than he intends. Thompson wilfully refuses to speak his fellows' speech, in order to speak a polysyllabic speech, made up out of all the periods of the English language – a speech which no one, certainly, has employed in just such a manner before, but which, all the same, does not become really individual. It remains, rather, a patchwork garb, flaming in all the colors, tricked out with barbaric jewels, and, for all its emphatic splendor, suggesting the second-hand dealer's.

In such a poem as *The Hound of Heaven*, in Thompson's former volume, there was a certain substratum of fine meaning, not obscured, or at all events not concealed, by a cloud of stormy words. But here I find no sufficing undercurrent of thought, passion, or reverie, nothing but fine fragments, splendid lines, glowing images. And of such fragments, however brilliant in themselves, no fine poetry can consist. Thompson declares of himself and his verse, with a really fervid sense of his own ardor:

And are its plumes a burning bright array?
They burn for an unincarnated eye.
A bubble, charioteered by the inward breath
    Which, ardorous for its own invisible lure,
Urges me glittering to aerial death,
    I am rapt towards that bodiless paramour;
Blindly the uncomprehended tyranny
    Obeying of my heart's impetuous might.

Scarcely could a single line express more concisely and more significantly the truth about Thompson than one of these lines. "Urges me glittering to aerial death:" how true that is in its confession of that fatal vagueness of aim, showiness of equipment and the toppling disaster of it all! Thompson has miscalculated his strength of flight. He is for ever straining after the heights, and there are moments when he seems to have reached them. But it is only that he has dazzled and confused our sight by the trick of some unfamiliar magic. And his magic, for the most part, is a magic of words. Those suggestions of a rare poetic vision, which, from the first, seemed nebulous rather than illuminated, have become little more than verbal sophistries. To have transposed a phrase until it becomes

To Naiad it through the unfrothing air

satisfies him as though it had been a vision or an invention. The frigid conceit of

The blushes on existence's pale face

satisfies him as though it were an imaginative conception. And such combinations of words as

The very hues
Which their conflagrant elements effuse

satisfy him as being effects of appropriate poetic novelty. The *Poems*, with all their faults, had suggestions of finer possibilities. In *Sister-Songs* none of these possibilities is realized. At the most it is a sort of fantastic world of waters (shall we say, at Thompson's suggestion?) where,

– like the phantasms of a poet pale,
    The exquisite marvels sail:
Clarified silver; greens and azures frail
As if the colours sighed themselves away,
And blent in supersubtile interplay
    As if they swooned into each other's arms;
        Repured vermilion,
        Like ear-tips 'gainst the sun;
And beings that, under night's swart pinion,
Make every wave upon the harbour bars
        A beaten yolk of stars.

But where day's glance turns baffled from the deeps,
    Die out those lovely swarms;
And in the immense profound no creature glides or creeps.

Francis Thompson's earlier volume of *Poems* attracted perhaps an undue amount of attention on account of its gorgeous and unusual qualities of diction, and a certain exuberant and extravagant fervor of mood. These are not indeed the characteristics of the highest kind of poetry, but they are characteristics which impress uncritical persons as being of the essence of poetic inspiration. To express a small thought by a large word is always impressive, and a certain excitement in the manner of it adds greatly to the effect of the performance. Thus, much writing which is merely feverish and blustering becomes admired for the quality of its defects, these defects being taken to be extraordinary merits; while writing which has all the quietness of true perfection passes unobserved or unrecognized. In particular it is forgotten that the expression of a thought should be like a well-fitting suit of clothes, following closely and gracefully the outlines of the body that informs it. Francis Thompson, alike in his former work and in the work which he has just brought out, is never content unless his thought is swathed in fold after fold of variegated drapery, cut after no recognized fashion and arranged on no consistent or indeed comprehensible plan. Take this passage, for instance, on page three of *Sister-Songs*:

Now therefore, thou who bring'st the year to birth,
    Who guid'st the bare and dabbled feet of May;
Sweet stem to that rose Christ, who from the earth
Suck'st our poor prayers, conveying them to Him;
    Be aidant, tender Lady, to my lay!
    Of thy two maidens somewhat must I say,
Ere shadowy twilight lashes, drooping, dim
Day's dreamy eyes from us;
Ere eve has struck and furled
The beamy-textured tent transpicuous,
    Of webbed coerule wrought and woven calms,
    Whence has paced forth the lambent-footed sun.

This is a fair, indeed a favorable, specimen of Thompson's way of "Making familiar things seem strange." His vocabulary is for the most part made up of an ingenious, and really novel, selection from the words that other people are ignorant of, or perhaps avoid if they know them: "battailously," for instance, or "illuminate and volute redundance," which will be found on a single page. He describes himself as a

Wantoner between the yet untreacherous claws
    Of newly-whelped existence;

while on another page he tells us:

The hours I tread ooze memories of thee, sweet!

He sees "blossoms mince it on river swells," and notices when

All the fair
Frequence swayed in irised wavers.

All this is surely a very artificial and unnecessary and inelegant way of expressing very ordinary matters. The same strain after a sort of exterior heightening of expression appears on every page. Often the language has a certain magnificence, and it is always employed in the service of a luxurious fancy, which not infrequently rises to the point of sheer imagination. But the whole book leaves no enduring impression on the mind, only the visual memory of flooding words, splashing in colored waves. As a piece of decoration, in this highly colored kind, it has qualities of extraordinary brilliance and audacity. And at times, becoming for a moment a little simpler than its wont, though still fantastic and freakish, it will present us with an effect like that in the following lines:

And thou, bright girl, not long shalt thou repeat
Idly the music from thy mother caught;

Not vainly has she wrought,
Not vainly from the cloudward-jetting turret
Of her aerial mind, for thy weak feet,
Let down the silken ladder of her thought.
　　She bare thee with a double pain,
　　Of the body and the spirit;
　　Thou thy fleshly weeds hast ta'en,
　　Thy diviner weeds inherit!

The precious streams which through thy young lips roll
　　Shall leave their lovely delta in thy soul.
　　　　Where sprites of so essential kind
　　　　　　Set their paces,
　　　　Surely they shall leave behind
　　　　　　The green traces
　　　　Of their sportance in the mind;
　　　　And thou shalt, ere we well may know it,
　　　　　　Turn that daintiness, a poet, –
　　　　　　　　Elfin-ring
　　　　Where sweet fancies foot and sing.

Such work as this comes strangely enough into the midst of contemporary verse, concerned as that for the most part is with other ends, and elaborated after quite another fashion. Always interesting, if never quite satisfying; too crowded, too loaded, rather than, as with most verse, meager and unfilled; curiously conceived, and still more curiously wrought out; it holds a unique position in the poetic literature of the day, if not, in Patmore's words concerning the earlier volume of *Poems*, "in the prominent ranks of fame, with Cowley and Crashaw." It is a book which no one else could have written, and in which no one can fail to admire, with however many reservations, the "illuminate and volute redundance" of an only too opulent talent.

For it is difficult to avoid the conviction that Thompson deliberately rejects simplicity, and even, at times, with an elaborate and conscious search after long and heavily colored words. There is in this book a translation of Victor Hugo's *Ce qu'on entend sur la Montagne*, a well known poem in the *Feuilles d'Automne*. In going carefully over Thompson's version and comparing it word for word with the original, we have found that where Victor Hugo – not a simple writer – is simple, Thompson embroiders upon him, and that where he is not simple, Thompson is always less so. For instance, in the very first couplet we have "let your tread aspirant rise" for *monté*; a few lines below,

> One day at least, whereon my thought, enlicensed to muse,
> Had drooped its wing above the beached margent of the ooze,

for

> *– un jour q'en rêve*
> *Ma pensée abattit son vol sur une grève.*

Further on,

> The one was of the waters; a be-radiant hymnal speech!

for

> *L'une venait des mers; chant de gloire; hymne heureux!*

And finally,

> And I made question of me, to what issues are we here,
> Whither should tend the thwarting threads of all this
> > ravelled gear,

in place of

> *Et je me demandai pourquoi l'on est ici,*
> *Quel peut être après tout le but de tout ceci.*

What could be more significant than this heaping up of long and extravagant and sometimes feeble words, instead of the direct language of Hugo, who in this poem, though not without a certain rhetoric, says exactly what he wants to say, and when, as in the last two lines quoted, he thinks that an almost bald simplicity will be in place, sets down his thoughts in terms of an almost bald simplicity? In this translation, Thompson has betrayed himself; he has allowed his critics to see him at work, substituting what is roundabout for what is straight-forward; what is lengthy for what is brief; what is elaborated for what is simple. Has not a similar process gone on in his own mind – how far consciously one can not tell – during the writing of his original poems?

III

The news comes to me on a little black-edged card that Francis Thompson died at dawn on November 13, 1907. He was a Roman Catholic, and we are asked to pray for his soul. It was a light that death could not put out, a torch that no wind could blow out in the darkness. From us indeed it is now turned away, and that little corner of the world to which the poet gives light is darkened.

For Francis Thompson was one of the few poets now or lately living in whom there was some trace of that divine essence which we best symbolize by fire. Emptiness he had and extravagances, but he was a poet, and he had made of many influences a form of new beauty. Much of his speech, which has a heaped imagery unique in our time, seems to have learned its technique from an almost indiscriminate quarrying among old quarries, and is sometimes so closely copied from that which was fantastically precise in Crashaw, Donne, Vaughan, that we wonder why it was not a few centuries ago that some one said:

Life is a coquetry
Of Death, which wearies me,
        Too sure
    Of the armour;

A tiring-room where I
Death's divers garments try,
      Till fit
    Some fashion sit.

No one since that time, when "conceits" could convey poetical substance, has touched so daintily on plain words, giving by the touch some transfiguring novelty. If it was a style learned, it was a style perfectly acquired, and at times equal to its original.

Words and cadences must have had an intoxication for him, the intoxication of the scholar; and "cloudy trophies" were continually falling into his hands, and half through them, in his hurry to seize and brandish them. He swung a rare incense in a censer of gold, under the vault of a chapel where he had hung votive offerings. The incense half obscures the offerings, and the dim figures of the saints painted on the windows. As he bows there in the chapel he seems to himself to be in "reverberant Eden-ways" or higher, at the throne of heaven, borne on "plumes night-tinctured, englobed and cinctured of saints." Passing beyond the world he finds strange shapes, full of pomp and wearing strange crowns; but they are without outline, and his words disguise, decorate, but do not reveal them.

When he chanted in his chapel of dreams, the airs were often airs which he had learned from Crashaw and Patmore. They came to life again when he used them, and he made for himself a music which was part strangely familiar and part his own, almost bewilderingly. Such reed-notes and such orchestration of sound were heard no where else; and people listened to the music, entranced as by a new magic.

When he put these dreams and this music into verse, with a craft which he had perfected for his own use, the poetry was for the most part a splendid rhetoric, imaginative and passionless, as if the moods went by, wrapped in purple, in a great procession. *The Hound of Heaven* has the harmonies of a symphony, and there are delicacies among its splendors, and, among instants of falsely fanciful sentiment, such august moments as this:

I dimly guess what Time in mists confounds;
Yet ever and anon a trumpet sounds
From the hid battlements of Eternity,
Those shaken mists a space unsettle, then
Round the half-glimpsed turrets slowly wash again.

It is full of fine and significant symbolism, it is an elaborate pageant of his own life, with all its miseries, heights, relapses, and flight after some eternity; but, as he writes it, it turns intellectual, and the voice is like that of one declaiming his confession. It was not thus that Christina Rossetti let us overhear a few of the deepest secrets of her soul.

The genius of Francis Thompson was oriental, exuberant in color woven into elaborate patterns, and went draped in old silken robes that had survived many dynasties. The spectacle of him was an enchantment; he passed like a wild vagabond of the mind, dazzling our sight. He had no message, but he dropped sentences by the way, cries of joy or pity, love of children, worship of the Virgin and saints and of those who were patron saints to him on earth; his voice was heard like a wandering music, which no one heeded for what it said, in a strange tongue, but which came troublingly into the mind, bringing it the solace of its old recaptured melodies. Other poets of his time have had deeper things to say, and a more flawless beauty; others have put more of their hearts into their song; but no one has been a torch waved with so fitful a splendor over the gulfs of our darkness.

COVENTRY PATMORE

The most austere poet of our time, Coventry Patmore, conceived of art as a sort of abstract ecstasy, whose source, limit and end are that supreme wisdom which is the innermost essence of love. Thus the whole of his work, those "bitter, sweet, few and veiled" songs, which are the fruit of two out of his seventy years, is love-poetry; and it is love-poetry of a quite unique kind. In the earlier of his two books, *The Angel in the House*, we see him, in the midst of a scientific generation (in which it was supposed that by adding prose to poetry you doubled the value of poetry) unable to escape the influence of his time, desperately set on doing the wrong thing by design, yet unable to keep himself from often doing the right thing by accident. In his later book, *The Unknown Eros*, he has achieved the proper recognition of himself, the full consciousness of the means to his own end; and it is by *The Unknown Eros* that he will love, if it is enough claim to immortality to have written the most devout, subtle and sublimated love-poetry of our century.

Patmore tells us in *The Angel in the House* that it was his intention to write

That hymn for which the whole world longs,
A worthy hymn in woman's praise.

But at that time his only conception of woman was the

conception of woman as the lady. Now poetry has nothing whatever to do with woman as the lady; it is in the novel, the comedy of manners, that we expect the society of ladies. Prose, in the novel and the drama, is at liberty to concern itself with those secondary emotions which come into play in our familiar intercourse with one another; with those conventions which are the "evening dress" by which our varying temperaments seek the disguise of an outward uniformity; with those details of life which are also, in a sense, details of costume, and thus of value to the teller of a tale, the actor on a stage. But the poet who endeavors to bring all this machinery of prose into the narrow and self-sufficing limits of verse is as fatally doomed to failure as the painter who works after photographs, instead of from the living model. At the time when *The Angel* was written, the heresy of the novel in verse was in the air. Were there not, before and after it, the magnificent failure of *Aurora Leigh*, the ineffectual, always interesting, endeavors of Clough, and certain more careful, more sensitive, never quite satisfactory, experiments of Tennyson? Patmore went his own way, to a more ingenious failure than any. *The Angel in the House* is written with exquisite neatness, occasional splendor; it is the very flower of the poetry of convention; and is always lifting the trivialities and the ingenuities to which, for the most part, it restricts itself, miraculously near to that height which, now and again, in such lines as *The Revelation*, it fully attains. But it is not here, it is in *The Unknown Eros* alone, that Patmore has given immortality to what is immortal in perishable things.

How could it be otherwise, when the whole force of the experiment lies in the endeavor to say essentially unpoetical things in a poetical manner?

> Give me the power of saying things
> Too simple and too sweet for words,

was his wise, reasonable, and afterward answered prayer.

Was it after the offering of such a prayer that he wrote of

Briggs,
Factotum, Footman, Butler, Groom?

But it is not merely of such "vulgar errors" as this that we have to complain, it is of the very success, the indisputable achievement, of all but the most admirable parts of the poem. The subtlety, the fineness of analysis, the simplified complexity, of such things as *The Changed Allegiance*, can scarcely be overpraised as studies in "the dreadful heart of woman," from the point of view of a shrewd, kindly, somewhat condescending, absolutely clear-eyed observer, so dispassionate that he has not even the privilege of an illusion, so impartial that you do not even do his fervor the compliment of believing it possible that his perfect Honoria had, after all, defects. But in all this, admirable as it is, there is nothing which could not have been as well said in prose. It is the point of view of the egoist, of the "marrying man," to whom

Each beauty blossomed in the sight
Of tender personal regard.

Woman is observed always in reference to the man who fancies she may prove worthy to be his "predestined mate," and it seems to him his highest boast that he is

proud

To take his passion into church.

At its best, this is the poetry of "being in love," not of love; of affection, not passion. Passion is a thing of flame, rarely burning pure, or without danger to him that holds that wind-blown torch in his hand; while affection, such as this legalized affection of *The Angel in the House*, is a gentle and comfortable warmth, as of a hearth-side. It is that excellent, not quite essential, kind of love which need endure neither pain nor revolt; for it has conquered the world on the world's terms.

Woman, as she is seen in *The Angel in the House*, is a delightful, adorable, estimable, prettily capricious child; demonstrably finite, capturable, a butterfly not yet Psyche. It is the severest judgment on her poet that she is never a mystery to him. For all art is founded on mystery, and to the poet, as to the child, the whole world is mysterious. There are experts who tell me that this world, and life, and the flowing of times past into times to come, are but a simple matter after all: the jarring of this atom against that, a growth by explicable degrees from a germ perhaps not altogether inexplicable. And there are the experts in woman, who will explain to me the bright disarray of her caprices, the strangeness of her moods, the unreason of her sway over man; assuring me that she is mysterious only because she is not seen through, and that she can never be seen through because into the depths of emptiness one can see but a little distance. Not of such is the true lover, the true poet. To him woman is as mysterious as the night of stars, and all he learns of her is but to deepen the mystery which surrounds her as with clouds. To him she is Fate, an unconscious part of what is eternal in things; and, being the liveliest image of beauty, she is to be reverenced for her beauty, as the saints are reverenced for their virtue. What is it to me if you tell me that she is but the creature of a day, prized for her briefness, as we prize flowers; loved for her egoism, as we love infants; marveled at for the exquisite and audacious completeness of her ignorance? Or what is it to me if you tell me that she is all that a lady should be, infinitely perfect in pettiness; and that her choice will reward the calculations of a gentleman? If she is not a flame, devouring and illuminating, and if your passion for her is not as another consuming and refining flame, each rushing into either that both may be commingled in a brighter ecstasy, you have not seen woman as it is the joy of the poet and the lover to see her; and your fine distinctions, your disentangling of sensations, your subtleties of interpretation, will be at the best but of the subject of prose, revealing to me what is transitory in the eternal rather than what is eternal in the transitory. The art of Coventry Patmore, in *The Angel in the House*, is an art founded on this scientific conception of woman. But the poet, who began by thinking of woman as being at her best a perfect lady, ended by seeing her seated a little higher than the angels, at the right hand of the Madonna, of whom indeed she is a scarcely lower symbol. She who was a bright and cherished toy in *The Angel in the House* becomes in *The Unknown Eros* pure spirit, the passionate sister of the pure idea. She is the mystical rose of beauty, the female half of that harmony of opposites which is God. She has other names, and is the Soul, the Church, the Madonna. To be her servant is to be the servant of all right, the enemy of all wrong; and therefore poems of fierce patriotism, and disdainful condemnation of the foolish and vulgar who are the adversaries of God's ordinances and man's, find their appropriate place among poems of tender human pathos, of ecstatic human and divine love.

And she is now, at last, apprehended under her most essential aspect, as the supreme mystery and her worship becomes an almost secret ritual, of which none but the adepts can fathom the full significance.

Vision, in *The Unknown Eros*, is too swift, immediate and far-seeing to be clouded by the delicate veils of dreams.

> Give me the steady heat
> Of thought wise, splendid, sweet,
> Urged by the great, rejoicing wind that rings
> With draught of unseen wings,
> Making each phrase, for love and for delight,
> Twinkle like Sirius on a frosty night:

that is his prayer, and it was not needful for him to

> remain
> Content to ask unlikely gifts in vain.

Out of this love-poetry all but the very essence of passion has been consumed; and love is seen to be the supreme wisdom, even more than the supreme delight. Apprehended on every side, and with the same controlling ardor, those "frightful nuptials" of the Dove and Snake, which are one of his allegories, lead upward, on the wings of an almost aerial symbolism, to those all but inaccessible heights where mortal love dies into that intense, self-abnegating, intellectual passion, which we name the love of God.

At this height, at its very highest, his art becomes abstract ecstasy. It was one of his contentions, in that beautiful book of prose, *Religio Poetae*, in which thought is sustained throughout at almost the lyrical pitch, that the highest art is not emotional, and that "the music of Handel, the poetry of Aeschylus, and the architecture of the Parthenon are appeals to a sublime good sense which takes scarcely any account of 'the emotions.'" Not the highest art only, but all art, if it is so much as to come into existence, must be emotional; for it is only emotion which puts life into the death-like slumber of words, of stones, of the figures on a clef. But emotion may take any shape, may inform the least likely of substances. Is not all music a kind of divine mathematics, and is not mathematics itself a rapture to the true adept? To Patmore abstract things were an emotion, became indeed the highest emotion of which he was capable; and that joy, which he notes as the mark of fine art, that peace, which to him was the sign of great art, themselves, the most final of the emotions, interpenetrated for him the whole substance of thought, aspiration, even argument. Never were arguments at once so metaphysical and so mystical, so precise, analytic and passionate as those "high arguments" which fill these pages with so thrilling a life.

The particular subtlety of Patmore's mysticism finds perhaps its counterpart in the writings of certain of the Catholic mystics: it has at once the clear-eyed dialectic of the Schoolmen and the august heat of Saint Theresa. Here is passion which analyzes itself, and yet with so passionate a complexity that it remains passion. Read, for instance, that eulogy of "Pain," which is at once a lyric rapture, and betrays an almost unholy depth of acquaintance with the hidden, tortuous and delightful way of sensation. Read that song of songs, *Deliciae Sapientiae de Amore*, which seems to speak, with the tongue of angels, all the secrets of all those "to whom generous Love, by any name, is dear." Read that other, interrupted song,

Building new bulwarks 'gainst the infinite,

"*Legem tuam dilexi.*" Read those perhaps less quintessential dialogues in which a personified Psyche seeks wisdom of Eros and the Pythoness. And then, if you would realize how subtle an argument in verse may be, how elegantly and happily expressed, and yet not approach, at its highest climb, the point from which these other arguments in verse take flight, turn to *The Angel in the House* and read "The Changed Allegiance." The difference is the difference between wisdom and worldly wisdom: wisdom being the purified and most ardent emotion of the intellect, and thus of the very essence of poetry; while worldly wisdom is but the dispassionate ingenuity of the intelligence, and thus of not so much as the highest substance of prose.

The word "glittering," which Patmore so frequently uses, and always with words which soften its sharpness, may be applied, not unsuitably, to much of his writing in this book: a "glittering peace" does indeed seem to illuminate it. The writing throughout is classical, in a sense in which perhaps no other writing of our time is classical. When he says of the Virgin:

Therefore, holding a little thy soft breath,
Thou underwent'st the ceremony of death;

or, of the eternal paradox of love:

Tis but in such captivity
The unbounded Heavens know what they be;

when he cries:

147

> O Love, that, like a rose,
> Deckest my breast with beautiful repose;

or speaks of "this fond indignity, delight;" he is, though with an entirely personal accent, writing in the purest classical tradition. He was accustomed always, in his counsels to young writers, to reiterate that saying of Aristotle, that in the language of poetry there should be "a continual slight novelty;" and I remember that he would point to his own work, with that legitimate pride in himself which was one of the fierce satisfactions of his somewhat lonely and unacknowledged old age. There is in every line of *The Unknown Eros* that continual slight novelty which makes classical poetry, certainly, classical. Learned in every meter, Patmore never wrote but in one, the iambic: and there was a similar restraint, a similar refusal of what was good, but not (as he conceived) the highest good, all strangeness of beauty, all trouble, curiosity, the splendor of excess, in the words and substance of his writing. I find no exception even in that fiercely aristocratic political verse, which is the very rapture of indignation and wrath against such things as seemed to him worthy to be hated of God.

Like Landor, with whom he had other points of resemblance, Coventry Patmore was a good hater. May one not say, like all great lovers? He hated the mob, because he saw in it the "amorous and vehement drift of Man's herd to hell." He hated Protestantism, because he saw in it a weakening of the bonds of spiritual order. He hated the Protestantism of modern art, its revolt against the tradition of the "true Church," the many heresies of its many wanderings after a strange, perhaps forbidden, beauty. Art was to him religion, as religion was to him the supreme art. He was a mystic who found in Catholicism the sufficing symbols of those beliefs which were the deepest emotions of his spirit. It was a necessity to him to be dogmatic, and he gave to even his petulances the irresistible sanction of the

Church.

Religio Poetae contains twenty-three short essays – many of them rather sermons than essays – on such topics as "Peace in Life and Art, Ancient and Modern Ideas of Purity, Emotional Art, Conscience, Distinction." There is nothing which marks it as of the present but an occasional personality, which we could wish absent, and a persistent habit of self-quotation. There is absolutely no popular appeal, no extraneous interest in the timeliness of subject, or the peculiarities of treatment; nothing, in fact, to draw the notice of the average reader or to engage his attention. To the average reader the book must be nothing but the vainest speculation and the dullest theory. Yet, in many ways, it is one of the most beautiful and notable works in prose that have appeared in recent years. It is a book, argumentative as it is, which one is not called on so much to agree with or dissent from as to ponder over, and to accept, in a certain sense, for its own sake. Patmore is one of the few surviving defenders of the faith, and that alone gives him an interesting position among contemporary men of letters. He is a Christian and a Catholic, that is to say the furthest logical development of the dogmatic Christian; but he is also a mystic; and his spiritual apprehensions are so vivid that he is never betrayed into dogmatic narrowness without the absolution of an evident vision and conviction. And, above all, he is a poet; one of the most essential poets of our time, not on account of the dinner-table domesticities of *The Angel in the House*, but by reason of the sublimated love-poetry of *The Unknown Eros*, with its extraordinary subtlety of thought and emotion, rendered with the faultless simplicity of an elaborate and conscious art. His prose is everywhere the prose of a poet. Thought, in him, is of the very substance of poetry, and is sustained throughout at almost the lyrical pitch. There is, in these essays, a rarefied air as of the mountain-tops of meditation; and the spirit of their pondering over things, their sometimes remote contemplation, is always, in one sense, as Pater has justly said of Wordsworth, impassioned. Each essay in itself may at once be said to be curiously incomplete or fragmentary, and yet singularly well related as a part to a whole, the effect of continuity coming from the fact that these are the occasional considerations of a mind which, beyond that of most men, is consistent and individual. Not less individual than the subject-matter is the style, which in its gravity and sweetness, its fine, unforbidding austerity, its smooth harmony – a harmony produced by the use of simple words subtly – is unlike that of any contemporary writer, though much akin to Patmore's own poetic style.

The subjects with which these essays deal may be grouped under three heads: religion, art and woman. In all Patmore's attitude is intensely conservative and aristocratic – fiercely contemptuous of popular idols and ideals, whenever he condescends to notice them. The very daring and very logical essay on "Christianity and Progress" is the clearest and most cogent statement of Christianity as an aristocracy, in opposition to the current modern view of it as a democracy, that has been made since the democratic spirit made its way into the pulpit. "Let not such as these," says Patmore,

> exalt themselves against the great Masters of the experimental science of Life, one of whom – St. Theresa, if I remember rightly – declares that more good is done by one minute of reciprocal communion of love with God than by the founding of fifty hospitals or of fifty churches.

It is from this point of view that Patmore writes:

> Many people doubt whether Christianity has done much, or even anything, for the "progress" of the human race as a race; and there is more to be said in defence of such doubt than most good people suppose. Indeed, the expression of this doubt is very widely considered as shocking and irreligious; and as condemnatory of Christianity altogether. It is considered to be equivalent to an assertion that Christianity has hitherto proved a "failure." But some who do not consider that Christianity has proved a failure, do, nevertheless, hold that it is open to question whether the race, as a race, has been much affected by it, and whether the external and

visible evil and good which have come of it do not pretty nearly balance one another.

It is with the same view of things, from the same standpoint, that Mr. Patmore states his ideal of the poetic art, and condemns what he considers the current misconception of the subject. "I may go further," he declares, in his vivacious attack on "Emotional Art,"

and say that no art can appeal "to the emotions only" with the faintest hope of even the base success it aspires to. The pathos of such art (and pathos is its greatest point) is wholly due to a more or less vivid expression of a vague remorse at its divorce from truth and order. The Dame aux Camelias sighs in all Chopin's music over her lost virtue, which, however, she shows no anxiety to recover, and the characteristic expression of the most recent and popular school of poetry and painting is a ray of the same sickly and in the most part hypocritical homage to virtue. Without some such homage even the dying and super-sensitive body of "emotional art" loses its very faintest pretensions to the name of art, and becomes the confessed carion of Offenbach's operas and the music-hall. Atheism in art, as well as in life, has only to be pressed to its last consequences in order to become ridiculous, no less than disastrous; and the "ideal," in the absence of an idea or intellectual reality, becomes the "realism" of the brothel and the shambles.

What, then, is the ideal, the proper substance and manner of poetry? It is thus defined in another essay, which contends that "Bad Morality is Bad Art:"

The poet, as a rule, should avoid religion altogether as a direct subject. Law, the rectitude of humanity, should be his only subject, as, from time immemorial, it has been the subject of true art, though many a true artist has done the Muse's will and knew it not. As all the music of verse arises, not from infraction, but inflection of the law of the set metre, so the greatest poets have been those the modulus of whose verse has been most variously and delicately inflected, in correspondence with feelings and passions which are the inflections of moral law in their theme. Masculine law is always, however obscurely, the theme of the true poet; the feeling and its correspondent rhythm, its feminine inflection, without which the law has no sensitive or poetic life. Art is thus constituted because it is the constitution of life, all the grace and sweetness of which arise from inflection of law, not from infraction of it, as bad men and bad poets fancy.

Again from the same standpoint, again with the same absolute and aristocratic outlook on the world, does Patmore "sing of the nature of woman" – the subject of his constant preoccupation as an artist, the one sufficing subject to which he has devoted all his art. The modern woman, one may suppose, is not likely to appreciate the precise manner in which Patmore exalts her sex. It is far too logical, too reasonable, too scrupulously according to nature; thus, for example, in a passage of characteristically delicate wit:

It is "of faith" that the woman's claim to the honour of man lies in the fact of her being the "weaker vessel." It would be of no use to prove what every Christian man and woman is bound to believe, and what is, indeed, obvious to the senses of any sane man or woman whatever. But a few words of random comment on the text may, by adding to faith knowledge, make man and woman – woman especially – more thankful than before for those conditions which constitute the chief felicity of her life and his, and which it is one of the chief triumphs of progress to render ever more and more manifest. The happiest result of the "higher education" of woman cannot fail to consist in the rendering of her weakness more and more daintily conspicuous. How much sweeter to dry the tears that flow because one cannot accede to some demonstrable fallacy in her theory of variable stars, than to kiss her into conformity to the dinner-hour or the fitness or unfitness of such-or-such a person to be asked to a picnic! How much more dulcet the *dulcis Amaryllidis ira* when Amaryllis knows Sophocles and Hegel by heart, than when her accomplishments extend only to a moderate proficiency in French and the pianoforte! It is a great consolation to reflect that, among all the bewildering changes to which the world is subject, the character of woman cannot be altered; and that, so long as she abstains from absolute outrages against nature – such as divided skirts, freethinking, tricycles, and Radical-ism – neither Greek, nor conic sections, nor political economy, nor cigarettes, nor athletics, can ever really do other than enhance the charm of that sweet unreasonableness which humbles the gods to the dust, and compels them to adore the lace below the last hem of her brocade!

Such, then, and so consistent, is Patmore's attitude in matters of religion, of art, and of the relation of man and woman. We are concerned neither to defend nor to contend against it, admitting only that, granted the premises (which, no doubt, can be taken on certain grave and ancient warrants), the deductions from those premises are strictly logical, and at the present day, as novel as they are logical. Patmore is inclined to be petulant, and he occasionally rides a hobby-horse so recklessly as to commit himself to incredible fallacies. But a book which attains perfection has never yet been produced, and Patmore's is close, very close indeed.

SIR WILLIAM WATSON

Why, I have sometimes asked myself, did not Pater say the right words on a writer greater than Mérimée – George Meredith? I imagine that he never admired his novels enough to try his hand on a subject not quite his own. Certain books, I confess, ought to have been launched at the British Philistine, like David's one convincing pebble, straight to the forehead. I confess also (my own fault it was in regard to Meredith) that to write about Carlyle, Swinburne or Meredith, without unconsciously reproducing some tricks of manner, is a feat of which any man might be proud.

The Egoist is a wonderful book, and in its elemental comedy it challenges Congreve and even Molière; but in the elemental tragedy of certain parts of *Rhoda Fleming* and *Richard Feverel*, he challenges Webster, or almost Shakespeare. Yet the uncouthness that disfigures certain pages in *Richard Feverel* is a mere after-taste of Arabian extravagance. It is a new kind of uncouthness that comes into prominence in *The Egotist* – that exaggeration of qualities which one sees in the later works of men who have a pronounced style, even in the case of Browning. No prose writer of our time has written finer or viler English than Meredith. It is a mistake to treat him as if he were stylist first, and novelist afterward, as Flaubert might almost be said to be. Meredith is a conscious artist always – as conscious as Goncourt, with whom he may be compared for his experimental treatment of language, his attempt to express what has never been expressed before by forcing words to say more than they are used to say. Sometimes they give his message, but ungraciously, like beaten slaves; sometimes the message seems to go astray. That is why Englishmen, forgetting triumph after splendid triumph of style, will sometimes tell you that Meredith can not write English, just as Frenchmen gravely assure one another that the novels of the Goncourts are written in any language but French.

That astonishing little volume, *Modern Love and Poems of the English Roadside*, published in 1862, has never received anything like justice except at the hands of such a fellow-craftsman as Swinburne. While I for one can not but feel that Meredith works more naturally, with a freer hand, in prose than in verse, that poem of *Modern Love* seems to me among the masterpieces of contemporary poetry. It is the most distinctly modern poem ever written. There has been nothing like it in English poetry: it brings into our literature something fundamentally new, essentially modern. Side by side with this super-subtle study of passion and sensation, we have the homely realism of "Juggling Jerry" – a poem which can only be compared with Burns' "Jolly Beggars" for triumphant success in perhaps the most difficult kind of literature.

So far I quote from an old article of mine, which was answered by William Watson. Here is part of his answer, printed in *The Academy*:

> Now I should like to ask, what has the British Philistine done that he should have a book shied at his head in the way Mr. Symons thinks desirable? As regards Meredith, it seems to me that the British Philistine has been most exemplary in what he would call the discharge of his duty. He has tried his very best to read Meredith, and has failed; or he has read Meredith, but has failed in the attempt to enjoy him. I fancy, however, that when Meredith's devotees speak of the British Philistine, they really mean the vast majority of the public, and it seems to me a little absurd, that because there is an author whose writings the public are comparatively indifferent to, it should be constantly assured that the only person not in the least

responsible for such indifference is the author. Other writers have achieved popularity before Meredith. Perhaps the best proof of the futility of trying to convert people into an attitude of admiration by "aiming" a book at them is afforded by Meredith's novels themselves. They are, in Mr. Symons' sense of the word, "aimed" at the British Philistine, if ever novels were. He has been pelted through, I do not know how many, volumes – but have the missiles converted him?

I leave all these questions unanswered, as they deserve no answer, after Time's verdict on Meredith. Now, what was, and is, the place of Sir William Watson in literature? The difference between literature and what is preeminently literary may be clearly illustrated on examination of his poems. No poems written in our time are more literary. They come to us asking to be received on account of their legitimate lineal descent from earlier poets, from Wordsworth and from Matthew Arnold for instance. "If," says the writer, frankly –

> If I be indeed
> Their true descendant, as the veriest hind
> May yet be sprung of kings, their lineaments
> Will out, the signature of ancestry
> Leap unobscured, and somewhat of themselves
> In me, their lowly scion, live once more.

Many of the poems are about poets, or about books; some are purely critical. And they are indeed, as they profess to be, in the tradition; they strike no unfamiliar note to any ears acquainted with the music of English poetry. Their range is limited, but within it they exhibit an unquestionable mastery of a particular kind of technique. Few lines are bad, all are careful, many are felicitous. Every poem has a certain neatness and order about it. The spirit of the whole work is orderly, reticent and dignified. Nothing has been left to chance, or to the appeal of lawless splendors. An artist has been at work. At work on what? At all events, not on the only really satisfactory material for the poet – himself. Watson tells us that he has chosen the best of himself for giving to the world:

> I have not paid the world
> The evil and the insolent courtesy
> Of offering it my baseness for a gift.

Well and good; but has he, in choosing among his selves, chosen really the essential one, base or not base, ignoble or not ignoble? He has chosen the self that loves good literature, thinks estimable thoughts, feels decorous emotions, and sets all this into polished and poetical verse. That is enough for the making of literary poetry, but not for poetry which shall be literature.

Watson, in his study of the great writers, seems never to have realized that what matters chiefly, what tells, is not the great phrase, but the personality behind the phrase. He has learned from many writers to make phrases almost as fine as those writers have made; his phrases are never meaningless in themselves, and they can be exquisite in their form. But the phrase, coming with nothing but its own significance behind it, a rootless flower, deriving no life from the soil, fails to convey to us more than an arid, unsatisfying kind of pleasure. There it is, a detached thing; to be taken, you may say, for what it is worth; only, live words will not be so taken. Compare Watson's "Ode to Autumn" with the "Ode to Autumn" of Keats. The poem is one of Watson's best poems; it is full of really poetical phraseology. But the ode of Keats means something in every word, and it means Keats quite as much as autumn. Watson's poem means neither autumn nor Watson; it represents Watson setting himself to describe autumn.

Take his "Hymn to the Sea." It is a long piece of exultant rhetoric, very finely imagined, full of admirable images; the most beautiful similes are gathered and brought together to represent the sea's multitudinous moods; but when the poem is finished, and you have admired it at leisure, you do not feel that this poet loves the sea. The poetry of Byron is assailable on many sides, but when he wrote those too rhetorical lines, now hackneyed almost out of recognition, beginning –

Roll on, thou deep and dark blue ocean, roll!

he wrote out of his heart, as nearly as he could, and the lines,
faulty as they are, have remained alive ever since. Mr. Watson's
verse is very much better verse, but will –

Grant, O regal in bounty, a subtle and delicate largess,

come back to men's lips as often, or for as long a time, as
those faulty lines of Byron's?

In his "Apologia," Watson replies to those who have
complained that he has brought nothing new into poetry –

I bring nought new
Save as each noontide or each Spring is new.
Into an old and iterative world.

And he asks –

Is the Muse
Fall'n to a thing of Mode, that must each year
Supplant her derelict self of yesteryear?

But he declines to see that the new thing which every
generation rightly asks of every new poet is by no means
"mode," or empty fashion of writing, but the one essential thing,
personality, which can never be twice the same. The reason why
you will not find any two poets writing in the same way is that
every genuine poet has to express himself in his own way,
whether it be by offering his own "baseness for a gift," like
Villon, or by building a new heaven and a new hell, like Dante.
The maker of literature puts this new thing into his work, in the
mere act of making it, and it stands out, as plainly as his
signature, in every line he writes. Not to find it is to have fallen
upon work which is but literary, "books made out of books." Walt
Whitman thought that such "pass away."

In that "Apologia" from which we have already quoted, Watson indignantly denounces those who think "all Art is cold" if "an ardor not of Eros' lips" is in it, and he attempts to indicate that state of vision in which man may know –

A deeper transport and a mightier thrill
Than comes of commerce with mortality.

Does he then,

In silence, in the visionary mood,

reach this ecstatic state? If so, it has left no impression on his poetry. In his poetry there is no vision, only speculation about vision; no ecstasy, only a reasonable meditation. He speaks of God, "the Whole," the "cosmic descant," and the large words remain empty. In such poems as *The Unknown God* and *The Father of the Forest* we seem to have been taught a lesson, read out in a resonant, well controlled voice; nothing has been flashed upon us, we have overheard nothing.

And, indeed, of how little of this poetry can we say, in the words of Mill's great definition, that it has been overheard! Its qualities, almost, though not quite, at the best, are the qualities of good oratory. Watson began by writing epigrams, admirable of their kind, with a more lyric nineteenth century handling of the sharp eighteenth century weapon. The epigram lies at the root of his work – that is to say, something essentially of the quality of prose. He is a Pope who has read Keats. Oratory or the epigram come into his most characteristic passages, as in the well known and much admired lines on the greatness and littleness of man:

Magnificent out of the dust we came
And abject from the Spheres.

Now that, striking and effective as it is, is an antithetical ingenuity which a really fine poet would have gone out of his way to avoid. It is oratory, not poetry, and it would make good oratory, for there point has need of all its sharpness; oratory is action.

It is through this oratorical quality of mind that Mr. Watson's style, though so ordered and measurably, often leaves an impression of having been deliberately heightened above the level of ordinary speech. The great things in poetry are song at the core, but externally mere speech. Think of some actual, anonymous Elizabethan song, and then read the piece which Watson has called "Song in Imitation of the Elizabethans." It is not merely that he has not captured the exact note of the period, but rather copied the note of a later period; such lines as

> Idly clanged the sullen portal,
> Idly the sepulchral door,

are not direct speech, and can therefore never become pure song. They are dressed in poetical phraseology, which is a very different thing.

It is curious to find this quality in a writer who is in every sense so critical. Behind a great deal of Watson's work there is the critical intelligence, not the poetical temperament. *Wordsworth's Grave* is written in discipleship to Matthew Arnold, and it is not Arnold when he is at his best – the Arnold of *Sohrab and Rustum* and *The Sick King in Bokhara* – that Watson has approached, but that half poet, half prose writer who wrote the Obermann poems. The foundation of those poems is prose, and a great deal of their substance is no more than rhymed prose. But at times the poet flashes out, transfiguring material and form for the moment, before he drops back into prose again. Watson's work is more on a level; he neither falls so low nor rises so high. But, even more than with Arnold, the substance of it is criticism, and the thinking and the style suggest the best kind of prose. Set the poem, with its finely chosen epithets and phrases – "Impassioned quietude, Thou wast home, Thou hadst, for weary feet, the gift of rest, the frugal note of Gray," and the like – beside Pater's essay on Wordsworth, and you will find many points of resemblance, and not only in the echo of "impassioned quietude" from Pater's "impassioned contemplation." Compare it with Matthew Arnold's essay on Wordsworth and you will again find many points of resemblance, not only in detail, which would not matter, but also in the whole way of approaching and handling the subject. Does the rhyme bring in any essential difference between specimens of fine prose and this poem, so well thought out, so poetically expressed? There lies the whole question, for if it does not bring such a difference, can it be accepted as poetry, as an adequate kind of poetry?

Criticism, though it may find place in a poem (as in Shelley's Letter to Maria Gisborne) can never be the basis of poetry. Pope tried to turn the current of English poetry into this narrow channel, but the sea-force soon had its way with the banks and dykes. Watson has tried to revive that heresy; he has disguised its principles under new terms, but it remains the same heresy. Poetry is even less a criticism of thought than it is a "criticism of life," it must be at all points creation, creation of life, creation of thought, if it is to be poetry in the true sense.

It is to Wordsworth, among many masters, that Watson tells us that he is most indebted. Wordsworth is not always a safe master, and it is apparently from him that Mr. Watson has accepted the main principles of his blank verse. Wordsworth's blank verse was more often bad than good; it was bad on principle, and good by the grace of a not infrequent inspiration. At its best, it is not among the great specimens of blank verse, or not for more than a very few lines at a time. It is without vitality, it is without that freedom in beauty which can come from vitality alone. Watson has learned from Wordsworth that it is possible to write grave and impressive lines, sweeping up to fine perorations, in which the pauses are measured, not by the vital pulses of the mood, but by a conscious, cultivated method. Some of Wordsworth's blank verse "The Prelude," though in itself tame and inefficient, takes hold of the reader through a personal warmth which makes him almost forget that he is reading verse at all. But we never feel personal warmth in Mr. Watson; he succeeds or fails as an artificer, and as an artificer only.

It is probably not too much to say that there is not a cadence in his verse which has not been heard before. By what miracle it is that out of the same number and order of syllables no two cadences of Shakespeare and of Browning, of Keats and of Herrick, of Crashaw and of Blake, can be precisely matched no man knows or will ever know – least of all the poet himself. He writes what comes to him, and he may work on his writing until hardly a word of the original stuff remains; and with all his care, or in spite of it, the thing turns doggedly into his own manner of speech, and comes to us with a cadence that we have never heard before. He may have read much or little, and it will make barely an appreciable difference. The music that is not learned in books comes from some unknown source which is as variable as the sea or the wind. Music learned from books, however much beauty may be breathed into it by the singer, keeps the taint of its source about it. It is by such music that the literary artist, not the artist in literature, is known.

William Watson's *Odes and Other Poems* is remarkable for precisely the qualities which have distinguished his work since the time when, in *Wordsworth's Grave*, he first elaborated a manner of his own. That manner has some of the qualities of eighteenth century verse – its sobriety, its strictness, its intellectual and critical interests; and it also has certain of the richer and more emotional elements of the nineteenth century revival of the Elizabethan passion, and splendor. The reader is reminded of Gray, of Wordsworth, of Matthew Arnold, at moments of Keats and of Rossetti. In spite of occasional and unaccountable blemishes, Watson's work is, in the main, the most careful work of any of the younger poets. Nor is it lacking in a poetic impulse. It does not seem to us that this impulse is a very strong one, or one of special originality, but it is there, undoubtedly; and Watson's verse, unlike that of most of the people now writing, justifies its existence. Take, for instance, these opening lines from the ode *To Arthur Christopher Benson*:

In that grave shade august
 That round your Eton clings,
To you the centuries must
 Be visible corporate things
And the high Past appear
Affably real and near,
 For all its grandiose airs, caught from the mien of Kings.
The new age stands as yet
 Half built against the sky
Open to every threat
 Of storms that clamor by:
Scaffolding veils the walls,
And dim dust floats and falls,
 As, moving to and fro, their tasks the masons ply.
But changeless and complete,
 Rise unperturbed and vast,
Above our din and heat,
 The turrets of the Past,
Mute as that city asleep,
Lulled with enchantments deep,
 Far in Arabian dreamland built where all things last.

The grave and equable sweep of this verse, so unlike most of the hot and flurried rhyming of contemporaries, has the excellence of form which gives adequate expression to a really poetic conception. Watson takes a very serious view of things, except in a few attempts at satire or playfulness, which are not quite fortunate either in idea or in execution. He has the laudable desire to enter into competition with the great masters on their own ground. And the result is by no means ludicrous, as it would be with most people. Only it is a little as if the accomplished copyist were to challenge comparison with the picture which he has, after all, copied. Work done in the manner, and under the influence, of previous writers may indeed, under certain circumstances, attain the virtue of originality; but only under certain circumstances. Chatterton, for instance, was original only when he copied, or when he fancied he was copying; Keats was absolutely himself even at the period when his form was entirely imitative. The personality of some men can find no home in the present, can wear no dress of modern fashion; can express itself only by a return to the ways of speech of an earlier age. But this sort of spiritual nostalgia can only become effective when it is a very deep and individual instinct, and not merely a general literary sympathy. Watson has learned more from his masters than he has brought to them. We have read his latest book with real appreciation of its many admirable qualities, but, on closing it, we have no more definite idea of Watson himself, of what he really is, apart from what he chooses to express, than we had before opening it. And yet the greater part of the book, in one sense, is quite personal. He tells us what he thought of Stevenson's *Catriona*, how he felt in Richmond Park, and of his friendly regard for one or two estimable men of letters. But the real man, the real point of view, the outlook on life, the deeper human sympathies: what do we learn of these? There is, indeed, one poem, among the finest in the book, in which a touch of more acute personal feeling gives a more intimate thrill to the verse – the poem called *Vita Nuova*, of which we may quote the greater part:

O ancient streams, O far-descended woods
Full of the fluttering of melodious souls;
O hills and valleys that adorn yourselves
In solemn jubilation; winds and clouds,
Ocean and land in stormy nuptials clasped,
And all exuberant creatures that acclaim
The Earth's divine renewal: lo, I too
With yours would mingle somewhat of glad song.
I too have come through wintry terrors – yea,
Through tempest and through cataclysm of soul
Have come, and am delivered. Me the Spring
Me also, dimly with new life hath touched,
And with regenerate hope, the salt of life;
And I would dedicate these thankful tears
To whatsoever Power beneficent,

Veiled though his countenance, undivulged his thought,
Hath led me from the haunted darkness forth
Into the gracious air and vernal morn,
And suffers me to know my spirit a note
Of this great chorus, one with bird and stream
And voiceful mountain, – nay, a string, how jarred
And all but broken! of that lyre of life
Whereon himself, the master harp-player.
Resolving all its mortal dissonance
To one immortal and most perfect strain,
Harps without pause, building with song the world.

But this poem stands alone in the volume as an expression of very interesting personal feeling, the rest being mainly concerned with generalities.

Like all Watson's volumes of verse, these *Odes and Other Poems* contain some excellent literary criticism, conveyed in the neatest and briefest fashion possible. In fact, Watson's verse is only too full of sane and measured criticism – an excellent quality no doubt, but hardly one quite compatible with poetry of a high order. But how fine, how exact, how discriminating, is this piece of criticism, for instance, in verse!

Forget not, brother singer! that though Prose
    Can never be too truthful or too wise,
Song is not Truth, not Wisdom, but the rose
Upon Truth's lips, the light in Wisdom's eyes.

It was in the epigram that Watson first did finished work, and his most typical work is certainly to be found in forms more or less akin to the epigram; in the sonnet, for example. There are so many good sonnets in this volume that choice is difficult; here is one called "Night on Curbar Edge":

No echo of man's life pursues my ears;
    Nothing disputes this Desolation's reign;
    Change comes not, this dread temple to profane,
Where time by aeons reckons, not by years,
Its patient form one crag, sole stranded, rears,

Type of whate'er is destined to remain
While yon still host encamped on night's waste plain
Keeps armed watch, a million quivering spears,
Hushed are the wild and wing'd lives of the moor;
The sleeping sheep nestle 'neath ruined wall,
Or unhewn stones in random concourse hurled;
Solitude, sleepless, listens at Fate's door;
And there is built and 'stablisht over all
Tremendous silence, older than the world.

The breadth of phrasing here is noticeable; and it is by such qualities as this, as well as by the careful accuracy with which every note is produced, that Watson is distinguished alike from older men of the type of Alfred Austin, and from younger men of such varying capacities as John Davidson and Yeats. If he has not the making of a great poet, he is already an accomplished poet; and if he does not possess the highest qualities, he possesses several of the secondary qualities in the highest degree.

Watson's *Ode on the Day of Coronation of King Edward the Seventh* is a fine piece of verse writing, and can hardly fail to remind the reader of great poetry. It is constructed with care, it flows, it has gravity, an air of amplitude, many striking single lines, and its sentiments are unexceptionable. When we read such lines as these:

All these, O King, from their seclusion dread,
And guarded palace of eternity,
Mix in thy pageant with phantasmal tread,
Hear the long waves of acclamation roll,
And with yet mightier silence marshal thee
To the awful throne thou hast inherited –

we feel that this is at least workman-like work, written by a man who has studied great masters, and who takes himself and his art seriously. There is not an undignified line in the whole poem, nor a break in the slow, deliberate movement. Watson has style, he is never facile or common. He has frequent felicities of phrase, but he subordinates separate effects to the effect of the whole, and he is almost the only living writer of verse of whom this could be said. His ode is excellently made, from every external point of view. Yet, after reading it over and over, with a full recognition of its technical qualities, we are unable to accept it as genuine poetry, as the equal of the thing which it resembles.

Great poetry is not often written for official occasions, but that it can be so written we need only turn to Marvell's *Horatian Ode upon Cromwell's Return from Ireland* to realize. Watson looks instinctively to public events for his inspiration, and there is something in his temper of mind and of style which seems to set him naturally apart as a commentator upon the destinies of nations. He has never put any vital part of himself into his work; he has told us nothing of what he is when he is not a writer. All his utterances have been themselves official, the guarded statement of just so much of his own thoughts and feelings as he cares to betray to the public. His kind is rather critical than creative, and it was by his epigrams that he first attracted attention. His technique is so accomplished that he seems very often to be thinking only of what he is saying, when it is evident, on a closer examination, that he is thinking much more of how he is saying it. For the poet who concerns himself with public events this might seem to be a useful part of his poetic equipment. Court ceremonies demand court dress. Undoubtedly, but the art of the courtier requires him to forget that he is dressed for an occasion, to forget everything but the occasion. Throughout the whole of his coronation ode Watson never forgets that he is celebrating an important ceremony. His costume is perfectly adjusted, he wears it with grace and dignity; his elocution, as he delivers his lines, is a model of clearness and discreet emphasis. Everything that he says is perfectly appropriate; good taste can go no further. But the occasion itself, the meaning, the emotion, of the occasion? That does not come into the poem; the poem tells us all about it.

Now look at Marvell's ode, and forget for the moment that it is a masterpiece of poetry. What a passion fires the hard, convincing thought! How the mere logic holds the attention!

▶ 167

Every word lives, and the cadences (creating a new form for themselves) do but follow the motions of the writer's bright, controlling energy. It is impossible to read the lines aloud without a feeling of exultation. In Watson's ode there is not a breath of life; what is said – admirable and sensible, and at times poetically conceived as it is – comes with no impetus from the mind that has conceived it coldly. And it is to be noted that, though thought and expression are fitted together with great skill and precision, the expression is always rather above the pitch of the thought. Take these lines:

> O doom of overlordships! to decay
> First at the heart, the eye scarce dimmed at all;
> Or perish of much cumber and array,
> The burdening robe of empire, and its pall;
> Or, of voluptuous hours the wanton prey;
> Die of the poisons that most sweetly slay;
> Or, from insensate height,
> With prodigies, with light
> Of trailing angers on the monstrous night,
> Magnificently fall.

There we find expression strained to a point to which the thought has not attained. In other words, we find rhetoric. Weight and resonance of verse do but drag down and deafen that which they should uplift and sound abroad, when, instead of being attendants upon greatness, they attempt to replace it.

EMIL VERHAEREN

The poetry of Emile Verhaeren, more than that of any other modern poet, is made directly out of the complaining voices of the nerves. Other writers, certainly, have been indirectly indebted to the effect of nerves on temperament, but Verhaeren seems to express only so much of a temperament as finds its expression through their immediate medium. In his early books *Les Flamandes, Les Moines* (reprinted, with *Les Bords de la Route*, containing earlier and later work, in the first of his two volumes of collected poems), he began by a solid, heavily colored, exterior manner of painting genre pictures in the Flemish style. Such poems as "Les Paysans," with its fury of description, are like a Teniers in verse; not Breughel has painted a kermesse with hotter colors, a more complete abandonment to the sunlight, wine and gross passions of those Flemish feasts. This first book, *Les Flamandes*, belongs to the Naturalistic movement; but it has already as in the similar commencements of Huysmans so ardent a love of color for its own sake, color becoming lyrical, that one realizes how soon this absorption in the daily life of farms, kitchens, stables, will give place to another kind of interest. And in *Les Moines*, while there is still for the most part the painting of exteriorities, a new sentiment, by no means the religious sentiment, but an artistic interest in what is less material, less assertive in things, finds for itself an entirely new scheme of color.

Here, for instance, was "Cuisson de Pain," in the first book:

Dehors, les grands fournils chauffaient leurs braises rouges,
Et deux par deux, du bout d'une planche, les gouges
Dans le ventre des fours engouffraient les pains mous.
Et les flammes, par les gueules s'ouvrant passage,
Comme une meute énorme et chaude de chiens roux,
autaient en rugissant leur mordre le visage.

But it is not until *Les Soirs* that we find what was to be the really individual style developing itself. It develops itself at first with a certain heaviness. Here is a poet who writes in images: good; but the images are larger than the ideas. Wishing to say that the hour was struck, he says:

"Seul un beffroi,
Immensément vêtu de nuit, cassait les heures."

And, indeed, everything must be done *immensément.* The word is repeated on every page, sometimes twice in a stanza. The effect of monotony in rhythm, the significant, chiming recurrence of words, the recoil of a line upon itself, the dwindling away or the heaping up of sound in line after line, the shock of an unexpected cæsura, the delay and the hastened speed of syllables: all these arts of a very conscious technique are elaborated with somewhat too obvious an intention. There is splendor, opulence, and, for the first time, "such stuff as dreams are made of." Description is no longer made for its own sake; it becomes metaphor. And this metaphor is entirely new. It may be called exaggerated, affected even; but it is new, and it is expressive.

"Les chiens du désespoir, les chiens du vent d'automne,
Mordent de leurs abois les échos noirs des soirs,
Et l'ombre, immensément, dans le vide, tâtonne
Vers la lune, mirée au clair des abreuvoirs."

In *Les Débâcles*, a year later, this art of writing in colored and audible metaphor, and on increasingly abstract and psychological subjects, the sensations externalized, has become more master of itself, and at the same time more immediately the servant of a more and more feverish nervous organization.

"*Tu seras le fiévreux ployé, sur les fenêtres.*
D'où l'on peut voir bondir la vie et ses chars d'or."

And the contemplation of this *fiévreux* is turned more and more in upon itself, finding in its vision of the outer world only a mirrored image of its own disasters. The sick man, looking down on his thin fingers, can think of them only in this morbid, monastic way:

"*Mes doigts, touchez mon front et cherchez, là,*
Les vers qui rongeront, un jour, de leur morsure,
Mes chairs; touchez mon front, mes maigres doigts, voilà
Que mes veines déjà, comme une meurtrissure
Bleuâtre, étrangement, en font la tour, mes las
Et pauvres doigts – et que vos longs ongles malades
Battent, sinistrement, sur mes tempes, un glas,
Un pauvre glas, mes lents et mornes doigts!"

Two years later, with *Les Flambeaux Noirs*, what was nervous has become almost a sort of very conscious madness: the hand on one's own pulse, the eyes watching themselves in the glass with an unswerving fixity, but a breaking and twisting of the links of things, a doubling and division of the mind's sight, which might be met with, less picturesquely, in actual madness. There are two poems, "Le Roc" and "Les Livres," which give, in a really terrifying way, the very movement of idea falling apart from idea, sensation dragging after it sensation down the crumbling staircase of the brain, which are the symptoms of the brain's loss of self-control:

C'est là que j'ai bâti mon âme,
– Dites, serai-je seul avec mon âme? –
Mon âme hélas! maison d'ébène,
Où s'est fendu, sans bruit, un soir,

▶ 171

Le grand miroir de mon espoir.

Dites, serai-je seul avec mon âme,
En ce nocturne et angoissant domaine?
Serai-je seul avec mon orgueil noir,
Assis en un fauteuil de haine?
Serai-je seul, avec ma pâle hyperdulie,
Pour Notre-Dame, la Folie?

In these poems of self-analysis, which is self-torture, there is something lacerating, and at the same time bewildering, which conveys to one the sense of all that is most solitary, picturesque and poignant in the transformation of an intensely active and keen-sighted reason into a thing of conflicting visionary moods. At times, as in the remarkable study of London called "Les Villes," this fever of the brain looks around it, and becomes a flame of angry and tumultuous epithet, licking up and devouring what is most solid in exterior space. Again, as in "Les Lois" and "Les Nombres," it becomes metaphysical, abstract, and law towers up into a visible palace, number flowers into a forest:

Je suis l'halluciné de la forêt des Nombres.

That art of presenting a thought like a picture, of which Verhaeren is so accomplished a master, has become more subtle than ever; and

ces tours de ronde de l'infini, le soir
Et ces courbes, et ces spirales,

of for the most part menacing speculations in the void, take visible form before us, with a kind of hallucination, communicated to us from that (how far deliberate?) hallucination which has created them. Gradually, in "Les Apparus dans mes Chemins," in "Les Campagnes Hallucinées," in "Les Villages Illusoires," in "Les Villes Tentaculaires," the hallucinations become entirely external: it is now the country, the village, the town, that is to say, the whole organized world, that agonizes among cloudy phantoms, and no longer a mere individual, abnormal brain. And so he has at once gained a certain relief from what had been felt to be too intimately a part of himself, and has also surrendered to a more profound, because a more extended, consciousness of human misery. Effacing himself, as he does, behind the great spectacle of the world, as he sees it, with his visionary eyes, in his own violent and lethargic country, he becomes a more hopeless part of that conspiracy of the earth against what man has built out of the earth, of what man has built out of the earth against the earth, which he sees developing silently among the grass and bricks. All these books are a sort of philosophy in symbols, symbols becoming more and more definite: "Le Donneur de Mauvais Conseils," who drives up to the farm gate:

La vieille carriole en bois vert-pomine
Qui l'emmena, on ne sait d'où,
Une folle la garda avec son homme
Aux carrefours des chemins mous.
Le cheval paît l'herbe d'automne,
Près d'une mare monotone,
Dont l'eau malade réverbère
Le soir de pluie et de misère
Qui tombe en loques sur la terre;

"Les Cordiers," the old man spinning his rope against the sky, weaving the past into the future:

Sur la route muette et régulière,
Les yeux fixés vers la lumière
Qui frôle en se couchant les clos et les maisons,
Le blanc cordier visionnaire,
Du fond du soir auréolaire,
Attire à lui les horizons;

and, finally, the many-tentacled towns, drawing to themselves all the strength and sap of the earth: "Les Spectacles,

La Bourse, Le Bazar," the monstrous and material soul of towns.

Contrast these poems with those early poems, so brutal, so Flemish, if you would see at a glance all the difference between the naturalistic and the symbolistic treatment. The subject-matter is the same; the same eye sees; there are the same

> *vers bâtis comme une estrade*
> *Pour la danse des mots et leurs belles parades.*

But at first there is merely an eye that sees, and that takes the visible world at its own valuation of itself. Later on, things are seen but to be readjusted, to be set into relation with other, invisible realities, of which they are no more than the wavering and tortured reflection. And with this poet, in his later manner, everything becomes symbol; the shop, the theater, the bank, no less than the old rope-maker weaving the horizons together.

> *Sur la Ville, d'où les affres flamboient,*
> *Règnent, sans qu'on les voie,*
> *Mais évidentes, les idées:*

as he can write, on the last page of *Les Villes Tentaculaires*, which points directly to *Les Aubes*, in which a sort of deliverance through ideas is worked out.

Verhaeren's second play, *Le Cloitre*, is much finer in every way than his first, *Les Aubes*, but it does not convince us that he is a dramatist, in the strict sense of the word. The only French poet of the present day who has really vivid energy, his energy is too feverish, too spasmodic, too little under the control of a shaping intellect, to be of precisely the quality required for the drama. The people of these brief and fiery scenes are like little broken bits of the savage forces of the world, working out their passionate issues under the quiet roofs of the cloister. All their words are cries, coming out of a half-delirious suffering; and these cries echo about the stage in an almost monotonous conflict. It seems to us that the form which suits Verhaeren best is the form which he has temporarily abandoned – a kind of fiery reverie, seen finally in his last book, *Les Visages de la Vie,*

Mon âme était anxieuse d'être elle-même
Elle s'illimitait en une âme suprême
Et violente, où l'univers se résumait; –

as he says in one of the poems of that book; and in all these poems, "La Foule, L'Ivresse, La Joie," and the rest, we see the poet sending his soul into the universe and becoming a vehement voice for all that he finds most passionate in it. It is, in its way, dramatizing of emotion, but, if one may say so, an abstract dramatizing. It is the crowd, not Dom Balthazar; joy itself, not some joyous human being for which he finds words; and his merits and his defects make him a better spokesman for disembodied than for embodied souls. Since the early period of Flemish realism he has been, while making his language more and more pictorial, making his interests more and more internal. He no longer paints landscapes, but the scenery of the soul, and in the same vast and colored images. He magnifies sensation until it becomes a sort of hallucination of which he seems always to be the victim. Now all this is so very personal, so clearly the vision of a not quite healthy temperament, that his neurotic monks in the cloister, with their heated and vehement speech, seem more like repetitions of a single type than individual characters. But he has certainly come nearer to dramatic characterization than in the *Shadowy Dawn*, and he has founded his play on a more emotionally human basis; on a basis, it would seem, partly suggested by the story which Browning tells in *Halbert and Hob.* And, taken as a poem, it is full of vigorous, imaginative writing, in which the religious passion finds eloquent speech. And, after all, is not this one of the most interesting, and not even one of the least successful, attempts at what a more extravagant imitator has lately called *La tragédie intérieure?* The actual tendency of art is certainly toward an abandonment of the heroic and amusing adventures which constituted so much of the art of the past, and a concentration upon whatever can be surmised of that soul which these adventures must doubtless have left so singularly indifferent. Ibsen has shown us destiny quietly at work in suburban drawing-rooms, among people who have rarely anything interesting to say, but whose least word becomes interesting because it is seen to knit one more mesh in the net of destiny. Maeterlinck has gone further, and shown us soul talking with soul, at first under almost pseudo-romantic disguises, among Leonardo landscapes, then more and more simply, as people who have no longer lost their crowns in a pool, but who, in Aglavaine and Selysette, might be any of our acquaintances, if we can imagine our acquaintances under a startling and revealing flash of light. Verhaeren falls into the movement, trying to give a more lyrical form to this new kind of drama, trying to give it a narrower and fiercer intensity. What he has so far achieved is a melodrama of the spirit, in which there is poetry, but also rhetoric. Will he finally be able to find for himself a form in which the "inner tragedy" can be externally presented without rhetoric? Then, perhaps, the poetry will make its own drama.

A NEGLECTED GENIUS:
SIR RICHARD BURTON

I

One hundred years ago, on March 19th, 1821, Sir Richard Burton was born; he died at Trieste on October 19th, 1890, in his seventieth year. He was superstitious; the fact that he was born and that he died on the nineteenth has its significance. On the night when he expired, as his wife was saying prayers to him, a dog began that dreadful howl which the superstitious say denotes a death. It was an evil omen; I have heard long after midnight dogs howl in the streets of Constantinople; their howling is only broken by the tapping of the bekjé's iron staff; it sounds like loud wind or water far off, waning and waxing, and at times, as it comes across the water from Stamboul, it is like a sound of strings, plucked and scraped savagely by an orchestra of stringed instruments.

In every age there have been I know not how many neglected men of genius, undiscovered, misunderstood, mocked at in the fashion Jesus Christ was mocked by the Jews, scorned as Dante was scorned when he was exiled from Florence, called a madman as Blake used to be called, censured as Swinburne was in 1866, for being "an unclean fiery imp of the pit" and "the libidinous Laureate of a pack of satyrs;" so the greatest as the least

– the greatest whose names are always remembered and the least whose names are invariably forgotten – have endured the same prejudices; have been lapidated by the same stones; such stones as Burton refers to when he writes in Mecca:

> On the great festival day we stoned the Devil, each man with seven stones washed in seven waters, and we said, while throwing the stones, "In the name of Allah – and Allah is Almighty – I do this in hatred of the Devil, and to his shame."

Burton was a great man, a great traveler and adventurer, who practically led to the discovery of the sources of the Nile; a wonderful linguist, he was acquainted with twenty-nine languages: he was a man of genius; only, the fact is, he is not a great writer. Continually thwarted by the English Government, he was debarred from some of the most famous expeditions by the folly of his inferiors, who ignorantly supposed they were his superiors; and, as Sir H. H. Johnston says in some of his notes, not only was Burton treated unjustly, but his famous pilgrimage to Mecca won him no explicit recognition from the Indian Government; his great discoveries in Africa, Brazil, Syria and Trieste were never appreciated; and, worst of all, he was refused the post of British Minister in Morocco; it was persistently denied him. He adds: "Had he gone there we might long since have known – what we do not know – the realities of Morocco."

Still, when Burton went to India, I do not imagine he was likely to suffer from any hostility on the part of the natives nor of the rulers. Lord Clive, who, in Browning's words, "gave England India," which was the result of his incredible victory in 1751 over the Nabob's army of 60,000 men, was never literally "loved" by the races of India; no more than Sir Warren Hastings. Still, Clive had genius, which he showed in the face of a bully he caught cheating at cards and in his mere shout at him: "You did cheat, go to Hell!" Impeached for the splendid service he had done in India he was acquitted in 1773; next year, having taken to opium, his own hand dealt himself his own doom. So he revenged himself on his country's ingratitude. So did Burton revenge himself – not in deeds, but in words, words, if I may say so, that are stupendous. "I struggled for forty-seven years, I distinguished myself honourably in every way I possibly could. I never had a compliment nor a 'Thank you,' nor a single farthing. I translated a doubtful book in my old age, and I immediately made sixteen thousand guineas. Now that I know the tastes of England, we need never be without money."

Burton first met Swinburne in 1861 at Lord Houghton's house, who, having given him *The Queen Mother*, said: "I bring you this book because the author is coming here this evening, so that you may not quote him as an absurdity to himself." In the summer of 1865 Swinburne saw a great deal of Burton. These two men, externally so dissimilar, had taken (as Swinburne said to me) a curious fancy, an absolute fascination, for each other. Virile and a mysterious adventurer, Burton was Swinburne's senior by sixteen years; one of those things that linked them together was certainly their passionate love of literature. Burton had also – which Swinburne might perhaps have envied – an almost unsurpassable gift for translation, which he shows in his wonderful version of *The Arabian Nights*. He used to say:

> I have not only preserved the spirit of the original, but the *mécanique*. I
> don't care a button about being prosecuted, and if the matter comes to
> a fight, I will walk into court with my Bible and my Shakespeare and
> my Rabelais under my arm, and prove to them that before they
> condemn me, they must cut half of *them* out, and not allow them to be
> circulated to the public.

In his Foreword to the first volume of his Translation, dated Wanderers' Club, August 15th, 1885, he says:

> This work, laborious as it may appear, has been to me a labor of love,
> an unfailing source of solace and satisfaction. During my long years
> of official banishment to the luxurious and deadly deserts of Western
> Africa, it proved truly a charm, a talisman against ennui and despon-
> dency. The Jinn bore me at once to the land of my predilection,

Arabia. In what is obscure in the original there are traces of Petronius Arbiter and of Rabelais; only, subtle corruption and covert licentiousness are wholly absent.

Therefore, in order to show the wonderful quality of his translation, I have chosen certain of his sentences, which literally bring back to me all that I have felt of the heat, the odor and the fascination of the East.

> So I donned my mantilla, and, taking with me the old woman and the slave-girl, I went to the Khan of the merchants. There I knocked at the door and out came two white slave-girls, both young, high-bosomed virgins, as they were Moons. They were melting a perfume whose like I had never before smelt; and so sharp and subtle was the odor that it made my senses drunken as with strong wine. I saw there also two great censers each big as a mazzar bowl, flaming with aloes, nard, perfumes, ambergris and honied scents; and the place was full of their fragrance.

The next quotation is from the Tale of the Fisherman and the Jinn:

> He loosened the lid from the jar, he shook the vase to pour out whatever might be inside. He found nothing in it; whereat he marvelled with an exceeding marvel. But presently there came forth from the jar a smoke which spread heavenwards into ether (whereat again he marvelled with mighty marvel) and which trailed along earth's surface till presently, having reached its full height, the thick vapors condensed, and became an Ifrit, huge of bulk, whose crest touched the clouds when his feet were on the ground.

I have before me Smithers' privately printed edition (1894) of *The Carmina of Valerius Catullus now first completely Englished into Verse and Prose, the Metrical Part by Capt. Sir Richard Burton, and the Prose Portion by Leonard C. Smithe*. Burton is right in saying that "the translator of original mind who notes the innumerable shades of tone, manner and complexion will not neglect the frequent opportunities of enriching his mother-tongue with novel and alien ornaments which shall justify the accounted barbarisms until formally naturalized and adopted. He must produce an honest and faithful copy, adding nought to the sense or abating aught of its *cachet.*" He ends his Foreword: "As discovery is mostly my mania, I have hit upon a bastard-urging to indulge it, by a presenting to the public of certain classics in the nude Roman poetry, like the Arab, and of the same date."

Certainly Burton leaves out nothing of the nakedness that startles one in the verse of Catullus: a nakedness that is as honest as daylight and as shameless as night. When the text is obscene his translation retains its obscenity; which, on the whole, is rare: for the genius of Catullus is elemental, primitive, nervous, passionate, decadent in the modern sense and in the modern sense perverse. In his rhymed version of the Attis Burton has made a prodigious attempt to achieve the impossible. Not being a poet, he was naturally unable to follow the rhythm – the Galliambic metre, in which Catullus obtains variety of rhythm; for, as Robinson Ellis says:

> It remains unique as a wonderful expression of abnormal feeling in a quasi-abnormal meter. Quasi-abnormal, however, only: for no poem of Catullus follows stricter laws, or succeeds in conveying the idea of a wild freedom under a more carefully masked regularity.

As one must inevitably compare two translations of the same original, I have to point out that Burton's rendering is, both metrically and technically, inaccurate; whereas, in another rendering, the translator has at least preserved the exact metre, the exact scansion, and the double endings at the end of every line; not, of course, in this case, employing the double rhymes Swinburne used in his translation from Aristophanes. These are Burton's first lines: –

O'er high deep seas in speedy ship his voyage Atys sped
Until he trod the Phrygian grove with hurried, eager tread,
And as the gloomy tree-shorn stead, the she-God's home he sought,
There sorely stung with fiery ire and madman's raging thought,
Share he with sharpened flint the freight wherewith his frame was
                                                    fraught.

These are the first lines of the other version: –

Over ocean Attis sailing in a swift ship charioted
When he reached the Phrygian forests, and with rash foot violently
Trod the dark and shadowy regions of the goddess, wood-
                                                    garlanded,
And with ravening madness ravished, and his reason abandoning
                                                    him,
Seized a pointed flint and sundered from his flesh his virility.

II

Burton himself admitted that he was a devil; for, said he: "the
Devil entered into me at Oxford." Evidently, also, besides his
mixture of races, he was a mixture of the normal and the
abnormal; he was perverse and passionate; he was imaginative
and cruel; he was easily stirred to rage. Nearly six feet in height,
he had, together with his broad shoulders, the small hands and
feet of the Orientals; he was Arab in his prominent cheek-bones;
he was gypsy in his terrible, magnetic eyes – the sullen eyes of a
stinging serpent. He had a deeply bronzed complexion, a
determined mouth, half-hidden by a black mustache, which hung
down in a peculiar fashion on both sides of his chin. This
peculiarity I have often seen in men of the wandering tribe in
Spain and in Hungary. Wherever he went he was welcomed by
the gypsies; he shared with them their horror of a corpse, of

death-scene, and of graveyards. "He had the same restlessness," wrote his wife, "which could stay nowhere long nor own any spot on earth. Hagar Burton, a Gypsy woman, cast my horoscope, in which she said: 'You will bear the name of our Tribe, and be right proud of it. You will be as we are, but far greater than we.' I met Richard two months later, in 1856, and was engaged to him." It is a curious fact that John Varley, who cast Blake's horoscope in 1820, also cast Burton's; who, as he says, had finished his *Zodiacal Physiognomy* so as to prove that every man resembled after a fashion the sign under which he was born. His figures are either human or bestial; some remind me of those where men are represented in the form of animals in Giovanni della Porta's *Fisonomia dell' Huomo* (Venice, 1668), which is before me as I write; Swinburne himself once showed to me his copy of the same book. Nor have I ever forgotten his saying to me – in regard to Burton's nervous fears: "The look of unspeakable horror in those eyes of his gave him, at times, an almost unearthly appearance." He added: "This reminds me of what Kiomi says in Meredith's novel: 'I'll dance if you talk of dead people,' and so begins to dance and to whoop at the pitch of her voice. I suppose both had the same reason for this force of fear: to make the dead people hear." Then he flashed at me this unforgettable phrase: "Burton had the jaw of a Devil and the brow of a God."

In one of his letters he says, I suppose by way of *persiflage* in regard to himself and Burton: "*En moi vous voyez Les Malheurs de la Virtu, en lui Les Prospérités du Vice.*" In any case, it is to entertain Burton when he writes: "I have in hand a scheme of mixed verse and prose – a sort of étude à la Balzac *plus* the poetry – which I flatter myself will be more offensive and objectionable to Britannia than anything I have done: *Lesbia Brandon.* You see I have now a character to keep up, and by the grace of Cotytto I will."

Swinburne began *Lesbia Brandon* in 1859; he never finished it; what remains of it consists of seventy-three galleys, numbered 25 to 97, besides four unprinted chapters. The first, "A Character," was written in 1864; "An Episode" in 1866; "Turris Eburnea" in 1886; "La Bohême Dédorée" must have been written a year or two later. Mr. Gosse gives a vivid description of Swinburne, who was living in 13, Great James Street, and who was never weary of his unfinished novel, reading to him parts of two chapters in June, 1877. "He read two long passages, the one a ride over a moorland by night, the other the death of his heroine, Lesbia Brandon. After reading aloud all these things with amazing violence, he seemed quite exhausted." It is possible to decipher a few sentences from two pages of his manuscript; first in "Turris Eburnea. 'Above the sheet, below the boudoir,' said the sage. Her ideal was marriage, to which she clung, which revealed to astonished and admiring friends the vitality of a dubious intellect within her. She had not even the harlot's talent of discernment." This is Leonora Harley. In *La Bohême Dédorée* we read:

> Two nights later Herbert received a note from Mr. Linley inviting him to a private supper. Feverish from the contact of Mariani and hungry for a chance of service, he felt not unwilling to win a little respite from the vexation of patience. The sage had never found him more amenable to the counsel he called reason. Miss Brandon had not lately crossed his ways. Over their evening Leonora Harley guided with the due graces of her professional art. It was not her fault if she could not help asking her younger friend when he had last met a darker beauty: she had seen him once with Lesbia.

III

In 1848 Burton determined to pass in India for an Oriental; the disguise he assumed was that of a half-Arab, half-Iranian, thousands of whom can be met along the northern shore of the Persian Gulf. He set out on his first pilgrimage as Mirza Abdulla the Bushiri, as a *buzzaz*, vendor of fine linen, muslins and *bijouterie*; he was admitted to the harems, he collected the information he required from the villagers; he won many women's hearts, he spent his evenings in the mosques; and, after innumerable adventures, he wended his way to Mecca. His account of this adventure is thrilling. The first cry was: "Open the way for the Haji who would enter the House!" Then:

> Two stout Meccans, who stood below the door, raised me in their arms, whilst a third drew me from above into the building. At the entrance I was accosted by a youth of the Benu Shazban family, the true blood of the El Hejaz. He held in his hand the huge silver-gilt padlock of the Ka'abeh, and presently, taking his seat upon a kind of wooden press in the left corner of the hall, he officially inquired my mother-nation and other particulars. The replies were satisfactory, and the boy Mohammed was authoritatively ordered to conduct me round the building and to recite the prayers. I will not deny that, looking at the windowless walls, the officials at the door, and a crowd of excited fanatics below –
>
> "And the place death, considering who I was,"
>
> my feelings were those of the trapped-rat description, acknowledged by the immortal nephew of his uncle Perez. A blunder, a hasty action, a misjudged word, a prayer or bow, not strictly the right shibboleth, and my bones would have whitened the desert sand. This did not, however, prevent my carefully observing the scene during our long prayer, and making a rough plan with a pencil upon my white *ihram*.

After having seen the howling Dervishes in Scutari in Asia, I can imagine Burton's excitement when in Cairo he suddenly left his stolid English friends, joined in the shouting, gesticulating circle, and behaved as if to the manner born: he held his diploma as a master Dervish. In Scutari I felt the contagion of these dancers, where the brain reels, and the body is almost swept into the orgy. I had all the difficulty in the world from keeping back the woman who sat beside me from leaping over the barrier and joining the Dervishes. In these I felt the ultimate, because the most animal, the most irrational, the most insane, form of Eastern ecstasy. It gave me an impression of witchcraft; one might have been in Central Africa, or in some Saturnalia of barbarians.

There can be no doubt that Burton always gives a vivid and virile impression of his adventures; yet, as I have said before, something is lacking in his prose; not the vital heat, but the vision of what is equivalent to vital heat. I have before me a letter sent from Hyderabad by Sarojini Naidu, who says: "All is hot and fierce and passionate, ardent and unashamed in its exulting and importunate desire for life and love. And, do you know, the scarlet lilies are woven petal by petal from my heart's blood, those quivering little birds are my soul made incarnate music, these heavy perfumes are my emotions dissolved into aerial essence, this flaming blue and gold sky is the 'Very You' that part of me that incessantly and insolently, yes, and a little deliberately, triumphs over that other part – a thing of nerves and tissues that suffers and cries out, and that must die tomorrow perhaps, or twenty years hence." In these sentences the whole passionate, exotic and perfumed East flashes before me – a vision of delight and of distresses – and, as it were, all that slumbers in their fiery blood.

"Not the fruit of experience," wrote Walter Pater, "but experience itself, is the end. A counted number of pulses only is given us of a variegated dramatic life. To burn always with this hard, gemlike flame, to maintain this ecstasy, is success in life." Alas, how few lives out of the cloud-covered multitude of existences have burned always with this flame! I have said somewhere that we can always, in this world, get what we want if we will it intensely enough. So few people succeed greatly because so few people can conceive a great end, and work toward that without tiring and without deviating. The adventurer of whom I am writing failed, over and over again, in spite of the fact that he conceived and could have executed great ends: never by his own fault, always by the fault of others.

IV

Richard Burton dedicated his literal version of the epic of Camões "To the Prince of the Lyric Poets of his Day, Algernon Charles Swinburne." He begins:

> My dear Swinburne, accept the unequal exchange – my brass for your gold. Your *Poems and Ballads* began to teach the Philistine what might there is in the music of language, and what marvel of lyric inspiration, far subtler and more ethereal than poetry, means to the mind of man.

In return for this Swinburne dedicated to him *Poems and Ballads*, Second Series.

> Inscribed to Richard F. Burton in redemption of an old pledge and in recognition of a friendship which I must always count among the highest honors of my life.

It was nine years before then, when they were together in the south of France, that Swinburne was seized by a severe illness; and, as he assured me, it was Burton who, with more than a woman's care and devotion, restored him to health. The pledge – it was not the covenant sealed between the two greatest, the two most passionate, lovers in the world, Iseult and Tristan, on the deck of that ship which was the ship of Life, the ship of Death, in the mere drinking of wine out of a flagon, which, being of the nature of a most sweet poison, consumed their limbs and gave intoxication to their souls and to their bodies – but a pledge in the wine Swinburne and Burton drank in the hot sunshine: –

> For life's helm rocks to windward and lee,
> And time is as wind, and waves are we,
> And song is as foam that the sea-waves fret,
> Though the thought at its heart should be deep as the sea

It was in July, 1869, that Swinburne joined the Burtons and

Mrs. Sartoris at Vichy. As I have never forgotten Swinburne's wonderful stories about Burton – besides those on Rossetti and Mazzini – I find in a letter of his to his mother words he might really have altered.

> If you had seen him, when the heat and the climb and the bothers of travelling were too much for me – in the very hot weather – helping, waiting on me – going out to get me books to read in bed – and always kind, thoughtful, ready, and so bright and fresh that nothing but a lizard (I suppose that is the most insensible thing going) could have resisted his influence – I feel sure you would like him (you remember you said you didn't) and then – love him, as I do. I never expect to see his like again – but him I do hope to see again, and when the time comes to see him at Damascus as H.B.M. Consul.

They traveled in carriages, went to Clermont-Ferrand, where Pascal was born; then to Le Puy-en-Velay. In 1898 I stayed with the Countess De la Tour in the Château de Chaméane, Puy de Dôme, and after leaving her I went to Puy-en-Velay. I hated it, the Burtons did not. Stuck like a limpet on a rock, the main part of the town seems to be clinging to the side of the hill on which the monstrous statue desecrates the sky. At night I saw its gilt crown merge into a star, but by day it is intolerably conspicuous, and at last comes to have an irrational fascination, leading one to the very corners where it can be seen best. And always, do what you will, you can not get away from this statue. It spoils the sky. The little cloister, with its ninth-century columns, is the most delightful spot in Le Puy; only the intolerable statue from which one can not escape showed me nature and humanity playing pranks together, at their old game of parodying the ideal. This is Swinburne's comment: –

> Set far between the ridged and foamless waves
> Of earth more fierce and fluctuant than the sea,
> The fearless town of towers that hails and braves,
> The heights that gild, the sun that brands Le Puy.

This year there has been a great Pardon at Le Puy. I have

seen several pilgrimages, in Moscow, for instance, at Serjevo, which is an annual pilgrimage to the Troitsa Monastery, and in these people there was no fervor, no excitement, but a dogged desire of doing something which they had set out to do. They were mostly women, and they flung themselves down on the ground; they lay there with their hands on their bundles, themselves like big bundles of rags. How different a crowd from this must have assembled at Le Puy; made so famous so many centuries ago by the visitations of Charlemagne and Saint Louis, who left, in 1254, in the Cathedral a little image of Horns and Isis. Then there was Jeanne d'Arc, who in 1429 sent her mother there instead of herself, being much too busy: she was on the way to Orléans.

As it is, Our Lady gets all the honors; only, there is a much older Chapel of Saint Michael, which is perched on the sheer edge of a rock; it is perhaps more original than any in France, with the exception of the Chapel of Saint Bonizel in Avignon. When I stood there and looked down from that great height I remembered – but with what a difference! – Montserrat in Spain, where the monastery seemed a part of the mountain; and from this narrow ledge between earth and heaven, a mere foothold on a great rock, I looked up only at sheer peaks, and down only into veiled chasms, or over mountainous walls to a great plain, ridged as if the naked ribs of the earth were laid bare.

V

I have been assured, by many who knew him, that Richard Burton had a vocabulary which was one of his inventions; a shameless one – as shameless as the vocabularies invented by Paul Verlaine and by Henri de Toulouse-Lautrec, which are as vivid to me as when I heard their utterance. These shared with Villiers de Isle-Adam that sardonic humor which is not so much satire as the revenge of beauty on ugliness, the persecution of the ugly: the only laughter of our generation which is as fundamental as that of Rabelais and of Swift. Burton, who had much the same contempt for women that Baudelaire imagined he had, only with that fixed stare of his that disconcerted them, did all that with deliberate malice. There was almost nothing in this world that he had not done, exulted in, gloried in. Like Villiers, he could not pardon stupidity; to both it was incomprehensible; both saw that stupidity is more criminal than even vice, if only because stupidity is incurable, if only because vice is curable. Burton, who found the Arabs, in their delicate depravity, ironical – irony being their breath of life – might have said with Villiers: "*L'Esprit du Siècle, ne l'oublions pas, est aux machines.*"

Every individual face has as many different expressions as the soul behind it has moods; therefore, the artist's business is to create on paper, or on his canvas, the image which was none of these, but which those helped to make in his own soul. I see, as it were, surge before me an image of Swinburne in his youth, when, with his passionate and pale face, with its masses of fiery hair, he has almost the aspect of Ucello's Galeazzo Malatesta. Burton's face has no actual beauty in it; it reveals a tremendous animalism, an air of repressed ferocity, a devilish fascination. There is almost a tortured magnificence in this huge head, tragic and painful, with its mouth that aches with desire, with those dilated nostrils that drink in I know not what strange perfumes.

EDGAR SALTUS

Edgar Saltus owes much of his bizarre talent to his mixed origin, for he is of Dutch and American extraction; indeed, for much of what I might call his rather unholy genius. His pages exhale a kind of exotic and often abnormal perfume of colors, color of sensations, of heats, of crowded atmospheres. He gives his women baneful and baleful names, such as Stella Sixmouth, Shorn Wyvell; these vampires and wicked creatures who ruin men's lives as cruelly as they ruin their own. His men have prodigious nerves, even more than his women; they commit all sorts of crimes, assassinations, poisonings, out of sheer malice and out of overexcited imaginations.

Of that most terrible of tragedies, the tragedy of a soul, he is for the most part utterly unconscious; and the very abracadabra of his art is in a sense – a curious enough and ultramodern sense – lifted from the Elizabethan dramatists. In them – as in many of his pages – a fine situation must have a murder in it, and some odious character removed by another more stealthy kind of obliteration. But, when he gives one a passing shudder, he leaves nothing behind it; yet in his perverted characters there can be found sensitiveness, hallucinations, obsessions; and some have that lassitude which is more than mere contempt. Some go solemnly on the path of blood, with no returning by a way so thronged with worse than memories. "No need for more crime," such men have cried, and for such reasons reaped the bitter harvest of tormenting dreams. Some have imagination that stands in the place of virtue; some, as in the case of Lady Macbeth, still keep the sensation of blood on their guilty hands.

Mary of Magdala (1891) is a vain attempt to do what Flaubert had done before Saltus in his *Hérodias*, and what Wilde has done after him in *Salome*, a drama that has a strange not easily defined fascination, which I can not dissociate from Beardsley's illustrations, in which what is icily perverse in the dialogue (it can not be designated drama) becomes in the ironical designs pictorial, a series of poses. To Wilde passion was a thing to talk about with elaborate and colored words. Salome is a doll, as many have imagined her, soulless, set in motion by some pitiless destiny, personified momentarily by her mother; Herod is a nodding mandarin in a Chinese grotesque.

In one page of Saltus's *Oscar Wilde: An Idler's Impressions* (1917) he evokes, with his cynical sense of the immense disproportion of things in this world and the next, the very innermost secret of Wilde. They dine in a restaurant in London and Wilde reads his MS. "Suddenly his eyes lifted, his mouth contracted, a spasm of pain – or was it dread? – had gripped him, a moment only. I had looked away. I looked again. Before me was a fat pauper, florid and over-dressed, who in the voice of an immortal, was reading the fantasies of the damned. In his hand was a manuscript, and we were supping on *Salome*."

Mr. Incoul's Misfortune seems to have its origin in some strange story of Poe's; for it gives one the sense of a monster, diabolical, inhuman, malevolent and merciless, who, after a mock marriage, abnormally sets himself to the devil's business of ruining his wife's lover's life, and of giving his wife a sudden death in three hideous forms: a drug to make her sleep, the gas turned on; and the door locked with "a nameless instrument."

The Truth about Tristan Varick (1888) is based on social problems of the most unaccountable kind. It has something strangely convincing in both conception and execution; it has suspense, ugly enough and uglier crises; and that the unlucky Varick is supposed to be partially insane is part of the finely woven plot, which is concerned with strange and perilous incidents and accidents; and which is based on his passionate pursuit of the ravishing Viola Raritan; the pursuit, really, of the chimera of his imagination.

And among the hazards comes one, of an evil kind – such as I have often experienced in foreign cities – that, in turning down one street instead of the next, a man's existence, and not his only, may be thereby changed. To have stopped one's rival's lying mouth and his lying life at the same instant is to have done something original – it is done by a poisoned pin's point. Then, this Orestes having found no Electra to return his love, but finding her vile, he lets himself disappear out of life in an almost incredible fashion, leaving the woman who never loved him to say, "I will come to see him sentenced:" a sentence which writes her down a modern Clytemnestra.

What Saltus says of Gonfallon can almost be said of Saltus: "With a set of people that fancied themselves in possession of advanced views and were still in the Middle Ages, he achieved the impossible: he not only consoled, he flattered, he persuaded and fascinated as well." Saltus can not console, he can sometimes persuade; but he can flatter and fascinate his public, as with

A breeze of fame made manifest.

The novelist is the comedian of the pen: it is his duty to amuse, to entertain – or else to hold his peace: to one in his trade nothing imaginable comes amiss. It is not sin that appeals him, but the consequences of sin; such as the fact that few sinners have ever turned into saints. In a word, he writes with his nerves.

Take, for instance, *A Transaction of Hearts* (1887), one of the queerest novels ever written and written with a kind of deliberate malice. Gonfallon, who becomes a bishop, falls passionately in love with an ardent and insolent girl who is his wife's sister; and before her beauty everything vanishes: virtue, genius, every-thing. "For a second that was an eternity he was conscious of her emollient mouth on his, her fingers intertwined with his own. For that second he really lived – perhaps he really lived." One wonders why Saltus uses so many ugly phrases – a kind of decadent French fashion of transposing words; such as the one I have quoted, together with "Ruedelapaixia" (meant to describe a dress), "Rafflesia, Mashed grasshoppers baked in saffron;" phrases chosen at random which are too frequently scattered in much too obvious a profusion over much too luxurious pages. I read somewhere that Oscar Wilde said to Amélie Rives: "In Edgar Saltus's work passion struggles with grammar on every page," which is certainly one of Wilde's finest paradoxes. I "cap this" – as Dowson often said to me in jest – with Léon Bloy's admirable phrase on Huysmans: "That he drags his images by the heels or the hair upside down the worm-eaten staircase of terrified syntax."

Imperial Purple (1906) shows the zenith of Saltus's talent, not in conceiving imaginary beings, but in giving modern conceptions of the most amazing creatures in the Roman Decadence, and in lyrical prose, which ought to have had for motto Victoria's stanza:–

> *Je suis l'Empire à la fin de la décadence,*
> *Qui regarde passer les grands Barbares blancs,*
> *En composant des acrostiches indolents,*
> *D'un style d'or où la langueur du soleil danse.*

Only Saltus is not Tacitus, in spite of having delved into his pages.

RECOLLECTIONS OF RÉJANE

NOTES ON THE ART OF THE GREAT FRENCH ACTRESS

Meilhac's play, *Ma Cousine*, which owed most of its success, when it was produced at the Variétés, October 27th, 1890, to the acting of Réjane, is one of those essentially French plays which no ingenuity can ever accommodate to an English soil. It is the finer spirit of farce, it is meant to be taken as a kind of intellectual exercise; it is human geometry for the masses. There are moments when the people of the play are on the point of existing for themselves, and have to be brought back, put severely in their places, made to fit their squares of the pattern. The thing as a whole has no more resemblance to real life than Latin verses have to a school-boy's conversation. Reality, that, after all, probably holds us in it, comes into it accidentally, in the form of detail, in little touches of character, little outbursts of temperament. The rest is done after a plan, it is an entanglement by rule; it exists because people have agreed to think that they like suspense; the tantalization of curiosity on the stage. We see the knot tied by the conjurer; we want to know what he will do with it. In France, and in such a piece as *Ma Cousine*, the conjurer is master of his trade; he gives us our illusions and our enlightenment in exactly the right doses.

And Réjane in this wittily artificial play suits herself perfectly to her subject, becomes everything there is in the character of Riquette; an actress who plays a comedy in real life, quite in the spirit of the stage. She has to save the situation from being taken too seriously, from becoming tragic: she has to take the audience into her confidence, to assure them that it is all a joke. And so we see her constantly overdoing her part, fooling openly. She does two things at once: the artificial comedy, which is uppermost in the play, and the character part which is implicit in it. And she is perfect in both.

The famous *Chahut*, which went electrically through Paris, when it was first given, in all its audacity, shows us one side of her art. The delicate by-plays with eyes and voice, or rather the voice and the overhanging eyelid of the right eye, shows us another. She is always the cleverest person on the stage. Her face in repose seems waiting for every expression to quicken its own form of life. When the face is in movement, one looks chiefly at the mouth, the thick, heavily painted lips, which twist upward, and wrinkle into all kinds of earthly subtleties. Her face is full of an experienced, sullen, chuckling gaminerie, which seems, after all, to be holding back something: it has a curious, vulgar undertone, a succulent and grossly joyous gurgle.

RÉJANE IN "MA COUSINE"

Here, in *Ma Cousine*, she abandons herself to all the frank and shady humors of the thing with the absolute abandonment of the artist. It is like a picture by Forain, made of the same material with the same cynicism and with the same mastery of line.

Ma Cousine, on seeing it a second time, is frankly and not too obviously amusing, a piece in which everybody plays at something, in which Réjane plays at being an actress who has a part to act in real life. *"Elle est impayable, cette Riquette!"* And it is with an intensely conscious abandonment of herself that she renders this good-hearted Cabotine, so worldly wise, so full of all the physical virtues, turned Bohemian. She has, in this part, certain guttural and nasal laughs, certain queer cries and shouts, which are after all a part of her *métier*; she runs through her whole gamut of shrugs and winks and nods. There is, of course, over again, the famous *Chahut*, in which she summarizes the whole art of the Moulin-Rouge; there is her long scene of pantomime, in which every gesture is at once vulgar and distinguished, vulgarly rendered with distinction. There are other audacities, all done with equal discretion.

I am not sure that Réjane is not at her best in this play: she has certainly never been more herself in what one fancies to be herself. There is all her ravishing gaminerie, her witty intelligence, her dash, her piquancy, her impudence, her mastery. I find that her high spirits, in this play, affect me like pathos: they run to a kind of emotion. I compared her art with the art of Forain; I said that here was a picture, made out of the same material, with the same cynicism, the same mastery of line. She suggested, in her costume of the Second Act, a Beardsley picture; there was the same kind of tragic grotesque, in which a kind of ugliness became a kind of beauty. The whole performance was of the best Parisian kind, with genius in one, admirably disciplined talent in all.

MELODRAMA WITH AN IDEA

Paul Hervieu's *La Course du Flambeau*, which was given by Réjane at the Vaudeville, April 17th, 1901, is first of all a sentimental thesis. It begins with an argument as to the duty of mother to child and of child to mother. A character who apparently represents the author's views declares life is a sort of *Lampadophoria*, or *La Course du Flambeau*, in which it is the chief concern of each generation to hand on the torch of life to the next generation. Sabine protests that the duty is equal, and offers herself as an example. "I," she says, "stand between mother and daughter; I love them myself; I could sacrifice myself equally for either." Maravan replies: "You do not know yourself. You do not know how good a mother you are, and I hope you will never know how bad a daughter." The rest of the play is ingeniously constructed to show, point by point, gradation by gradation, the devotion of Sabine to her daughter and the readiness with which she will sacrifice, not only herself, but her mother.

The only answer to the author's solution is to reinstate the problem in terms of precisely contrary facts; we have another solution, which may be made in terms no less inevitable. The play itself proves nothing, and it seems to me that the writer's persistence in arguing the point in action has given a somewhat needless and unnatural air of melodrama to his piece. It is a melodrama with an idea, a clue, but it is none the less a melodrama, because the idea and the clue are alike so arbitrary. One is never left quietly alone with nature; the showman's hand is always visible, around the corner of the curtain, pulling the strings. Whenever one sees a human argument struggling to find its way through the formal rhetoric of the speaker, it is the French equivalent of sentiment.

The piece is really the comedy of a broken heart, and what Réjane has to do is to represent all the stages of the slow process of heartbreak. She does it as only a great artist could do; but she allows us to see that she is acting. She does it consciously, deliberately, with method.

She has forced herself to become bourgeois; she takes upon herself the bourgeois face and appearance, and also the bourgeois soul. The wit and bewildering vulgarity have gone out of her, and a middle-class dignity has taken their place. She shows us the stage picture of a mother marvelously: that is to say, she interprets the play according to the author's intentions; when she is most effective as an actress she is not content with the simplicity of nature, as in the tirade in the third act. She brings out the melodramatic points with the finest skill; but the melodrama itself is a wilful divergency from nature; and she has few chances to be her finest self. She proves the soundness of her art as an actress by the ability to play such a part finely, seriously, effectively. Her own temperament counts for nothing; it is not even a hindrance: it is all the skill of a *métier*, the mastery of her art.

"MADAME SANS-GÊNE"

In 1893 Réjane created, at the Vaudeville, the woman whose part she had to act, in *Madame Sans-Gêne*. For some reason unknown to me, Réjane is best known in England by her performances in this thoroughly poor play, which shows us Sardou working mechanically, and for character effects of a superficial kind. There are none of the ideas, none of the touches of nature of *La Parisienne*; none of the comic vitality of *Ma Cousine*; none of the emotional quality of *Sapho*. It is full of piquancies for acting, and Réjane makes the most of them. Her acting is admirable, from beginning to end; it has her distinguished vulgarity; her gross charm; she is everything that Sardou meant, and something more.

But all that Sardou meant was not a very interesting thing,

and Réjane can not make it what it is not. She brightens her part, she does not make a different thing of it. There were moments when it seemed to me as if she played it with a certain fatigue. The thing is so artificial in itself, and yet pretends to be nature; it is so palpably ingenious, so frank an appeal to the stage! It has about it an absurd air of honest simplicity, a pretense of being bourgeois in some worthy sense.

Réjane plays her game with the thing, shows her impeccable cleverness, makes point after point, carries the audience with her. But I find nowhere in it what seems to me her finest qualities, at most no more than a suggestion of them. It is a picture painted so sweepingly that every subtlety would be out of place in it. She plays it sweepingly, with heavy contrasts, an undisguised exaggeration; one eye is always on the audience. That is, no doubt, the way the piece should be played; but I must complain of Sardou while I justify Réjane.

THE IRONIC COMEDY OF BECQUE

La Parisienne of Henri Becque, like most of his plays, has never lost its interest, like the topical plays of that period. It is a hard, ironical piece of realism, founded on a keen observation of life and on certain definite ideas. It is called a comedy, but there is no straightforward fun in it, as in *Ma Cousine*, for instance; it has all that transposed sadness which we call irony. It shows us rather a mean gray world, rather contemptuously; and it leaves us with a bitter taste in the mouth. That is, if one takes it seriously. Part of the actor's art in such a piece is to prevent one from taking it too seriously.

Throughout Réjane is the faultless artist, and her acting is so much of a piece that it is difficult to praise it in detail. A real woman lives before one, seems to be overseen on the stage at certain moments of her daily existence. We see her life going on, not, as with Duse, a profound inner life, but the life of the character, a vivid, worldly life, hard, selfish, calculating, deceiving naturally, naturally wary, the woman of the world, the Parisian. Compare Clotilde with Sapho and you will see two opposite types rendered with an equal skill; the woman in love, to whom nothing else matters, and the woman with lovers, the (what shall I say?) business woman of the emotions.

There is a moment near the beginning where Lafont asks Clotilde if she has been to see her milliner or her dressmaker, and she answers sarcastically: "Both!" Her face, as she submits to the question, has an absurd stare, a stare of profound dissimulation, with something of a cat who waits. Her whole character, her whole plan of campaign are in that moment; they but show themselves more pointedly, later on, when her nerves get the better of her through all the manifestations of her impatience, up to the return into herself at the end of the second act, when she stands motionless and speechless, while her lover entreats her, upbraids her, finally insults her. Her face, her whole body, endures, wearied into a desperate languor, seething with suppressed rage and exasperation; at last, her whole body droops on itself, as if it Can no longer stand upright. Throughout she speaks with that somewhat discontented grumbling tone which she can make so expressive; she empties her speech with little side shrugs of one shoulder, her sinister right eye speaks a whole subtle language of its own. The only moments throughout the play when I found anything to criticize are the few moments of pathos, when she becomes Sarah at second hand.

After *La Parisienne* came *Lolotte*, a one-act play of Meilhac and Halévy. It is amusing, and it gives Réjane the opportunity of showing us little samples of nearly all her talents. She is both canaille and bonne fille; above all she is triumphantly, defiantly clever. Again I was reminded of a Forain drawing: for here is an art which does everything that it is possible to do with a given material, and what more can one demand of an artist?

"LA ROBE ROUGE"

A greater contrast could hardly be imagined than that between these two plays and Brieux's sombre argument in the drama *La Robe Rouge*. Unlike *Les Avariés*, where the argument swamps the drama, *La Robe Rouge* is at once a good argument and a good play. There are perhaps too many points at issue, and the story is perhaps too much broken into section, but the whole thing takes hold of one, and, acted as it is acted by Réjane, and her company, it seems to lift one out of the theater into some actual place where people are talking and doing good or evil and suffering and coming into conflict with great impersonal forces; where, in fact, they are living. Without ever becoming literature, it comes, at times, almost nearer to every-day reality than literature can permit itself to come. There is not a good sentence in the play, or a sentence that does not tell. It is the subject and the hard, unilluminated handling of the subject that makes the play, and it is a model of that form of drama which deals sternly with actual things. It gives a great actress, who is concerned mainly with being true to nature, an incomparable opportunity, and it gives opportunities to every member of a good company. The second act tortures one precisely as such a scene in court would torture one. Its art is the distressingly, overwhelmingly real.

  La Robe Rouge is a play so full of solid and serious qualities that it is not a little difficult not to exaggerate its merits or to praise it for merits it does not possess. The play deals with vital questions, and it does not deal with them, as Brieux is apt to do, in a merely argumentative way. It is not only that abstract question: What is justice? May the law not be capable of injustice?

but the question of conscience in the lawyer, the judge, the administration of which goes by the name of justice. It is tragedy within tragedy. How extremely admirably the whole thing acts, and how admirably it was acted! After seeing this play, I realize what I have often wondered, that Réjane is a great tragic actress, and that she can be tragic without being grotesque. She never had a part in which she was so simple and so great. When I read the play I found many passages of mere rhetoric in the part of Zanetta; by her way of saying them Réjane turned them into simple natural feeling. I can imagine Sarah saying some of these passages, and making them marvelously effective. When Réjane says them they go through you like a knife. After seeing La *Robe Rouge*, I am not sure that of three great living actresses, Duse, Sarah, and Réjane, Réjane is not, as a sheer actress, the greatest of the three.

Réjane has all the instincts, as I have said, of the human animal, of the animal woman, whom man will never quite civilize. Réjane, in *Sapho* or in *Zaza* for instance, is woman naked and shameless, loving and suffering with all her nerves and muscles, a gross, pitiable, horribly human thing, whose direct appeal seizes you by the throat. In *Sapho* or *Zaza* she speaks the language of the senses, no more; and her acting reminds you of all that you may possibly have forgotten of how the senses speak when they speak through an ignorant woman in love. It is like an accusing confirmation of some of one's guesses at truth, before the realities of the flesh and of the affections of the flesh. Skepticism is no longer possible: the thing is before you, abominably real, a disquieting and irrefutable thing, which speaks with its own voice, as it has never spoken on the stage through any other actress.

In *Zaza*, a play made for Réjane by two playwrights who had set themselves humbly to a task, the task of fitting her with a part, she is seen doing *Sapho* over again, with a difference. Zaza is a vulgar woman, a woman without instruction or experience; she has not known poets and been the model of a great sculptor; she comes straight from the boards of a *café-concert* to the kept woman's house in the country. She has caught her lover vulgarly, to win a bet; and so, to the end, you realize that she is, well, a woman who would do that. She has no depth of passion, none of Sapho's roots in the earth; she has a "beguin" for Dufresne, she will drop everything else for it, such as it is, and she is capable of good hearty suffering. Réjane gives her to us as she is, in all her commonness. The picture is full of humor; it is, as I so often feel with Réjane, a Forain. Like Forain, she uses her material without ever being absorbed by it, without relaxing her impersonally artistic energy. In being Zaza, she is so far from being herself (what is the self of a great actress?) that she has invented a new way of walking, as well as new tones and grimaces. There is not an effect in the play which she has not calculated; only, she has calculated every effect so exactly that the calculation is not seen. When you watch Jane Hading, you see her effects coming several seconds before they are there; when they come, they come neatly, but with no surprise in them, and therefore with no conviction. There lies all the difference between the actress who is an actress equally by her temperament and by her brain and the actress who has only the brain (and, with Jane Hading, beauty) to rely on. Everything that Réjane can think of she can do; thought translates itself instantly into feeling, and the embodied impulse is before you.

When Réjane is Zaza, she acts and is the woman she acts; and you have to think, before you remember how elaborate a science goes to the making of that thrill which you are almost cruelly enjoying.

THE RUSSIAN BALLETS

I

The dance is life, animal life, having its own way passionately. Part of that natural madness which men were once wise enough to include in religion, it began with the worship of the disturbing deities, the gods of ecstasy, for whom wantonness and wine, and all things in which energy passes into evident excess, were sacred. From the first it has mimed the instincts; but we lose ourselves in the boundless bewilderments of its contradictions.

As the dancers dance, under the changing lights, so human, so remote, so desirable, so evasive, coming and going to the sound of a thin heady music which marks the rhythm of their movements like a kind of clinging drapery, they seem to sum up in themselves the appeal of everything in the world that is passing and colored and to be enjoyed. Realizing all humanity to be but a mask of shadows, and this solid world an impromptu stage as temporary as they, it is with a pathetic desire of some last illusion, which shall deceive even ourselves, that we are consumed with this hunger to create, to make something for ourselves, if at least the same shadowy reality as that about us. The art of the ballet awaits us, with its shadowy and real life, its power of letting humanity drift into a rhythm so much of its own, and with ornament so much more generous than its wont. And, as all this is symbolical, a series of living symbols, it can but reach the brain through the eyes, in the visual and imaginative way, so that the ballet concentrates in itself a great deal of the modern ideal in matters of artistic impression.

I am avid of impressions and sensations; and in the Russian Ballet at the Coliseum, certainly, there is a new impression of something not easily to be seen elsewhere. I need not repeat that, in art, rhythm means everything. And there can be a kind of rhythm even in scenery, such as one sees on the stage. Convention, even here, as in all plastic art, is founded on natural truth very closely studied. The rose is first learned, in every wrinkle of its petals, petal by petal, before that reality is elaborately departed from, in order that a new, abstract beauty may be formed out of these outlines, all but those outlines being left out.

So, in these Russian Ballets, so many of which are founded on ancient legends, those who dance and mime and gesticulate have at once all that is humanity and more than is in humanity. And their place there permits them, without disturbing our critical sense of the probability of things, to seem to assume a superhuman passion; for, in the Art of the Ballet, reality must fade into illusion, and then illusion must return into a kind of unreal reality.

The primitive and myth-making imagination of the Russians shows a tendency to regard metaphors as real and to share these tendencies with the savage, that is to say with the savagery that is in them, dependent as they are on rudimentary emotions. Other races, too long civilized, have accustomed themselves to the soul, to mystery. Russia, with centuries of savagery behind it, still feels the earth about its roots, and the thirst in it of the primitive animal. It has lost none of its instincts, and it has just discovered the soul. So, in these enigmatical dancers, the men and the women, who emerge before us, across the flaming gulf of the footlights, who emerge as they never did in any ballet created by Wagner, one finds the irresponsibility, the gaiety, the sombreness, of creatures who exist on the stage for their own pleasure and for the pleasure of pleasing us, and in them something large and lyrical, as if the obscure forces of the earth half-awakened had begun to speak. And these live, perhaps, an exasperated life – the life of the spirit and of the senses – as no others do; a life to most people inconceivable; to me, who have traveled in Russia, conceivable.

In what is abstract in Russian music there is human blood. It does not plead and implore like Wagner's. It is more somber, less carnal, more feverish, more unsatisfied in the desire of the flesh, more inhuman, than the ballet music in *Parsifal*. Even in that music, though shafts of light sometimes pierce the soul like a sword, there is none of the peace of Bach; it has the unsatisfied desire of a kind of flesh of the spirit. But in Tchaikovsky's music the violins run up and down the scales like acrobats; and he can deform the rhythms of nature with the caprices of half-civilized impulses. In your delight in finding any one so alive, you are inclined to welcome him without reserve, and to forget that a man of genius is not necessarily a great artist, and that, if he is not a great artist, he is not a quite satisfactory man of genius.

When I heard his music in *The Enchanted Princess* I was struck by the contrast of this ballet music with the overture to *Francesca da Rimini* I had heard years before. The red wind of hell, in which the lovers are afloat, blows and subsides. There is a taste of sulphur in the mouth as it ends, after the screams and spasms. Scrawls of hell-fire rush across the violins into a sharpened agony; above all, not Dante's; always hell-fire, not the souls of unhappy lovers who have loved too well.

Lydia Lopokova is certainly a perfect artist, whose dancing is a delight to the eyes, as her miming appeals to the senses. She has passion, and of an excitable kind; in a word, Russian passion. She can be delicious, malicious, abrupt in certain movements when she walks; she has daintiness and gaiety; her poses and poises are exquisite; there is an amazing certainty in everything she does. A creature of sensitive nerves, in whom the desire of perfection is the same as her desire for fame, she is on the stage and off the stage essentially the same; and in her conversations with me I find imagination, an unerring instinct, an intense thirst for life and for her own art; she has *la joie de vivre*.

Her technique, of course, is perfect; and, as in the case of every artist, it is the result of tireless patience. Technique and the artist: that is a question of interest to the student of every art. Without technique, perfect of its kind, no one is worth consideration in any art. The rope-dancer or the acrobat must be perfect in technique before he appears on the stage at all; in his case, a lapse from perfection brings its own penalty, death perhaps; his art begins when his technique is already perfect. Artists who deal in materials less fragile than human life should have no less undeviating a sense of responsibility to themselves and to art. So Ysaye seems to me the type of the artist, not because he is faultless in technique, but because he begins to create his art at the point where faultless technique leaves off.

Lubov Tchernicheva is a snake-like creature, beautiful and hieratic, solemn; and in her aspect, as in her gestures, a kind of Russian Cleopatra. Swinburne might have sung of her as he sang of the queen who ruled the world and Antony: –

Her mouth is fragrant as a vine,
    A vine with birds in all its boughs;
Serpent and scarab for a sign
    Between the beauty of her brows
And the amorous deep lids divine.

And it is a revelation to our jaded imaginations of much less jaded imaginations. These may be supposed to be characters in themselves of little interest to the world in general; to have come by strange accident from the ends of the world. Yet these are thrown into chosen situations, apprehended in some delicate pauses of life; they have their moments of passion thrown into relief in an exquisite way. To discriminate them we need a cobweb of illusions, double and treble reflections of the mind upon itself, with the artificial light of the stage cast over them and, as it were, constructed and broken over this or that chosen situation – on how fine a needle's point that little world of passion is balanced!

II

Apart from the loveliness of *Manfred* – the almost aching loveliness of Astarte – and the whole of the *Carnival, Kreisleriana,* and several other pieces, I have never been able to admire Schumann's music. When I wrote on Strauss I said that he has many moments in which he tries to bring humor into music. Turn from the "Annie" motive in *Enoch Arden* to the "Eusebius" of the *Carnival,* and you will readily see all the difference between two passages which it is quite possible to compare with one another. The "Annie" motive is as pretty as can be; it is adequate enough as a suggestion of the somewhat colorless heroine of Tennyson's poem; but how lacking in distinction it is, if you but set it beside the "Eusebius," in which music requires nothing but music to be its own interpreter. But it is in his attempts at the grotesque that Schumann seems at times actually to lead the way to Strauss. It is from Schumann that Strauss has learned some of those hobbling rhythms, those abrupt starts, as of a terrified peasant, by which he has sometimes suggested his particular kind of humor in music.

Schumann, like Strauss, reminds me at one time of De Quincey or Sydney Dobell, at another of Gustave Moreau or of Arnold Bocklin, and I know that all these names have had their hour of worship. All have some of the qualities which go to the making of great art; all, in different ways, fail through lack of the vital quality of sincerity, the hard and wiry line of rectitude and certainty. All are rhetorical, all produce their effect by an effort external to the thing itself which they are saying or singing or painting.

On seeing the *Carnival* for the second time I am more than ever struck by the fact that the ballet is a miracle of moving motion. In the dance of Columbine and Harlequin – they danced and mimed like living marionettes – I recalled vividly my impression on seeing a ballet, a farce and the fragments of an opera performed by the marionettes at the Costanzi Theatre in Rome. I was inclined to ask myself why we require the intervention of any less perfect medium between the meaning of a piece, as the audience conceived it, and that other meaning which it derives from our reception of it. In those inspired pieces of living painted wood I saw the illusion that I always desire to find, either in the wings of the theater or from a stall. In our marionettes, then, we get personified gesture, endless gesture, like all other forms of emotion, generalized. The appeal in what seems to you those childish maneuvers is to a finer, because to a more innately poetic sense of things than the rationalistic appeal of very modern plays. If at times we laugh – as one must in this ballet – it is with wonder at seeing humanity so gay, heroic and untiring. There is the romantic suggestion of magic in this beauty. So, in Harlequin, I find the personification of grace, of *souplesse*, in his miming and dancing; and when he is grotesque, I find a singular kind of beauty. A sinister gaiety pervades the ballet; a malevolent undercurrent of subtle meanings gives one the sense of an intricate intrigue; and I almost forgive the fact that the music is German!

I am, on the whole, disappointed with the *Cleopatra* ballet; for the scenery certainly does not suggest Egypt; but, to my mind, suggests rather the scenery used in Paris when I saw Alfred Jarry's *Ubu Roi*, a symbolist farce, given under strange conditions. The action took place in the land of nowhere; and the scenery was painted to represent by adroit conventions temperate and torrid zones at once. Then there were closed windows and a fireplace, containing an alchemist's crucible. These were crudely symbolical, but those in the Coliseum were not. In our search for sensation we have exhausted sensation; and, in that theater, before a people who have perfected the fine shades to their vanishing point, who have subtilized delicacy of perception into the annihilation of the very senses through which we take in ecstasy, I heard a literary Sans-culotte shriek for hours that unspeakable word of the gutter which was the refrain of this comedy of masks. Just as the seeker after pleasure whom pleasure has exhausted, so the seeker after the material illusions of a literary artifice turns finally to that first, subjugated, never quite exterminated element of cruelty which is one of the links which bind us to the earth.

The Russians have cruelty enough, but not this kind of cruelty; they are more complex than cruel, and why credit them with any real sense of morality? They are gifted with a kind of sick curiosity which makes them infinitely interesting to themselves. And – to concern myself again with these Russian dancers – they live in a prodigious illusion; their life in them is so tremendous that they are capable of imagining anything. And, in the words of Gorki, "in every being who lives there is hidden a vagabond more or less conscious of himself;" but – for all those who revolt – he has one phrase: *l'Épouvante du mal de vivre.*

Now, Lubov Tchernicheva, who looked Cleopatra and was dressed after Cleopatra's fashion, had nothing whatever to do, except to be repellent and attractive. She was given no chance to show that the queen she represented was one of those diabolical creatures whose coquetry is all the more dangerous because it is susceptible of passion; one in whom passion was at times like a will-o'-the-wisp that is suddenly extinguished after having given light to a conflagration.

Scheherazade is barbaric and gorgeous in *décor*, and in costume exotic and tragic and Oriental as the Russian music is; only, to me, the music is not quite satisfying; it has rather an irritating effect on the nerves. The dances are bewildering, intricate and elaborate, and intensely alive with animal desire. It is really a riot in color, amid an ever-moving crowd of revellers; in which Massine shows himself as the personification of lust, as he makes – with furious and too convulsive leaps in the air and with too obvious gestures and grimaces – frantic love to Zobeide, mimed by Tchernicheva, who has the stateliness of a princess, who glides mysteriously and is wonderful in the plastic quality of her movements, which I can only image as that of a tiger-cat.

Carlo Goldoni has been compared as a great comic dramatist with Pietro Longhi, who, in his amazingly amusing pictures, reflects also the follies and revels and miseries of the period. Longhi used to tell Goldoni that they – the painter and the playwright – were brethren in art; and one of Goldoni's sonnets records this saying: –

> Longhi, tu che la mia musa sorella
> Chiami del tuo pennel che cerca il vero.

It seems that their contemporaries were alive to the similar qualities and the common aims of the two men; for Gasparo Gozzi drew a parallel between them in a number of his Venetian *Gazzetta*.

It struck me, as I saw the Goldoni ballet and heard the music of Domenico Scarlatti, that all of the costumes and much of the effect of the miming – which were the most delicious and capricious that I have ever seen – had been designed after Longhi's paintings and drawings; for in many of these he gives a wonderful sense of living motion; but certainly nothing of what is abominably alive in the great and grim and sardonic genius of Hogarth.

In Venice I have often spent delightful hours before, for instance, such innumerable drawings of his as: painters at the easel, ballet girls with castanets, maid-servants holding trays, music and dancing masters (indeed, is not Enrico Cecchetti in the ballet a most admirable and most Italian dancing master?), tavern-keepers, street musicians, beggars, waiters; the old patrician lolling in his easy-chair and toying with a fan; the cavaliere in their fantastic dresses; the women with their towering head-dresses. The whole sense of Venice returned to me as I saw Lydia Lopokova – always so bird-like, so like a butterfly with painted wings, so witty in gestures, so absolutely an artist in every dance she dances, in every mime she mimics, in her wild abandonment to the excitement of these shifting scenes, where all these masked and unmasked living puppets have fine nerves and delicate passions – putting powder on the face of the Marquise Silvestra and mocking her behind her back. I saw then Casanova's favorite haunts: the *ridotti*, the gambling-houses, the *cafés* in San Marco's, the carnivals, the masked balls, the intrigues; the *traghetti* where I seemed to see mysterious figures flitting to and fro in wide miraculous *route* beneath the light of flickering flambeaux.

I see before me, as I write, the night when I went from the Giddecca to the Teatro Rossini, where a company of excellent Italian comedians gave one of Goldoni's comedies, and, as when the chatter in the gallery ends, the chatter begins on the stage, I found for once the perfect illusion; there is no difference between the one and the other. Voluble, living Venice, with its unchanging attitude toward things, the prompt gaiety and warmth of its temperament, finds equal expression in the gallery, and in the interpretation of Goldoni, on that stage. Going to the theater in Venice is like a fantastic overture to the play, and sets one's mood properly in tune. You step into the gondola, which darts at once across a space of half-lighted water, and turns down a narrow canal between walls which seem to reach more than half-way to the stars. Here and there a lamp shines from a bridge or at the water-gate of a house, but with no more than enough light to make the darkness seen. You see in flashes: an alley with people moving against the light, the shape of a door or balcony, seen dimly and in a wholly new aspect, a dark church-front, a bridge overhead, the water lapping against the green stone of a wall which your elbow all but touches, a head thrust from a window, the gondola that passes you, sliding gently and suddenly alongside, and disappearing into an unseen quiet.

Sadko is simply a magical and magnificent pantomime, and Rimski-Korsakov's ballet music gives me the sense of the swirl and confusion, of the bewilderments and infinite changes in the realm of the sea-king. And, apart from the riotous Russian dancing, most of the ballet is made of nervous gestures of the hands and arms, that have an exciting effect on the nerves, and that recall to my memory certain aspects of the sea; as when I saw a deadly sluggish sea, a venomous serpent coil and uncoil inextricable folds; symbols of something suddenly seen on the sea-surface in contrast with a wizard transmutation of colors. But, most of all, one aspect of curdling thick green masses of colors under a curdling green sea. In that instant I saw all the beauty of corruption. Then the underworld became visible, close under the sea: with palaces (like Poe's); streets, people, ruins; forests thick with poisonous weeds, void spaces, strange shifting shapes: symbols I could not fathom. Then came a stealthy, slow, insidious heaving of the reluctant waves. Then, again, the surging and swaying; and, always motionless, yet steadily changing in shape, the somber and unholy underworld.

In Tchernicheva I saw an actual Princess of the Sea, gorgeously dressed, and enchanting. Yet, all of the spectacle was not beautiful; it was singularly inhuman and, at times, unnatural. Nothing but beauty should exist on the stage. Visible beauty comes with the ballet, an abstract thing; gesture adds pantomime, with which drama begins; and then words bring in the speech by which life tries to tell its secret. Still, in the two extremes, pantomime and the poetic drama, the appeal is to the primary emotions, and with an economy and luxuriance of means, each of which is in its own way inimitable. Pantomime addresses itself, by the artful limitations of its craft, to universal human experiences, knowing that the moment it departs from those broad lines it will become unintelligible.

Pantomime, in its limited way, is no mere imitation of nature: it is a transposition. It can appeal to the intellect for its comprehension, and, like ballet, to the intellect through the eyes. To watch it is like dreaming. And as I watched this ballet I felt myself drawn deep into an opium-dream, as when I wrote of:

> This crust, of which the rats have eaten part,
>> This pipe of opium; rage, remorse, despair;
> This soul at pawn and this delirious heart.

Then, as the spell tightened closer and closer around me, I seemed to have taken hashish, of which I wrote: –

> Behold the image of my fear;
> O rise not, move not, come not near!
>> That moment, when you turned your face,
>> A demon seemed to leap through space;
> His gesture strangled me with fear.

> Who said the world is but a mood
> In the eternal thought of God?
>> I know it, real though it seem,
>> The phantom of a hashish dream
> In that insomnia which is God.

Does not every one know that terrifying impossibility of speaking which fastens one to the ground for the eternity of a second? Exactly that sensation came over me, the same kind of suspense, seeming to hang over the silent actors in the pantomime, giving them a nervous exaltation which has its subtle, immediate effect upon us, in comic or tragic situations.

III

The English theater with its unreal realism and its unimaginative pretenses toward poetry left me untouched and unconvinced. I found the beauty, the poetry, that I wanted only in two theaters, the Alhambra and the Empire. The ballet seemed to me the subtlest of the visible arts, and dancing a more significant speech than words. I could have said as Verlaine said to me, in jest, coming away from the Alhambra: "*J'aime Shakespeare, mais – j'aimes mieux le ballet!*" A ballet is simply a picture in movement. It is a picture where the imitation of nature is given by nature itself; where the figures of the composition are real, and yet, by a very paradox of travesty, have a delightful, deliberate air of unreality. It is a picture where the colors change, re-combine, before one's eyes; where the outlines melt into one another, emerge, and are again lost in the mazes of the dancing.

The most magical glimpse I ever caught of a ballet was from the road in front, from the other side of the road, one night when two doors were suddenly thrown open as I was passing. In the moment's interval before the doors closed again I saw, in that odd, unexpected way, over the heads of the audience, far off in a sort of blue mist, the whole stage, its brilliant crowd drawn up in the last pose, just as the curtain was beginning to go down.

I liked to see a ballet from the wings, a spectator, but in the midst of the magic. To see a ballet from the wings is to lose all sense of proportion, all knowledge of the piece as a whole, but, in return, it is fruitful in happy accidents, in momentary points of view, in chance felicities of light and movement and shade. It is almost to be in the performance one's self, and yet passive, with the leisure to look about one.

The front row of the stalls, on a first night, has a character of its own. It is entirely filled by men, and the men who fill it have not come simply from an abstract esthetic interest in the ballet. They have friends on the other side of the footlights, and their friends on the other side of the footlights will look down, the moment they come on, to see who are in the front row, and who are standing by the bar on either side. The standing room by the bar is the reserve of the first-nighters with friends who could not get a seat in the front row. On such a night the air is electrical. A running fire of glances crosses and re-crosses, above the indifferent, accustomed heads of the gentlemen in the orchestra; whom it amuses, none the less, to intercept an occasional smile, to trace it home. On the faces of the men in the front row, what difference in expression. Here is the eager, undisguised enthusiasm of the novice, all eyes on one; here is the wary practised attention of the man who has seen many first nights, and whose scarcely perceptible smile reveals nothing, compromises nobody, rests on all.

And there is a charm, not wholly imaginary, in that form of illusion known as make-up. To a face really charming it gives a new kind of exciting savor; and it has, to the remnant of Puritan conscience that is the heritage of us all, a certain sense of dangerous wickedness, the delight of forbidden fruit. The very phrase, painted women, has come to have an association of sin, and to have put paint on her cheeks, though for the innocent necessities of her profession, gives to a woman a kind of symbolic corruption. At once she seems to typify the sorceries and entanglements of what is most deliberately enticing in her sex, with all that is most subtle, least like nature, in her power of charm. *Maquillage*, to be attractive, must, of course, be unnecessary.

The art of the ballet counts for much in the evolution of many favorite effects of contemporary drawing, and not merely because Degas – who meant to me everything when I was writing on the ballets, standing in the wings, writing verses in which I was conscious of transgressing no law or art in taking that scarcely touched material for new uses – has drawn dancers, with his reserved, essentially classical mastery of form. By its rapidity of flight within bounds, by its bird-like and flowerlike caprices of color and motion, by that appeal to the imagination which comes

▶ 217

from its silence (to which music is but like an accompanying shadow, so closely, so discreetly does it follow the feet of the dancers), by its appeal to the eyes and to the senses, its adorable artificiality, the ballet has tempted almost every draughtsman, as the interiors of music-halls have also been singularly tempting, with their extraordinary tricks of light, their suddenness of gesture, their fantastic humanity. And pantomime, too, in the French and correct, rather than in the English and incorrect sense of that word, has had its significant influence. And the point of view is the point of view of Pierrot –

"*Le subtil génie*
De sa malice infinie
De poète-grimacier" –

Verlaine's *Pierrot Gamin.*

Watteau, the Prince of Court Painters, is the only painter of *la galanterie* who has given seriousness to the elegance of that passing moment, who has fixed that moment in an attitude which becomes eternal. In a similar gravity in the treatment of "light" subjects, and for a similar skill in giving them beauty and distinction, we must come down to Degas. In Degas the ballet and the *café* replace the Italian comedy of masks and the afternoon conversation in a park. But in Degas there is the same instantaneous notation of movement and the same choice and strange richness of color; with a quite comparable fondness for seizing what is true in artificial life, and for what is sad and serious in humanity at play. But Watteau, unlike Degas, is never cruel.

Never, as Watteau, "a seeker after something in the world, that is there in no satisfying measure or not at all," Degas, implacably *farouche*, the inexorable observer of women's flesh, in the wings of music-halls, in *café-concerts*, loves and hates and adores this strange mystery of women's flesh which he evokes, often curiously poisonous, but always with a caressing touch, a magic atmosphere that gives heat and life and light to all his pictures. Where Renoir is pagan and sensual, Degas is sensuous and a moralist. In the purity of his science, the perhaps impurity of his passion, he is inimitable. Is not his style – for painters have their own styles – the style of sensation – a style which is almost entirely made of sensations? He flashes on our vision *vrai vérité* of things, the very essence of them – not so much the essence of truth as of what appears in the visible world to the eyes that see it.

No one ever painted *maquillage* as he does, nor the strokes of light that shine in a dancer's eyes, nor the silk of her rose-colored tights that outline her nervous legs; nor the effects – sudden and certain – of what I have seen for years from the stage: silhouettes and faces and bodies and patches of light, a cigarette in a man's mouth; and, in the wings, miracles of change, of caprice, of fantasy, and of what seems and is not an endless motion of the dancers. I have always felt that the rhythm of dancing is a kind of arrested music, which Degas has certainly given us, as in the feet that poise, the silent waves of wandering sound of the dancer's moving melody, and her magic. A man of singular, but not universal, genius, Degas, his work being done, leaves behind him a sense of intense regret; for he created a new art in painting, that is to say, in painting the sex he adored, without pity and without malice.

ON HAMLET AND HAMLETS

I have seen many Hamlets. I have seen romantic, tragic, passionate, morbid, enigmatical, over-subtle and over-exceptional Hamlets, the very bells on the cap of "Fortune's fool." And as almost every actor has acted this part, every one of them gives a different interpretation: that is to say, from the time of Shakespeare to our own age. One knows that Shakespeare, besides other of the dramatists, acted at least one part, which seems to have surprised his audience: the Ghost in *Hamlet*. And as Shakespeare put more of his inner self into Hamlet's mouth than into the mouth of any of his other characters, it is not to be forgotten that perhaps the most wonderful prose in our language is spoken by Hamlet in that famous scene with the Players. Take, for instance, this speech:

> I have of late – but wherefore I know not – lost all my mirth, foregone all custom of exercise; and indeed it goes so heavily with my dis-position that this goodly frame, the earth, seems to me a sterile promontory, that most excellent canopy, the air, look you, this brave over-hanging firmament, this majestical roof fretted with golden fire, why, it appears no other thing to me than a foul and pestilent congreg-ation of vapors. What a piece of work is a man! How noble in reason! how infinite in faculty! in form and moving how express and admirable: in action how like an angel! in appearance how like a god! The beauty of the world! the paragon of animals! And yet to me, what is this quintessence of dust? Man delights not me: no, nor woman neither, though by your smiling you seem to say so.

If any prose is immortal, this is; and creative also, and imaginative, and lyrical: it has vision, and it has the sense of the immense contrast between "this majestical roof" and "this quintessence of dust" to which we are all reduced at the end.

I have always felt that a play of Shakespeare, seen on the stage, should give one the impression of assisting at "a solemn music." The rhythm of Shakespeare's art is not fundamentally different from that of Beethoven, and *Romeo and Juliet* is a suite, *Hamlet* a symphony. To act either of these plays with whatever qualities of another kind, and to fail in producing this musical rhythm from beginning to end, is to fail in the very foundation. It has been said that Shakespeare will sacrifice his drama to his poetry, and even *Hamlet* has been quoted against him. But let *Hamlet* be rightly acted, and whatever has seemed mere meditation will be realized as a part of that thought which makes or waits on action. The outlines of the tragedy are crude, irresistible melodrama, still irresistible to the gallery; and the greatness of the play, though it comes to us by means of its poetry, comes to us legitimately as a growth out of melodrama.

I have often asked myself this question, when I have sat in the stalls watching a play, and having to write about it: is the success of this piece due to the playwright's skill or to the skill of the actors? Nor is any question more difficult to answer than this; which Lamb certainly does his best to answer in one of his underlined sentences, in regard to the actor. "*He must be thinking all the while of his appearance, because he knows that all the while the spectators are judging of it.*" And again when he says: "In fact, the things aimed at in theatrical representations are to arrest the spectator's eye upon the form and the gesture, and to give a more favorable hearing to what is spoken: it is not what the character is, but how he looks; not what he says, but how he speaks it." Was anything more fundamentally true ever said on what the actor *ought* to do? Lamb answered it again, in his instinctive fashion of aiming his arrow straight at the mark, when he said of a performance of Shakespeare in which there were two great actors, that "it seemed to embody and realize conceptions which had hitherto assumed no distinct shape," but that "when the novelty is past, we find to our cost that instead of realizing an idea, we have only materialized and brought down a fine vision to the standard of flesh and blood."

Every artist who has the sense of the sublime knows that the pure genius is essentially silent, and that his revelation has in it more of vision than of reality. For when he deigns to appear, he is constrained, under penalty of extinction, to lessen himself so as to pass into the Inaccessible. He creates; if he fails in creation, he is of necessity condemned to the utter darkness. He is the ordinator of chaos: he calls and disposes of the blind elements; and when we are uplifted in our admiration before some sublime work, it is not that he creates an idea in us: it is that, under the divine influence of the man of genius, this idea, which was in us, obscure to itself, is reawakened.

I am confronted now with Villiers de l'Isle Adam in his conjectures in regard to certain questions – never yet settled – in *Hamlet*. A modern man of taste might ask what Shakespeare would have answered if the actor who played Hamlet's part were to interrogate the Specter "escaped from hideous Night" as to whether he had seen God's face, whether he wanted to be concerned with, not the eternal mysteries, but with what he had seen in hell and what he hated seeing on earth; and, if he had come only to utter absurdities, really, why need he have died at all?

The Ghost, by the mere fact of being there, seems, at first sight, an absurdity; but if he has really seen God and the Absolute and if he has entered into them – which is impossible – the sublimity of his words might seem to be superfluous; and yet the incoherencies that he utters are all the more terrifying because of their incomprehensibility. "The secret of the Absolute cannot be expressed with syntax, and therefore one cannot ask the ghost to produce more than an *impression*." The Specter, for Shakespeare, is not a human being: he is obsession. Had he wanted Hamlet really to perceive the ghost and had he thought this dramatic effect ought to seize on the imagination of the audience, it was because he was certain that every one of them, in the ghost perceived by Hamlet, would see the familiar ghost that actually haunts himself.

Hamlet's soliloquy "To be or not to be" is a magnificent disavowal – on the part of Shakespeare. And if one excuses the contradiction by supposing that Hamlet tried to deliver himself from the obsession, to doubt, one can only reply that he never doubts the Ghost itself, but the nature of this ghost; for he says at the end of the second act:

> The spirit I have seen
> May be the devil: and the devil hath power
> To assume a pleasing shape; yea, and perhaps,
> Out of my weakness and my melancholy,
> (As he is very potent with such spirits),
> Abuses me to damn me.

Therefore if we compare the motive and the spirit of those sickly phrases with those of the soliloquy, we shall realize that this has *no relation whatsoever* with the superstitious character of Hamlet; even more so, because every single word of them is in flagrant contradiction with the entire drama.

I have no intention of discussing either Mr. Martin Hervey's representation of Hamlet or the somber and sinister Hamlet acted by Josef Keinz in Berlin; or the performance of Tree, or of Forbes-Robertson; or of any one's, with the exception of that given by Edward Sothern. He is by no means the only Hamlet, for there are always – to quote Browning – "points in Hamlet's soul unseized by the Germans yet." Sothern had depth in his acting; and there was nothing fantastic in his grave, subdued, powerful, and piteous representation, in which no symbol, no figment of a German brain, no metaphysical Faust, loomed before us, but a man more to be pitied and not less to be honored than any man in Elsinore. Yet when one considers what Hamlet actually was – and there is no getting at the depths of his mystery – one finds, for one thing, a man too intensely restless to make up his mind on any question of thought, of conduct, and that he does for the most part the opposite of what he says. The pretense of madness is an almost transparent pretense, and used often for a mere effect of malicious wit, in the confusion of fools, or at the prompting of mere nerves. To me Hamlet seems to be cursed with the veritable genius of inaction. Always he is alone, even when he is in a crowd; he is the most sensitive of all Shakespeare's creations; his nerves are jarred, when knaves would play on him as one plays on an instrument; his blood is feverish, infected with the dark melancholy that haunts him. Does he love Ophelia? I see in him no passion for loving: to him passion is an abstract thing. In any case, irresolution is baneful to him; irresolution that loses so many chances, for which no one forgives himself. This Swinburne denies, supposing that the signal characteristic of Hamlet's inmost nature "is by no means irresolution or hesitation or any form of weakness, but rather the strong conflux of contending forces;" adding, what is certainly true, that the compulsory expedition of Hamlet to England and his hot-headed daring prove to us his almost unscrupulous resolution in time of practical need. Only, when all Hamlet's plans of revenge have been executed, with the one exception of his unnecessary death, before he utters his last immortal words "The rest is silence," the thought of death to him is as if a veil had been withdrawn for an instant, the veil which renders life possible, and, for that instant, he has seen.

LEONARDO DA VINCI

I

What counts, certainly, for much of what is so extraordinary in the genius of Leonardo da Vinci – who died exactly five hundred years ago – is the fact that the noble blood he inherited (the so-called dishonor that hangs over his birth being in his case a singular honor) is curiously like the stain of some strange color in one of his paintings; he being the least of all men to whom there could be anything poisonous in the exotic flowers of evil that germinated in Milan; where, as in Venice and in Rome, moved a changeful people who, in the very midst of their exquisite and cruel amusements, committed the most impossibly delicious sins, and without the slightest stings of conscience. Savonarola, from whom, in the last years of his life, Botticelli caught the contagion of the monk's fanaticism, was then endeavoring to strip off one lovely veil after another from the beauty of mortal things, rending them angrily; for which, finally, he received the baptism of fire. Rodrigo Borgia – a Spaniard born in Xàtiva – then Pope Alexander VI, was fortunate enough to possess in his son, Cesare, a man of sinister genius – cruel, passionate, ardent – who had the wonderful luck of persuading Leonardo to wander with him in their wild journey over Central Italy in 1502, as his chief engineer, and as inspector of strongholds. Not even the living pages of Machiavelli can give us more than a glimpse of what those conversations between two such flame-like creatures must have been; yet, we are aware of Cesare being condemned by an evil fate, as evil as Nero's, to be slain at the age of thirty-one, and of Leonardo, guided by his good genius, living to the age of sixty-seven.

The science of the Renaissance was divided, as it were, by a thousand refractions of things seen and unseen; so that when Leonardo, poring over his crucibles, desires no alchemist's achievement, but the achievement of the impossible, his vision is concentrated into infinite experiences, known solely to himself; exactly as when, in his retirement in the villa of the Melzi, his imagination is stirred feverishly as he writes detached notes, as he dashes off rapid drawings; and always not for other men's pleasure, but simply for his own; careless, as I think few men of genius have ever been, of anything but the moment's work, the instant's inspiration. And, what is also certain is that Da Vinci like Shakespeare created, ambiguously for all the rest of the world, flesh that is flesh and not flesh, bodies that are bodies and not bodies, by something inexplicable in their genius; something nervous, magnetic, overwhelming; and, to such an extent, that if one chooses to call to mind the greatest men of genius who have existed, this painter and this dramatist must take their places beside Aeschylus and beside Balzac.

Of Leonardo da Vinci, Pater has said: "Curiosity and the desire of beauty – these are the two elementary forces in his genius; curiosity often in conflict with the desire of beauty, but generating in union with it, a type of subtle and curious grace." Certainly the desire of perfection is, in Da Vinci, organic; so much so that there remains in him always the desire, as well as the aim, of attaining nothing less than finality, which he achieves more finally than any of the other Italian painters; and, mixed with all these, is that mystery which is only one part of his magic.

Is all this mystery and beauty, then, only style, and acquired style? Fortunate time, when style had become of such subtlety that it affects us, to-day, as if it were actually a part of the soul! But was there not, in Leonardo, a special quality, which goes some way to account for this? Does it not happen to us, as we look at one of his mysterious faces, to seem to distinguish, in the eyes reluctant to let out their secret, some glimpse, not of the soul of *Monna Lisa*, nor of the Virgin of the Rocks, but of our own retreating, elusive, not yet recognized soul? Just so, I fancy, Leonardo may have revealed their own souls to Luini and to Solario, and in such a way that for those men it was no longer possible to see themselves without something of a new atmosphere about them, the atmosphere of those which Leonardo had drawn to him out of the wisdom of secret and eternal things. With men like Leonardo style is, really, the soul, and their influence on others the influence of those who have discovered a little more of the unknown, adding, as it were, new faculties to the human soul.

Raphael, I have said elsewhere, could "correct" Michelangelo, could make Michelangelo jealous; Raphael, who said of him that he "treats the Pope as the King of France himself would not dare to treat him," that he goes along the streets of Rome "like an executioner;" Raphael who for the remaining years of his life paces the same streets with that grim artist; of Raphael, may it not be asked: who in the Vatican has not turned away from the stanza a little weary, as one turns aside out of streets or rooms thronged with men and women, happy, vigorous, and strangers: and has not gone back to the Sistine Chapel, and looked at the ceiling on which Michelangelo has painted a world that is not this world, men and women as magnificent as our dreams, and has not replunged into that abyss with a great sense of relief, with a supreme satisfaction?

Is this feeling of a kind of revulsion, before so many of his pictures, really justifiable? Is it, I ask myself, reasonable to complain, as I was obliged to complain in Rome, that his women have no strangeness in their beauty: that they do not brood over mysteries, like *Monna Lisa*? Might it not be equally reasonable to complain of the calm, unthinking faces of Greek statues, in which the very disturbance of thought – not of emotion – is blotted out, as it might be among beings too divine for any meaner energy than that of mere existence, "ideal spectators" of all that moves and is restless?

II

Two men of genius, in our own generation, have revealed for all time the always inexplicable magic of Leonardo da Vinci: Walter Pater in his prose and Dante Gabriel Rossetti in his sonnet. It is impossible not to quote this lyrical prose.

> The presence that thus so strangely rose beside the waters is express-ive of what in the ways of a thousand years men had come to desire. Here is the head upon which all "the ends of the world are come," and the eyelids are a little weary. It is a beauty wrought out from within upon the flesh, the deposit, little cell by cell, of strange thoughts and fantastic reveries and exquisite passions. All the thoughts and experience of the world have been etched and moulded there in that which they have of power to refine and make expressive the outward form, the animalism of peace, the lust of Rome, the reverie of the Middle Ages with its spiritual ambition and imaginative loves, the return of the Pagan world, the sins of the Borgias. She is older than the rocks among which she sits; like the vampire, she has been dead many times, and learned the secrets of the grave; and has been a diver in deep seas, and keeps their fallen day about her; and trafficked for strange webs with Eastern merchants; and, as Leda, was the mother of Helen of Troy, and, as Saint Anne, the mother of Mary; and all this has been to her but as the sound of lyres and flutes, and lives only in the delicacy with which it has moulded the changing lineaments and tinged the eyelids and the hands.

Rossetti, whose criticisms on poets are as direct and inevitable as his finest verse, was always his own best critic. He who said finally: "The life-blood of rhymed translation is this – that a good poem shall not be turned into a bad one," was as finally right on himself, as he was on others, in his unsurpassable revision of one of the most imaginative sonnets ever written: "A Venetian Pastoral by Giorgione." Certainly no poem of his shows more plainly the strength and wealth of the workman's lavish yet studious hand. And, in this sonnet as in the one on Leonardo, there is the absolute transfusion of a spirit that seemed incommunicable from one master's hand to another's. Only in the Leonardo, which I shall quote, there is none of the sovereign oppression of absolute beauty and the nakedness of burning life that I find in the *Fête Champêtre*. For in this divine picture the romantic spirit is born, and with it modern art. Here we see Whistler and the Japanese: a picture content to be no more than a picture: "an instant made eternity," a moment of color, of atmosphere, of the noon's intense heat, of faultless circumstance. It is a pause in music, and life itself waits, while men and women are for a moment happy and content and without desire; these, content to be beautiful and to be no more than a strain of music; to those others, who are content to know only that the hour is music.

Here, then, is Rossetti's version of the beauty of mysterious peace which broods over the *Virgin of the Rocks*.

Mother, is this the darkness of the end,
The Shadow of Death? and is that outer sea
Infinite imminent Eternity?
And does the death-pang by man's seed sustained
In Time's each instant cause thy face to bend
Its silent prayer upon the Son, while he
Blesses the dead with his hand silently
To his long day which hours no more offend?

Mother of grace, the pass is difficult,
Keen as these rocks, and the bewildered souls
Throng it like echoes, blindly shuddering through.
Thy name, O Lord, each spirit's voice extols,
Whose peace abides in the dark avenue
Amid the bitterness of things occult.

So Leonardo, who said "that figure is not good which does not express through its gestures the passions of its soul," becomes, more than any painter, the painter of the soul. He has created, not only in the *Gioconda*, a clairvoyant smile, which is the smile of mysterious wisdom hidden in things; he has created the motion of great waters; he has created types of beauty so exotic that they are fascinating only to those who are drawn into the unmirrored depths of this dreamless mirror. He invents a new form of landscape, subtle and sorcerous, and a whole new movement for an equestrian statue; besides inventing – what did not this miraculous man invent! – the first quite simple and natural treatment of the Virgin and Child. So, as he was content to do nothing as it had been done before, he creates in the *Gioconda* a new art of portrait painting; and, in her, so disquieting, that her eyes, as they follow you persistently, seem to ask one knows not what impenetrable and seductive question, on which all one's happiness might depend. Mysterious and enigmatical as she is, there is in her face none of the melancholy – which is part of the melancholy of Venice – that allures one's senses in a famous picture in the Accademia; where, the feast being over, and the wine drunk, something seems to possess the woman, setting those pensive lines about her lips, which will smile again when she has lifted her eyelids.

III

The sinister side of Leonardo da Vinci's genius leads him to the execution of the most prodigious caricatures ever invented; that is to say, before the malevolent and diabolical and macabre and malignant creations in this genre of Goya. In his *Caprichos* one sees the man's immense arrogance, his destructive and constructive genius, his rebellion – perhaps even more so than Leonardo's – against old tradition; which he hated and violated. Dramatic, revolutionary, visionary in his somber Spanish fashion, it seems to me that this – one of the supreme forms of his art – is, in the same sense as Villon's *Grand Testament*, his Last Testament: for in both poet and painter the nervous magnificence seen equally in the verse and in the painting is created, almost literally, out of their life-blood.

Only, in Leonardo, visions shape themselves into strange perversities – not the pensive perversities of Perugino – and assume aspects of evasive horrors, of the utmost ugliness, and are transformed into aspects of beauty and of cruelty, as the artist wanders in the hot streets of Florence to catch glimpses of strange hair and strange faces, as he and they follow the sun's shadow. He seizes on them, furiously, curiously, then he refines upon them, molding them to the fashion of his own moods; but always with that unerring sense of beauty which he possesses supremely – beauty, often enough, in its remoteness from actual reality. With passion he tortures them into passionate shapes; with cruelty he makes them grimace; abnormally sensitive (as Rodin often enough was) he is pitiless on the people he comes in contact with, setting ironical flames that circle round them as in Dante's Inferno, where the two most famous lovers of all time, Francesca and Paolo, endure the painted images of the fires of hell, eternally unconsumed. When he seeks absolute beauty there are times when it is beyond the world that he finds it; when he seeks ignominy, it is a breath blowing from an invisible darkness which brings it to his nerves. In evoking singular landscapes, he invents the *bizarre*. When he is concerned with the tragic passions of difficult souls, he drags them suddenly out of some obscure covering, and seems, in some of his extravagances, to set them naked before us.

As it is Pater who says that inextricably mingled with those qualities there is an element of mockery, "so that, whether in sorrow or scorn, he caricatures Dante even," I am reminded of certain of Botticelli's designs for Dante's *inferno*, in which I find the element of caricature; as, for instance, when the second head grows on Dante's shoulders, looking backward; as, in the face of Beatrice, which is changed into a tragic mask, because in the poem she refrains from smiling, lest the radiance of the seventh heaven, drawn into her eyes, shall shrivel Dante into ashes.

Nearest to Leonardo in the sinister quality of his genius is El Greco. I have never forgotten his *Dream of Philip II*, in the Escurial, where there is a painted hell that suggests the fierce material hells of Hieronymus von Bosch: a huge fanged mouth wide open, the damned seen writhing in that red cavern, a lake of flame awaiting those beyond, where the king, dressed in black, kneels at the side. It is almost a vision of madness, and as if this tormented brain of the fanatic, who built these prison walls about himself, and shut himself living into a tomb-like cell, and dead into a more tomb-like crypt, had wrought itself into the painter's brain; who would have found something not uncongenial to himself in this mountainous place of dust and gray granite, in which every line is rigid, every color ashen, in a kind of stony immobility more terrible than any other of the images of death.

I am tempted to bring in here, by way of comparison with these two artists, Jacques Callot, a painter of extraordinary genius, born at Nancy, in Lorraine, in 1592; who, in many of his works, created over again ancient dragons and devils: created them with the fury of an invention that never rested. In his engraving of the hanged men there is that strangeness in beauty which takes away much of the horror of the actual thing; and in his monstrous and malignant *Fantasie*, where two inhuman creatures – in all the splendor of caricature – grind I know not what poison, in a wide-mouthed jar, plumed and demoniacal.

La Tentation de Saint Antoine, done in 1635, is stupendous. High in the sky is the enormous figure of a reptile-faced Satan, who vomits out of his mouth legions of evil spirits; he is winged with ferocious wings that extend on both sides hugely; one of his clawed hands is chained, the right hurls out lightning. There is Chaos in this composition; it is imaginative in the highest degree of that satanical quality that produces monstrosities. There are clawed creatures that swim in the air, unicorns with stealthy glances. And, with his wonderful sense of design, the saint is seen outside his cave, assailed by legions of naked women, winged and wanton, shameless and shameful. And what is the aim, what is the desire of these evil creatures? To seduce Saint Antony of the Temptations.

Another picture painted on the same subject is that of Gruneweld in the Cologne Museum, which represents a tortured creature who has floated sheer off the earth in his agony, his face drawn inward, as it were, with hideous pains; near him a crew of red and green devils, crab-like, dragon-like, who squirm and gnaw and bark and claw at him, in an obscene whirl and fierce orgy of onslaught. Below, a strange bar of sunset and at the side a row of dripping trees; behind, a black sky almost crackling with color. In some of the other monstrous pictures I saw suggestions of Beardsley; as in the child who kisses the Virgin with thrust-out lips; in those of Meister van S. Severin, in which I found a conception of nature as unnatural and as rigid as that of the Japanese, but turned hideous with hard German reality, as in the terrifying dolls who are meant to be gracious in the Italian manner. And in this room I was obliged to sit in the midst of a great heat, where blood drips from all the walls, where tormented figures writhe among bright-colored tormentors; where there is a riot of rich cloths, gold and jewels, of unnatural beasts, of castles and meadows, in which there is nothing exquisite; only an unending cruelty in things. The very colors cry out at one; they grimace at you; a crucified thief bends back over the top of the cross in his struggles; all around monsters spawn out of every rock and cavern and there is hell fire.

To turn from these to the Cranachs in Vienna is to be in another world of art: an art more purposely perverse, more curiously unnatural; but, where his genius is shown at its greatest, is in an exquisite Judith holding the head of Holofernes, which lies, open-eyed, all its red arteries visible, painted delicately. She wears orange and red clothes, with collars and laces, and slashed sleeves through which many rings are seen on her fingers; she has a large red hat placed jauntily on her head. She is all peach-blossom and soft, half-cruel sweetness with all the wicked indifference of her long narrow eyes, the pink mouth and dimpled chin. She is a somnambulist, and the sword she holds is scarcely stained. There are two drops of blood on the table on which she rests the great curled head with its open eyes; her fingers rest on the forehead almost caressingly. She is *Monna Lisa*, become German and bourgeoise, having certainly forgotten the mysterious secret of which she still keeps the sign on her face.

Writing in Florence on Leonardo da Vinci I used by way of comparison two Greek marbles I had seen in London; one, the head of an old man, which is all energy and truth – comparable only in Greek work, with the drunken woman in Munich, and, in modern art, with *La Vieille Heaulmière* of Rodin; the other, a woman's head, which ravishes the mind. The lips and eyes have no expression by which one can remember them; but some infinitely mysterious expression seems to flow through them as through the eyes and lips of a woman's head by Leonardo. And all this reminds me of certain unforgettable impressions; and, most of all, when in Bologna I saw, in the Museo Civico, the spoils of Etruscan sepulchres, that weighed on me heavily; and, at the same time, I felt an odor of death, such as I had not even felt in Pompeii; where in so frightful a step backward of twenty centuries, the mind reels, clutching at that somewhat pacifying thought, for at least its momentary relief. Here were the bodies of men and women, molded for ever in the gesture of their last moment, and these rigid corpses are as vivid in their interrupted life as the damp corpses in the morgue. In Bologna, as I was pursued by the sight of the hairpins of dead women, there flashed on me this wonderful sentence of Leonardo: "Helen, when she looked in her mirror, seeing the withered wrinkles made in her face by old age, wept and wondered why she had twice been carried away."

But, as I walked back at night in those desolate streets – so essentially desolate after the warmth of Naples – on my way back to the hotel where Byron lived, before his evil genius hurried him to an early death, I remembered these two sentences in his letters; one, when in Florence, he returns from a picture-gallery "drunk with beauty"; one, where, as he sees the painted face of a learned lady, he cries: "This is the kind of face to go mad for, because it can not walk out of its frame." There, it seems to me, that Byron, whose instinct was uncertain, has, by instinct, in this sentence, anticipated a great saying of Whistler's. It was one of his aims in portrait painting to establish a reasonable balance between the man as he sits in the chair and the image of the man reflected back to you from the canvas. "The one aim," he wrote, "of the unsuspecting painter is to make his man 'stand out' from the frame – never doubting that, on the contrary, he should, and in truth absolutely does, stand within the frame – and at a distance behind it equal to the distance at which the painter has seen it. The frame is, indeed, the window through which the painter looks at his model, and nothing could be more offensively inartistic than this brutal attempt to thrust the model on the hither-side of this window!" He never proposed, in a picture, to give you something which you could mistake for reality: but frankly, a picture, a thing which was emphatically not nature, because it was art; whereas, in Degas, the beauty is a part of truth, a beauty which our eyes are too jaded to distinguish in the things about us.

In the Ambrosiane in Milan, beside two wonderful portraits, once attributed to Leonardo, and coming near to being worthy of him, are his grotesque drawings that are astonishing in their science, truth and naked beauty. Each is a quite possible, but horrible and abnormal, exaggeration of one or another part of the face, which becomes bestial and indeed almost incredible, without ceasing to be human. It is this terrible seriousness that renders

▶ 235

them so dreadful: old age, vice and disease made visible.

In another room there are many of his miraculously beautiful drawings – the loveliest drawings in the world. Note, for instance, the delicious full face drawing of a child with an enchanting pout. The women's faces are miracles. After these all drawings, and their method, seem obvious. The perfect love and understanding with which he follows the outline of a lovely cheek, or of a bestial snout; there is equal beauty, because there is equal reverence, in each. After this the Raphael cartoon (for the Vatican *School of Athens*) seems merely skilful, a piece of consummate draughtsmanship; supremely adequate but entirely without miracle.

In one of Leonardo's drawings in Florence there is a small Madonna and Child that peeps sidewise in half reassured terror, as a huge griffin with bat-like wings – stupendous in invention – descends suddenly from the air to snatch up a lion wandering near them. This might perhaps have been one of his many designs for the famous *Medusa* – *Aspecta Medusa* – in the Uffizi; for to quote Pater's interpretation of this corpse-like creation, "the fascination of corruption penetrates in every line its exquisitely finished beauty. About the dainty lines of the cheek the bat flies unheeded. The delicate snakes seem literally to strangle each other in terrified struggle to escape the Medusa brain. The hue which violent death brings with it is in the features." It is enough to compare any grotesque or evil head in the finest of Beardsley's drawings with Leonardo's head of Judas in the Windsor Library, or with one of those malevolent and malignant heads full of the energy of the beasts he represents and of insane fury which he scatters over the pages of his sketchbook, to realize that, in Beardsley, the thing drawn must remain ugly through all the beauty of the drawing and must hurt.

It hurts because he desires to hurt every one except himself, knowing, all the time, that he was more hated than loved. Sin is to him a diabolical beauty, not always divided against itself. Always in his work is sin – Sin conscious of sin, of an inability to escape from itself; transfigured often into ugliness and then transfigured from ugliness back to beauty. Having no convictions, he can when he chooses make patterns that assume the form of moral judgments.

IV

Leonardo da Vinci's unfinished *Saint Jerome*, in the Vatican at Rome, is exactly like intarsia work; the ground almost black, the men and the lion a light brown. This particular way of painting reminds me of the intarsia work in the halls in Santo Spirito in Bergamo by Fra Damiano in 1520; done just one year after Leonardo died. Here, in this supple and vigorous work in wood, I saw what could be done by a fine artist in the handling of somewhat intractable material. The work was broad or minute at will, with splendid masses and divisions of color in some designs which seemed to represent the Deluge, sharp, clear, firmly outlined in the patterns of streets and houses; full of rich color in the setting of wood against wood, and at times almost as delicate as a Japanese design. There was the head of John the Baptist laid on a stone slab, which was like a drawing of Daumier. And, in the whole composition of the design, with its two ovals set on each side like mirrors for the central horror, there was perfect balance. San Acre, this superb intarsia work of Fra Damiano, seemed a criticism on Lotto, the criticism of a thing, comparatively humble in itself, but in itself wholly satisfying, upon the failure of a more conspicuous endeavor, which has made its own place in art, to satisfy certain primary demands which one may logically make upon it.

In the Jerome, as in his finished work, one sees Leonardo's undeviating devotion to the perfect achievement of everything to which he set his hand; and how, after a long lapse of time, in the heat of the day, he crosses Florence to mount the scaffold, adds two or three touches to a single figure, and returns forthwith. Never did Michelangelo paint in such various ways as Leonardo; for, in his frescoes in the Sistine Chapel, art ceases to approach one directly, through this sense or that, through color, or some fancied outlook of the soul; only, one seems to be of the same vivid and eternal world as these meditative and joyous beings, joyous even in hell, where the rapture of their torment broods in eyes and limbs with the same energy as the rapture of God in creation, of the women in disobedience.

Certainly, however, in the Jerome there is a glimpse of background in which I find already the suggestion of the magical rocks of the *Virgin* and of *Monna Lisa*; only it is sketched in green, and in it there are gaunt brown rocks, which seem to open on another glimpse in yellow. All of the outline is gaunt, both the saint and his rocky cave; only not the lion, who is the most ample and living beast I have ever seen attendant on any Jerome. All the lines are outlined; the painful but not grotesque anatomy of the saint and of the sharp angles of the rocks, are painted in dim, almost uniform, tones. Is the picture rhetorical, like the other Saint Jeromes, or does it in some subtle fashion escape? It seems to me to escape, retaining only the inevitable violence of gesture and the agony of emotion in body and face; together with an immense dignity, loneliness and obscure suffering.

Leonardo, who was in Venice in 1500, certainly must have seen Titian's early *Annunciation* in the Scuola di San Rocco; which is a rebuke to Tintoretto's explosive *Crucifixion*. Before this picture it struck me that Tintoretto is the Zola of painting. Here, in this immense drama of paint, is a drama in which the central emotion is lacking; Christ is no more than the robber who is being nailed to the cross or the robber whose cross is being hoisted. Every part of the huge and bustling scene has equal interest, equal intensity; and it is all an interest and intensity of execution – which in its way is stupendous. But there is no awe, no religious sense. The beauty of detail is enormous, the energy overwhelming; but there is no nobility, no subtlety; it is a tumultuous scene painted to cover a wall.

In the Old Pinakothek in Munich the finest piece of paint in the Gallery is the *Scourging of Christ* by Titian. The modern point of view, indeed most modern art, has come out of it – equally in Watts and in Monticelli and in the Impressionists. We see Titian breaking the achieved rules, at the age of ninety, inventing an art absolutely new, a new way, a more immediate way of rendering what he sees, with all that moving beauty of life in action: lights, colors, and not forms merely, all in movement. The depth and splendor of a moment are caught, with all the beauty of every accident in which color comes or changes, and in the space of a moment. Color is no longer set against color, each for itself, with its own calm beauty; but each tone rushes with exquisite violence into the embrace of another tone; there are fierce adulteries of color unheard of till now. And a new, adorable, complete thing is born, which is to give life to all the painting that is to come after it It seems as if paint at last had thoroughly mastered its own language.

I have always believed that Giorgione, born in 1478, one year before the birth of Titian, played in the development of Venetian Art a part exactly the same as that played by Marlowe, born in the same year as Shakespeare, in the history of tragic Drama. Shakespeare never forgot Marlowe, Titian never forgot Giorgione; only the influence of his predecessor on Shakespeare was a passing one; that of Giorgione on Titian was, until he finally escaped from his influence, immense. It is from Andrea del Verrocchio that Leonardo begins to learn the art of painting; soon surpasses him; but, as Pater supposes, catches from him his love of beautiful toys. Giorgione possesses perfection without excess; Leonardo's absolute perfection often leads him into passionate excesses. He adored hair; and certainly hair, mostly women's hair, is the most mysterious of human things. No one ever experimented in more amazing ways than he did; but his experiment in attempting to invent a medium of using oils in the painting of frescoes failed him in what might have been his masterpiece, *The Last Supper*, painted on the damp wall of the refectory, oozing with mineral salts, of the Chaedo Vinciano in Milan. One looks at it as through a veil, which Time seems to have drawn over it, even when it is most cracked and chipped. Or it is as if it had soaked inward, the plaster sullenly absorbing all the color and all but the life. It is one of the few absolute things in the world, still; here, for once, a painter who is the subtlest of painters has done a great, objective thing, a thing in the grand style, supreme, and yet with no loss of subtlety. It is in a sense the measure of his greatness. It proves that the painter of *Monna Lisa* means the power to do anything.

IMPRESSIONISTIC WRITING

Impressionistic writing requires the union of several qualities; and to possess all these qualities except one, no matter which, is to fail in impressionistic writing. The first thing is to see, and with an eye which sees all, and as if one's only business were to see; and then to write, from a selecting memory, and as if one's only business were to write. It is the interesting heresy of a particular kind of art to seek truth before beauty; but in an impressionistic art concerned, as the art of painting is, with the revelation, the re-creation, of a colored and harmonious world, which (they tell us) owes its very existence to the eyes which see it, truth is a quality which can be attained only by him who seeks beauty before truth. The truth impressionist may be imagined as saying: "Suppose I wish to give you an impression of the Luxembourg Gardens, as I see them when I look out of my window, will it help to call up in your mind the impression of those glimmering alleys and the naked darkness of the trees, if I begin by telling you that I can count seven cabs, half another at one end, and a horse's head at the other, in the space between the corner of the Odéon and the houses on the opposite side of the street; that there are four trees and three lamp-posts on the pavement; and that I can read the words 'Chocolat Menier,' in white letters, on a blue ground, upon the circular black kiosk by the side of the second lamppost? I see those things, no doubt, unconsciously, before my eye travels as far as the railings of the garden; but are they any essential part of my memory of the scene afterward?"

I have turned over page after page of clever, ingenious summarizing of separate detail in a certain book, but I have found nowhere a page of pure beauty; all is broken, jagged, troubled, in this restless search after the broken and jagged outlines of things. It is all little bits of the world seen without atmosphere, and, in spite of many passages which endeavor to draw a moral from clouds, gas, flowers and darkness, seen without sentiment. When the writer describes to us "the old gold and scarlet of hanging meat; the metallic green of mature cabbages; the wavering russet of piled potatoes; the sharp white of fly-bills, pasted all awry;" we can not doubt that he has seen exactly what he describes, exactly as he describes it, and, to a certain extent, we too see what he describes to us. But he does not, as Huysmans does in the *Croquis Parisiens*, absolutely force the sight of it upon us, so that we see it, perhaps with horror, but in spite of ourselves we see it. Nor does he, when some vague encounter on the road has called up in him a "sense of the ruthless nullity of life, of the futile deception of effort, of bitter revolt against the extinction of death, a yearning after faith in a vague survival beyond," convey to us the impression which he has felt in such a way that we, too, feel it, and feel it to be the revelation of the inner meaning of just that landscape, just that significant moment. He has but painted a landscape, set an inexpressive figure in the background, and ticketed the frame with a motto which has nothing to do with the composition.

In this book the writer has not, it seems to me, succeeded in his intention; but I have a further fault to find with the intention itself. It is one of the discreditable signs of the haste and heedlessness of our time that artists are coming to content themselves, more and more, with but sketching out their pictures, instead of devoting themselves to the patient labor of painting them; and that they are anxious to invent an excuse for their idleness by proclaiming the superiority of the unfinished, instinctive first draught over the elaborated, scarcely spontaneous work of finished art. A fine composition may, in the most subtle and delicate sense, be slight: a picture of Whistler, for example, a poem of Verlaine. To be slight, as Whistler, as Verlaine, is slight, is to have refined away, by a process of ardent, often of arduous, craftsmanship, all but what is most essential in outward form, in intellectual substance. It is because a painter, a poet of this kind, is able to fill every line, every word, with so intense a life, that he can afford to dispense with that amplification, that reiterance, which an artist of less passionate vitality must needs expend upon the substance of his art. But it is so easy to be brief without being concise; to leave one's work unfinished, simply because one has not the energy to finish it! This book, like most experiments in writing prose as if one were writing sonnets, is but a collection of notes, whose only value is that they may some day be worked into the substance of a story or an essay. It has not yet been proved – in spite of the many interesting attempts which have been made, chiefly in France, in spite of *Gaspard de la Nuit*, Baudelaire's *Petits Poèmes en Prose*, and Mallarmé's jeweled fragments – that prose can, quite legitimately, be written in this detached, poetic way, as if one were writing sonnets. It seems to me that prose, just because it is prose, and not poetry – an art of vaguer, more indeterminate form, of more wandering cadences – can never restrict itself within those limits which give the precision of its charm to verse, without losing charm, precision, and all the finer qualities of its own freedom.

In France, as in England, there are two kinds of poetical reputation, and in France these two kinds may be defined as the reputation of the Latin Quarter and the reputation of the boulevards. In England a writer like Francis Thompson was, after all, known to only a very narrow circle, even though many, in that circle, looked on him as the most really poetical poet of his generation. In France, Vielé-Griffin is greatly admired by the younger men, quite as much, perhaps, as De Régnier, but he is not read by the larger outside public which has, at all events, heard of De Régnier. These fine shades of reputation are not easily recognized by the foreigner; they have, indeed, nothing to do with the question of actual merit; but they have, all the same, their interest, if only as an indication of the condition and tendency of public opinion.

If we go further, and try to compare the actual merit of the younger French and English poets, we shall find some difficulty in coming to any very definite conclusion. To certain enthusiasts for exotic things, it has seemed as if the mere fact of a poem being written in French gives it an interest which it could not have had if it had been written in English. When the poem was written by Verlaine or by Mallarmé, yes; but now that Verlaine and Mallarmé are gone? Well, there is still something which gives, or seems to give, French verse an advantage over English. The movement which began with Baudelaire, and culminated in Verlaine, has provided, for every young man who is now writing French verse, a very helpful kind of tradition, which leaves him singularly free within certain definite artistic limits. It shows him, not a fixed model, but the suggestion of innumerable ways in which to be himself. All modern French verse is an attempt to speak straight, and at the same time to speak beautifully. "*L'art, mes enfants, c'est d'être absolument soi-même,*" said Verlaine, and all these poets who are writing vers libre, and even those who are not writing *vers libre*, are content to be absolutely themselves, and to leave externalities perhaps even too much alone. What we see in England is exactly the contrary. We have had our traditions, and we have worn them out, without discovering a new form for ourselves. When we try to be personal in verse, the personal emotion has to mold anew every means of expression, every time; and it is rarely that we succeed in so difficult a task. For the most part we write poems for the sake of writing poems, choosing something outside ourselves to write about, and bringing it into permanent relation with ourselves. Our English verse-writers offer us a ballad, a sonnet, an eclogue; and it is a flower without a root, springing from no deep soil in the soul. The verse is sometimes excellent verse, but it is not a personal utterance; it is not a mood of a temperament, but something outside a temperament. In France, it is true, we often get the temperament and nothing else. And, in France, all these temperaments seem stationary; they neither change nor develop; they remain self-centered, and in time we become weary of seeing their pale reflections of themselves. Here, we become weary of poets who see everything in the world but themselves, and who have no personal hold upon the universe without. Between the too narrowly personal and a too generalized impersonality, there remains, in France and in England, a little exquisite work, which is poetry. Is it important, or even possible, to decide whether there is a little more of it to be found in the books of English or of French poets?

PARADOXES ON POETS

The great period of English poetry begins half-way through the sixteenth century, and lasts half-way into the seventeenth. In the poetry strictly of the sixteenth century, before the drama had absorbed poetry into the substance of its many energies, verse is used as speech, and becomes song by way of speech. It was the age of youth, and rejoiced, as youth does, in scarcely tried strength and in the choice of adventure. And it was an adventure to write. Soldiers and voyagers, Sidney, Raleigh, led the way as on horses and in ships. It is Raleigh, in the preface to a deeply meditated "History of the World," who speaks gallantly of "leisure to have made myself a fool in print." New worlds had been found beyond the sea, and were to be had for the finding in all the regions of the mind. There were buried worlds of the mind which had lately been dug up, lands had been newly colonized, in Italy and in France; à kind of second nature, it seemed to men in those days, which might be used not less freely than nature itself. And, just as the Renaissance in Italy was a new discovery of the mind, through a return to what had been found out in antiquity and buried during the Middle Ages, so, in England, poetry came to a consciousness of itself by way of what had already been discovered by poets like Petrarch and Ronsard, and even their later apes and mimics, Serafino or Desportes, among those spoils. Poetry had to be reawakened, and these were the messengers of dawn. Once awakened, the English tongue could but sing, for a while, to borrowed tunes; yet it sang with its own voice, and the personal accent brought a new quality into the song. Song-writers and sonnet-writers, when they happened to be poets, found out themselves by the way, and not least when they thought they were doing honor to a foreign ideal.

And it was an age of music. Music, too, had come from Italy, and had found for once a home there. Music, singing and dancing made then, and then only, the "merry England" of the phrase. And the words, growing out of the same soil as the tunes, took equal root. Campion sums up for us a whole period, and the song-books have preserved for us names, but for them unknown, of perfect craftsmen in the two arts. Every man, by the mere feeling and fashion of the time, took care

to write
Worthy the reading and the world's delight.

It was an age of personal utterance; and men spoke frankly, without restraint, too nice choosing, or any of the timidities or exaggerations of self-consciousness. The personal utterance might take any form; whether Fulke Greville wrote "treatises" on the mind of man, or Drayton pried into the family affairs of the fairies, or Samuel Daniel thought out sonnets to Delia, or Lodge wantoned in cadences and caprices of the senses. It might seem but to pass on an alien message, in as literal a translation as it could compass of a French or Italian poem. In the hand of a poet two things came into the version: magic, and the personal utterance, if in no other way, through the medium of style.

Style, to the poets of the sixteenth century, was much of what went to the making of that broad simplicity, that magnificently obvious eloquence, which seems to us now to have the universal quality of the greatest poetry. The poets of the nineteenth century are no nearer to nature, though they seem more individual because they have made an art of extracting rare emotions, and because they take themselves to pieces more cunningly. Drayton's great sonnet is the epilogue, and Spenser's great poem the epithalamium, for all lovers; but it needs another Shelley to find out love in the labyrinth of "Epipsychidion." All that is greatest in the poetry of the sixteenth century is open to all the world, like a wood, or Arcadia, in which no road is fenced with prohibitions, and the flowers are all for the picking.

And when, in the nineteenth century, poetry began again, it was to the poets of the sixteenth century that the new poets looked back, finding the pattern there for what they were making over again for themselves. A few snatches from Elizabethan song-books were enough to direct the first awakenings of song in Blake; Wordsworth found his gnomic and rational style, as of a lofty prose, in Samuel Daniel; Keats rifled the best sweets of Lodge's orchard; and Shelley found in the elegies of Michael Drayton the model of his incomparable style of familiar speech in verse, the style of the *Letter to Maris Gisborne*. Every reader of modern verse will find something contemporary in even the oldest of these poems; partly because modern verse is directly founded on this verse of the sixteenth century, and partly because the greatest poetry is contemporary with all ages.

Byron is to be judged by the whole mountainous mass of his world and not by any fragment of colored or glittering spar which one's pick may have extricated from the precipitous hillside. His world is a kind of natural formation, high enough to climb, and wide enough to walk On. There is hard climbing and heavy walking, but, once there, the air braces and the view is wide.

In making a selection from this large and uneven mass of poetry, it is difficult to do justice to a writer who was almost never a really good writer of verse, except in a form of what he rightly defined as "nondescript and ever-varying rhyme." The seriocomic ottava rima of *Don Juan* and *The Vision of Judgment* is the only meter which Byron ever completely mastered; and it is only in those unique poems, in which Goethe detected, for the first time in modern poetry, a "classically elegant comic style," that Byron is wholly able to express the new quality which he brought into English literature in a wholly personal, or at all satisfying, way. From the first he was a new force, but a force unconscious of direction, with all the uncouthness of nature in convulsions. He had a strong, direct, and passionate personality, but we find him, even in the better parts of *Childe Harold*, putting rhetoric in the place of that simplicity which he was afterward to discover by accident, as in jest; we find him, throughout almost the whole of the poetical romances, a mere masquerader in Eastern frippery, which is scarcely the better because it happened to have been bought on the spot; we find him, in his serious reflections, either quite sensible and quite obvious, or, as in addresses to the ocean, and the like, straining on tiptoe toward heights that can only be reached by wings. His lyric verse was always without magic, and only now and then, and chiefly in the lines beginning "When we two parted," was he able to turn speech into a kind of emphatic and intense chant, into which poetry comes as a kind of momentary suspension of the emphasis. His rendering of actual sensation, as in parts of *Mazeppa*, is the nearest approach to poetry which he made in those poems which were supposed to be the very voice of passion. Everything that he wrote in blank verse, and consequently the whole of the plays, is vitiated by his incapacity to handle that meter, or indeed to distinguish it, in any vital or audible way, from prose. Now and again personal feeling flung off the ill-fitting and constraining clothes of rhetoric, and stood up naked; sentiments of resentment, against his wife, or against the world, or against himself, made poetry sometimes. Then, as it was to be under other conditions in the later work, his flame is the burning of much dross: excellent food for flames.

And yet, out of all this writing which is hardly literature, this poetry which is hardly verse, there comes, even to the reader of to-day, for whom "the grand Napoleon of the realms of rhyme" is as dead and buried as Napoleon, some inexplicable thrill, appeal, potency; Byron still lives, and we shall never cease to read almost his worst work, because some warmth of his life comes through it.

Almost everything that he wrote was written for relief, and its effect on us is due to something never actually said in it; it is a kind of wild dramatic speech of some person in a play, whose words become weighty, tragic and pathetic because of the fierce light thrown upon them by a significant character and by transfiguring circumstances.

When Byron wrote to Murray, "You might as well want a midnight all stats as rhyme all perfect," he was theorizing over his own failure to achieve sustained excellence on any one level Luckily he carried the theory, in his own downright way, into practise, and, in the "versified Aurora Borealis" of the great comic poems, the defect turns into a quality, and creates what is really a new poetical form. Byron is a heroical Buffoon, the great jester of English poetry; and he is this because he is the only English poet who is wholly buoyant, arrogant and irresponsible. "I never know the word which will come next," he boasts, in *Don Juan*, and for once, improvisation becomes a means to an end, almost an end in itself. It is in the comic verse, strangely enough, that the first real mastery over form shows itself: a genius for rhyme which becomes a new music and decoration, as of cap and bells on the head of sober marching verse, and a genius for plain statement which leaves prose behind in mere fighting force, and glorifies fighting force with a divine natural illumination.

A NOTE ON ARTHUR SYMONS

By Jeremy Mark Robinson

Arthur William Symons (Feb 28, 1865, Milford Haven, Wales - Jan 22, 1945, Wittersham, Kent) is best-known now for his poetry and criticism, and his contributions to the evaluation of modernist and Symbolist poetry (which influenced Eliot, Joyce, Pound, Yeats *et al*). Symons' literary studies included monographs on Aubrey Beardsley, Joseph Conrad, Algernon Swinburne, Robert Browning, William Blake, Dante Gabriel Rossetti, Elizabethan drama, Charles Baudelaire and Walter Pater. Symons also wrote extensively on painting, art, theatre and music (and topics such as Leonardo da Vinci, Auguste Rodin, Impressionism and Symbolism). He was associated with several magazines of the late 19th century period, including the *Yellow Book,* the *Athenaeum,* the *Saturday Review,* the *Fortnightly Review* and the short-lived *Savoy* (which he edited). He was a member of the Rhymer's Club (poets in the group included the founder W.B. Yeats, Lionel Johnson and Ernest Dowson).

Arthur Symons grew up in Wales (his parents were Cornish, and his father was a minister), was educated in Devon, and moved to London at 16. He was educated privately (and somewhat sporadically). Symons was known as the 'blond angel', a vagabond poet, clearly in the Bohemian/ French tradition of

Baudelaire, Verlaine and Rimbaud (Verlaine was a strong influence on his poetry). It's no surprise that Symons gravitated towards living in France and Italy – his passion for French culture (and for Parisian life) is obvious in any of his critical studies. In Paris he attended the famous Tuesday evenings with Stéphane Mallarmé.

Arthur Symons knew many of the key artists and writers of the day, including Aubrey Beardsley, Joseph Conrad, W.B. Yeats, Edmund Gosse and Walter Pater. Symons bought a house (Island Cottage) in Wittersham, Kent, a pleasant village on the Kent-Sussex border, in 1906 (where he died in 1945).

Arthur Symons suffered a major breakdown in 1908, when he was living in Italy (it took two years for him to recover; some say he never fully recovered, and it affected his literary reputation). He later wrote about the experience in the 1930 book *Confessions: A Study In Pathology*.

In his books of literary criticism, Arthur Symons discussed many figures of the late 19th century and early 20th century, including Baudelaire, Pater, Rossetti, Verlaine, Rimbaud, Mallarmé, Conrad, Poe, Ibsen, Patmore, Hardy, Meredith, Zola, Flaubert, Villiers and Maeterlinck. Symons was especially fond of French literature, and Symbolist and Decadent poetry in particular: Verlaine, Rimbaud, Laforgue, Baudelaire, Lautréamont, and Symbolist/ *fin de siècle* authors such as Wilde, Rossetti, Swinburne and Huysmans. Symons' 1899 book *The Symbolist Movement In Literature*[1] was an important early study of *fin de siècle* poetry.

Arthur Symons' poetry included books such as *Days and Nights* (his first book of poetry, published in 1889), *Silhouettes* (1892), *London Nights* (1895), *Amor Victima* (1897), *Images of Good and Evil* (1899), *Poems* (1902), *Lyrics* (1903), *The Fool of the World* (1906), *Poems By Arthur Symons* (1911), *Knave of Hearts* (1913) and *Jezebel Mort* (1931). Symons also translated a good deal of poetry, including Verlaine, Baudelaire, Verhaeren, D'Annunzio,

1 It developed out of an essay published in *Harper's Magazine* in Nov, 1893: *The Decadent Movement In Literature*.

▶ 253

Mallarmé, etc. Symons' plays included *The Minister's Call* (1892), *The Toy Cart* (1916), and *Tristan and Iseult* (1917).

FURTHER READING

K. Beckson. *Arthur Symons*, Oxford University Press, 1987
N. Freeman. *Arthur Symons*, Modern Humanities Research
    Association, Cambridge, 2017
S. Hayes. *Arthur Symons*, Brimstone, Shaftesbury, 2007
J. Munro. *Arthur Symons*, Twayne, New York, 1969
J. Wainwright. *Poets On Poets*, Carcanet Press, Manchester, 1997

CRESCENT MOON PUBLISHING

web: www.crmoon.com e-mail: cresmopub@yahoo.co.uk

ARTS, PAINTING, SCULPTURE

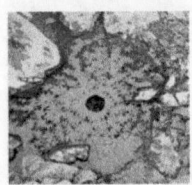

The Art of Andy Goldsworthy

Andy Goldsworthy: Touching Nature
Andy Goldsworthy in Close-Up
Andy Goldsworthy: Pocket Guide
Andy Goldsworthy In America

Land Art: A Complete Guide
The Art of Richard Long
Richard Long: Pocket Guide
Land Art In the UK
Land Art in Close-Up
Land Art In the U.S.A.
Land Art: Pocket Guide
Installation Art in Close-Up
Minimal Art and Artists In the 1960s and After
Colourfield Painting
Land Art DVD, TV documentary
Andy Goldsworthy DVD, TV documentary

The Erotic Object: Sexuality in Sculpture From Prehistory to the Present Day
Sex in Art: Pornography and Pleasure in Painting and Sculpture
Postwar Art
Sacred Gardens: The Garden in Myth, Religion and Art
Glorification: Religious Abstraction in Renaissance and 20th Century Art
Early Netherlandish Painting
Leonardo da Vinci
Piero della Francesca
Giovanni Bellini
Fra Angelico: Art and Religion in the Renaissance
Mark Rothko: The Art of Transcendence
Frank Stella: American Abstract Artist
Jasper Johns
Brice Marden
Alison Wilding: The Embrace of Sculpture
Vincent van Gogh: Visionary Landscapes
Eric Gill: Nuptials of God
Constantin Brancusi: Sculpting the Essence of Things
Max Beckmann
Caravaggio
Gustave Moreau
Egon Schiele: Sex and Death In Purple Stockings
Delizioso Fotografico Fervore: Works In Process 1
Sacro Cuore: Works In Process 2
The Light Eternal: J.M.W. Turner
The Madonna Glorified: Karen Arthurs

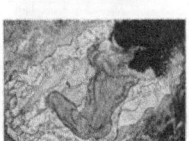

LITERATURE

J.R.R. Tolkien: The Books, The Films, The Whole Cultural Phenomenon
J.R.R. Tolkien: Pocket Guide
Tolkien's Heroic Quest
The *Earthsea* Books of Ursula Le Guin
Beauties, Beasts and Enchantment: Classic French Fairy Tales
German Popular Stories by the Brothers Grimm
Philip Pullman and *His Dark Materials*
Sexing Hardy: Thomas Hardy and Feminism
Thomas Hardy's *Tess of the d'Urbervilles*
Thomas Hardy's *Jude the Obscure*
Thomas Hardy: The Tragic Novels
Love and Tragedy: Thomas Hardy
The Poetry of Landscape in Hardy
Wessex Revisited: Thomas Hardy and John Cowper Powys
Wolfgang Iser: Essays and Interviews
Petrarch, Dante and the Troubadours
Maurice Sendak and the Art of Children's Book Illustration
Andrea Dworkin
Cixous, Irigaray, Kristeva: The *Jouissance* of French Feminism
Julia Kristeva: Art, Love, Melancholy, Philosophy, Semiotics and Psychoanalysis
Hélene Cixous I Love You: The *Jouissance* of Writing
Luce Irigaray: Lips, Kissing, and the Politics of Sexual Difference
Peter Redgrove: Here Comes the Flood
Peter Redgrove: Sex-Magic-Poetry-Cornwall
Lawrence Durrell: Between Love and Death, East and West
Love, Culture & Poetry: Lawrence Durrell
Cavafy: Anatomy of a Soul
German Romantic Poetry: Goethe, Novalis, Heine, Hölderlin
Feminism and Shakespeare
Shakespeare: Love, Poetry & Magic
The Passion of D.H. Lawrence
D.H. Lawrence: Symbolic Landscapes
D.H. Lawrence: Infinite Sensual Violence
Rimbaud: Arthur Rimbaud and the Magic of Poetry
The Ecstasies of John Cowper Powys
Sensualism and Mythology: The Wessex Novels of John Cowper Powys
Amorous Life: John Cowper Powys and the Manifestation of Affectivity (H.W. Fawkner)
Postmodern Powys: New Essays on John Cowper Powys (Joe Boulter)
Rethinking Powys: Critical Essays on John Cowper Powys
Paul Bowles & Bernardo Bertolucci
Rainer Maria Rilke
Joseph Conrad: *Heart of Darkness*
In the Dim Void: Samuel Beckett
Samuel Beckett Goes into the Silence
André Gide: Fiction and Fervour
Jackie Collins and the Blockbuster Novel
Blinded By Her Light: The Love-Poetry of Robert Graves
The Passion of Colours: Travels In Mediterranean Lands
Poetic Forms

POETRY

Ursula Le Guin: Walking In Cornwall
Peter Redgrove: Here Comes The Flood
Peter Redgrove: Sex-Magic-Poetry-Cornwall
Dante: Selections From the Vita Nuova
Petrarch, Dante and the Troubadours
William Shakespeare: Sonnets
William Shakespeare: Complete Poems
Blinded By Her Light: The Love-Poetry of Robert Graves
Emily Dickinson: Selected Poems
Emily Brontë: Poems
Thomas Hardy: Selected Poems
Percy Bysshe Shelley: Poems
John Keats: Selected Poems
Joh n Keats: Poems of 1820
D.H. Lawrence: Selected Poems
Edmund Spenser: Poems
Edmund Spenser: Amoretti
John Donne: Poems
Henry Vaughan: Poems
Sir Thomas Wyatt: Poems
Robert Herrick: Selected Poems
Rilke: Space, Essence and Angels in the Poetry of Rainer Maria Rilke
Rainer Maria Rilke: Selected Poems
Friedrich Hölderlin: Selected Poems
Arseny Tarkovsky: Selected Poems
Arthur Rimbaud: Selected Poems
Arthur Rimbaud: A Season in Hell
Arthur Rimbaud and the Magic of Poetry
Novalis: Hymns To the Night
German Romantic Poetry
Paul Verlaine: Selected Poems
Elizaethan Sonnet Cycles
D.J. Enright: By-Blows
Jeremy Reed: Brigitte's Blue Heart
Jeremy Reed: Claudia Schiffer's Red Shoes
Gorgeous Little Orpheus
Radiance: New Poems
Crescent Moon Book of Nature Poetry
Crescent Moon Book of Love Poetry
Crescent Moon Book of Mystical Poetry
Crescent Moon Book of Elizabethan Love Poetry
Crescent Moon Book of Metaphysical Poetry
Crescent Moon Book of Romantic Poetry
Pagan America: New American Poetry

MEDIA, CINEMA, FEMINISM and CULTURAL STUDIES

J.R.R. Tolkien: The Books, The Films, The Whole Cultural Phenomenon
J.R.R. Tolkien: Pocket Guide
The *Lord of the Rings* Movies: Pocket Guide
The Cinema of Hayao Miyazaki
Hayao Miyazaki: *Princess Mononoke*: Pocket Movie Guide
Hayao Miyazaki: *Spirited Away*: Pocket Movie Guide
Tim Burton : Hallowe'en For Hollywood
Ken Russell
Ken Russell: *Tommy*: Pocket Movie Guide
The Ghost Dance: The Origins of Religion
The Peyote Cult
Cixous, Irigaray, Kristeva: The *Jouissance* of French Feminism
Julia Kristeva: Art, Love, Melancholy, Philosophy, Semiotics and Psychoanalysis
Luce Irigaray: Lips, Kissing, and the Politics of Sexual Difference
Hélene Cixous I Love You: The *Jouissance* of Writing
Andrea Dworkin
'Cosmo Woman': The World of Women's Magazines
Women in Pop Music
HomeGround: The Kate Bush Anthology
Discovering the Goddess (Geoffrey Ashe)
The Poetry of Cinema
The Sacred Cinema of Andrei Tarkovsky
Andrei Tarkovsky: Pocket Guide
Andrei Tarkovsky: *Mirror*: Pocket Movie Guide
Andrei Tarkovsky: *The Sacrifice*: Pocket Movie Guide
Walerian Borowczyk: Cinema of Erotic Dreams
Jean-Luc Godard: The Passion of Cinema
Jean-Luc Godard: *Hail Mary*: Pocket Movie Guide
Jean-Luc Godard: *Contempt*: Pocket Movie Guide
Jean-Luc Godard: *Pierrot le Fou*: Pocket Movie Guide
John Hughes and Eighties Cinema
Ferris Bueller's Day Off: Pocket Movie Guide
Jean-Luc Godard: Pocket Guide
The Cinema of Richard Linklater
Liv Tyler: Star In Ascendance
Blade Runner and the Films of Philip K. Dick
Paul Bowles and Bernardo Bertolucci
Media Hell: Radio, TV and the Press
An Open Letter to the BBC
Detonation Britain: Nuclear War in the UK
Feminism and Shakespeare
Wild Zones: Pornography, Art and Feminism
Sex in Art: Pornography and Pleasure in Painting and Sculpture
Sexing Hardy: Thomas Hardy and Feminism

The Light Eternal is a model monograph, an exemplary job. The subject matter of the book is beautifully
organised and dead on beam. (Lawrence Durrell)
It is amazing for me to see my work treated with such passion and respect. (Andrea Dworkin)

CRESCENT MOON PUBLISHING
P.O. Box 1312, Maidstone, Kent, ME14 5XU, Great Britain. www.crmoon.com

cresmopub@yahoo.co.uk   www.crescentmoon.org.uk